CAN'T BE
FADED

CAN'T BE FADED

Twenty Years in the New Orleans Brass Band Game

Stooges Brass Band and Kyle DeCoste

University Press of Mississippi / Jackson

The University Press of Mississippi is the scholarly publishing agency of
the Mississippi Institutions of Higher Learning: Alcorn State University,
Delta State University, Jackson State University, Mississippi State University,
Mississippi University for Women, Mississippi Valley State University,
University of Mississippi, and University of Southern Mississippi.

www.upress.state.ms.us

The University Press of Mississippi is a member
of the Association of University Presses.

First printing 2020

∞

Library of Congress Cataloging-in-Publication Data

Names: Stooges Brass Band, author. | DeCoste, Kyle, author.
Title: Can't be faded : twenty years in the New Orleans brass band game /
Stooges Brass Band and Kyle DeCoste.
Other titles: American made music series.
Description: Jackson : University Press of Mississippi, 2020. | Series:
American made music series | Includes bibliographical references and
index.
Identifiers: LCCN 2020017650 (print) | LCCN 2020017651 (ebook) | ISBN
9781496830036 (hardback) | ISBN 9781496830043 (trade paperback) | ISBN
9781496830067 (epub) | ISBN 9781496830050 (epub) | ISBN 9781496830074
(pdf) | ISBN 9781496830081 (pdf)
Subjects: LCSH: Stooges Brass Band. | Brass bands—Louisiana—New Orleans.
| African American musicians—Louisiana—New Orleans.
Classification: LCC ML421.S816 S76 2020 (print) | LCC ML421.S816 (ebook)
| DDC 784.906/076335—dc23
LC record available at https://lccn.loc.gov/2020017650
LC ebook record available at https://lccn.loc.gov/2020017651

British Library Cataloging-in-Publication Data available

To the memory of

Andrew Baham Jr.
Ersel Bogan Jr.
Sharon Gerdes
Demetrie R. Harris
Arian "Fat Boy" Macklin
Joseph "Shotgun Joe" Williams

CONTENTS

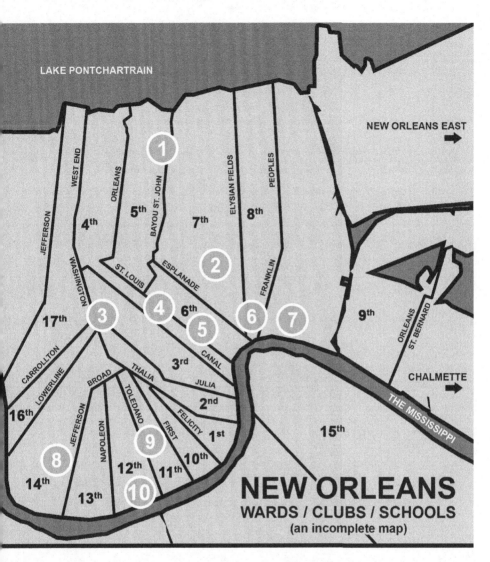

LAKE PONTCHARTRAIN

NEW ORLEANS EAST →

WEST END

JEFFERSON

ORLEANS

BAYOU ST. JOHN

ELYSIAN FIELDS

PEOPLES

4th

5th

7th

8th

WASHINGTON

ST. LOUIS

ESPLANADE

FRANKLIN

17th

6th

9th

ORLEANS

ST. BERNARD

CARROLLTON

LOWERLINE

BROAD

THALIA

3rd

CANAL

JULIA

CHALMETTE →

16th

JEFFERSON

TOLEDANO

2nd

THE MISSISSIPPI

NAPOLEON

FIRST

FELICITY

1st

15th

14th

12th

11th

10th

13th

NEW ORLEANS
WARDS / CLUBS / SCHOOLS
(an incomplete map)

1. JOHN F. KENNEDY HIGH SCHOOL
2. ST. AUGUSTINE HIGH SCHOOL
3. LIVIN SWELL STUDIOS
4. FAMILY TIES
5. THE WELL / CLUB N'FINITY

6. THE HI-HO
7. GOODY'S
8. NOCCA (OLD LOCATION)
9. BABY'S
10. THE ROCK BOTTOM

Map of wards and significant locations in the book. By Kyle DeCoste.

Making "The Stooges Book"

Coming up on their twentieth anniversary in 2016, the Stooges Brass Band sought to document their careers and lives in music. Al Growe ("Uncle Al"), the sentimental old soul of the band and an uncle in the brass band community, was the first to suggest a book. Playing the ever-determined bandleader, Walter Ramsey ran with the project. He had previously been interviewed by my mentor, Matt Sakakeeny, and approached him first about writing a "Stooges book." With his plate already overflowing, Matt proposed the idea to me. I'm a trumpet player who grew up in Nova Scotia, an East Coast Canadian province with a rich Black history, in which my small, deindustrializing hometown of New Glasgow played a prominent role.[1] I first fell in love with brass band music while still living in Canada and found my way down here by way of that interest. When Matt approached me about the book, I had lived in New Orleans for two years while getting my master's degree at Tulane University. Under Matt's advisory, I wrote about the city's only all-woman brass band, the Original Pinettes, and I eventually published some of that work in an article in the journal *Ethnomusicology*,[2] but this was the first time I'd ever written a book. Ditto for the Stooges. Matt introduced me to Walter, and after an introductory group interview, I began attending performances, getting to know everyone, and coordinating interviews with a handful of the band's fifty-something past and present members.

In true Stooges fashion, we meticulously did our homework, and Walter and I both got copies of William Germano's *Getting It Published: A Guide for*

Scholars and Anyone Serious About Serious Books. With some naiveté and much enthusiasm, we attempted to churn out the manuscript in a year, but by the fall of 2016, with it far from finished, I left for New York City, where I began a PhD program in ethnomusicology (the critical study of music and sound) at Columbia University.[3] Our writing was then mostly limited to the four months out of the year when I was on summer break, though the project was kept alive by regular texts, calls, and the Stooges' annual sojourn to play in New York.

In the five years it's taken to publish *Can't Be Faded*, the Stooges have welcomed me into their family as something of a white, Canadian adoptee.[4] They've become big brothers, colleagues, or friends, and entrusted me with preserving their stories for their families and for generations of future musicians. Our relationships vary and are too numerous to state here, but the ways they've changed and grown over the course of the book's writing are made evident in the varying degrees of emotional vulnerability and closeness found in our dialogue in this book. The stoic barriers that are typical of men at times broke down to reveal moments of emotional honesty and even tears on a few occasions. When I first circulated tomes of compiled interview transcripts to the band, some learned things that had long gone unspoken between them—not because of any preternatural interview skills on my part, but rather because the book and the interviews that went into it afforded a rare opportunity to reflect on their careers and relationships in depth.

Can't Be Faded is a coproduction. The band gave me significant control over the book's form, often exclaiming, "You're the writer!" when I sought editorial input. I tried to follow their lead and they tried to follow mine, sometimes leading to moments of writerly stagnation. I probably checked in a bit *too* much—to the extent that it became a joke. Trombonist Garfield Bogan, the wisecracking troublemaker of the band, teased me about my incessant checking in. After I made a Facebook page to promote the book, he texted our group message, saying, "You don't think you should've asked before you did it? Lol," to the laughter of a few of the other band members. When I called to ask him about it, he assured me he was just joking, and I learned that it's okay to be a bit more decisive. Although our individual areas of expertise dictated that I do the transcription, inscription, and much of the editing, I frequently checked in to share writing samples (and eventually the entire manuscript) with the Stooges, and we conducted each formal interview with the book and its audience(s) in mind. While it's true that I'm the one sitting at a computer typing these words, the book is cowritten. Writing is not solely the act of putting words on a page, but includes a scope of activities the Stooges have partaken in, without which this book would not exist: creating and recounting the stories in the book, photo documentation, writing brief autobiographies, cosigning paperwork for the press, and nudging me in different directions with the manuscript.[5]

A group photo from the final meeting for *Can't Be Faded*, June 30, 2019. *Left to right:* Mike Jones, Ersel "Garfield" Bogan, John Cannon, Walter Ramsey (seated), Kyle DeCoste, Al Growe, Que'Dyn Growe, John Perkins (seated), Virgil Tiller, Kai Carter, Javan Carter, Kaiza Carter, Ellis Joseph. Photo by Pableaux Johnson, with apologies for photoshopping Eric's head onto Garfield's shirt.

While our division of labor necessitated that I did the bulk of what is traditionally considered writing, my aim has been to allow the Stooges to speak for themselves as much as possible while also providing a cohesive, unifying narrative to their story. By this, I don't mean a narrative void of tension that irons out difference or flattens our voices.[6] To the contrary, I view the interpersonal differences in the text as a source of strength, one which, following poet Audre Lorde, "is enriching rather than threatening to the defined self, when there are shared goals."[7] We've worked closely and collaboratively in the writing of this book, and we share a love of the music and many people in the brass band community. At the same time, I'm also an imperfect intermediary for the book. The stories and content of the book are the product of the things I chose to focus on in interviews and reflect my experiences just as they do those of the band members. I'm a thirty-year-old, white, working-class/upwardly mobile, trumpet-playing scholar from Nova Scotia, and my experiences often differ from those of the Stooges in that they're complicated by differences in age, race, nationality, and occupation. All of our lives have been differently shaped by our identities and their structural correlates in racism, economic exploitation, and citizenship.[8] Bridging the personal and political narratives among those featured in this book has been a guiding principle throughout its writing. We

each hold different experiences, musical backgrounds, and ways of understanding our own stories, and *Can't Be Faded* attends to these differences and their
negotiation, allowing our voices to speak at times harmoniously, at other times
in productive tension, and always as honestly as possible.

Can't Be Faded is not written exclusively—or even primarily—to academic
audiences. Al made it clear to me early in the process that "it would be nice for
all of us to be able to go up and show our grandkids a book of our story," and
I've done my best to follow his request. The book, we think, caters to multiple
audiences, a possibility afforded by my writing it outside graduate programs in
the humanities, where coauthored work isn't typically incentivized.[9] This book
is addressed to scholars and fans, but also to the city's music community, the
band's family members, and future generations of brass band musicians.[10] We
also see *Can't Be Faded* as an effort at public-facing scholarship, a contribution
to discussions about broader social and political topics that have relevance
beyond the specificity of the Stooges' experiences: "what we were going through
with some sort of social commentary," as philosophically minded founding
trumpeter Drew Baham (a.k.a. "Da Phessah") put it. Accordingly, the book
speaks to racist policing, the connections between social class and musical
genre, masculinity, the value of music education, and music as labor, among
other things. If not always done *explicitly* in the interviews, I've attempted
to provide some political/contextual scaffolding in the introduction to each
chapter so that the book not only represents the musicians it's about, but also
represents their *interests*.[11] The book follows Drew and Al's aims in its address
to multiple audiences and its claims for the social significance of its stories.[12]

The book is organized in a loose chronology and is divided into four parts
that follow generations of the band: "Part I: The First Generation," "Part II: The
Second Generation," "Part III: The Street Kings Generation," and "Part IV: The
Stage Band Generation." These divisions, which the band uses to narrate their
story, follow personnel changes and defining moments in the band's career.
Each part contains three chapters that begin with an episode immersing the
reader in the spaces I've followed the Stooges into, followed by a synthesis/
analysis of the chapter's material. These episodes take you from the potholed
streets of the city to barroom stages, from practice spaces and studios to the
stuffy confines of a tour van. Each chapter then moves into dialogue between
me and the band members that we've edited and curated from our interviews
over the past few years. The book's appendix, which features autobiographies
of each band member featured, is meant to supplement the main text. If you
find yourself confused by who is who or simply want to learn more about
individual band members, the appendix is there to be used as a resource. Each
autobiography therein was either written by the band members and sent to

me or dictated to me and then collaboratively edited at my computer during writing sessions.

Whether you're a friend or family member of the Stooges; a young brass band musician; a fan of New Orleans music; a scholar of race, class, gender, and culture; or simply perusing the shelves of a bookstore, we hope this book offers you a critical and heartfelt view of the past twenty-plus years of the New Orleans brass band scene. Through a combination of first-person narrative and dialogue, we illuminate the struggles, joys, and brotherhoods forged and fortified by musicians working to make a living in the city and abroad. Let's go!

ACKNOWLEDGMENTS

THE STOOGES: We want to thank God for allowing us the opportunity to be musicians, the opportunity to create the Stooges, and for what the Stooges are today. We would also like to thank all our families and friends for their loving support. We would like to thank all the life mentors we had throughout school; a special thanks to Walter "Doc" Harris, Clyde Kerr Jr., Edwin "Hamp" Hampton, and Lloyd Harris.

We want to thank all the musicians before us in brass bands: the Dirty Dozen, the Rebirth, the Soul Rebels, the Lil Rascals, and the Treme brass bands, in particular. Thanks also goes to the young brass bands. A special shout-out to Philip Frazier and Kermit Ruffins from the Rebirth Brass Band for giving us our first start to the streets by allowing us to play for their fifteenth anniversary. We would like to give Kermit Ruffins thanks for allowing us to play in Tuba Fats Square every Tuesday when we were young and didn't know how to play music at all. Thank you to all of the Stooges band members that have helped us grow this business and love for this music for over twenty years.

Thank you to the Stoogerettes. We would like to acknowledge all the social aid and pleasure clubs and the different clubs we've played over the years (Baby's, Family Ties, Goody's, the Hi-Ho, Club N'Finity, the Blue Nile, the Rock Bottom, Kisses, Club Caribbean).

Thanks to all of our families, including Walter's mama, Demetrie R. Harris (RIP), for allowing us to tear up her living room set over decades of rehearsing in her house; Ersel's daddy, Ersel Bogan Jr. ("Mr. B.," RIP), who used to play cowbell for us; Uncle Ronnie (RIP), who was Flash before Flash; Walter's grandparents, Ashton and Ruby Ramsey, for letting us practice at their house back when we started (upstairs for seven days a week); Pat Baham, our first manager; and Sharon Gerdes (RIP). An extra special thank-you to the band members' spouses for putting up with us for years. It's not easy dealing with a member of the band as a wife or whatever. They have really had to deal with a lot of stressful stuff.

Thanks to Conrad Wyre and Mookie Square (RIP), who have photographed us over the years. We also would like to thank the Stooges' management company, Hypersoul, and Tony Ciaccio and Donna Santiago from Hypersoul. Without them backing us, we would not be able to travel the world. We'd like to thank the Mardi Gras Indians, who are too numerous to mention. We'd like to thank the radio DJs who have spun our music: LBJ, who first played our record on 102.9; DJ Papa Smurf; and Captain Charles. We'd also like to thank Kyle for his dedication and hard work. It's been an amazing journey and you've been the writer and director of that journey. Lastly, thank you to the future musicians (especially Dorian Jones and Que'Dyn Growe) and all of our kids for being the motivation for us to continue playing music.

KYLE: Firstly, I'd like to thank all of the Stooges for being generous and open while I learned about their lives and careers over numerous interviews. Thank you for welcoming me into the Stooges family, looking out for me over the years, and being patient and kind throughout the book-writing process. I hope the fruits of our labor are worth it. I'm particularly grateful for the time of Walter Ramsey, Al Growe, Garfield Bogan, Drew Baham, Virgil Tiller, Mike Jones, Eric Gordon, Chris Cotton, Arian Macklin (RIP), Chad Honore, Flash Jackson, John Perkins, Spug Smith, Ellis Joseph, John Cannon, J'mar Westley, Abdule Muhammad, Elliot Slater, and Javan Carter. An extra special thank-you goes out to Al Growe for being the driving force behind this book, as well as to his wife, Shawn Goffner-Growe, for being a warm and friendly person to hang out with at Stooges shows. Thanks for driving me and my bicycle home numerous times—you both saved the people who care about me lots of worry!

Thank you to Karen Lozinski, Pableaux Johnson, Michael Mastrogiovanni, Conrad Wyre, Ashton Ramsey, Greg Rhoades, and Lisa Palumbo for graciously donating photos for this book. I'm grateful for your artistry and documentation of brass band history. Thanks also go to Jerin "Jerk" Beasley for creating the custom artwork for the cover.

The New Orleans Center for the Gulf South (NOCGS) supported the creation of this book through a Global South Research Grant that provided honorariums for the Stooges' writing. At NOCGS, I'm thankful to Rebecca Snedecker, Denise Frazier, and Regina Cairns for their continued support, kindness, and generosity.

I am indebted to the two anonymous readers who spent time with the manuscript and offered advice that I believe has made this book much stronger than it would be otherwise. I would especially like to thank Bruce Boyd Raeburn, the first reader, for his encouragement throughout my career and his careful attention to the manuscript. I am indebted also to Will Buckingham, Jasmine Henry, and Matt Sakakeeny for graciously reviewing the manuscript, offering helpful advice, and providing thorough comments. Special thanks go to Matt Sakakeeny for his support of this book throughout its creation and for introducing me to the Stooges in the first place. Thanks also go out to my best friends and brothers, Alex MacNeil and Adam Johnson, for reading through early versions of material used in the book proposal, as well as to my colleague and friend Jesse Chevan, for reading and offering suggestions on a grant proposal for the book.

I would like to thank the *entire* team at the University Press of Mississippi for bringing this book to fruition. In particular, I am grateful to our editor, Craig W. Gill, for believing in this project from the beginning and being supportive and accommodating throughout; Carlton W. McGrone for cutting his editorial teeth on this book; Emily Snyder Bandy for supporting the book in its early stages; Todd Lape and his team for designing the book and patiently working with us on the cover; Valerie Jones for seeing the book through the entire process; and Nick Bergin for his careful and considerate copyediting.

Thank you to Dr. Debra S. Karhson, who lovingly made sure I took care of my business and helped me organize my time between my PhD program and this book project. She was honest in her critique and generous with advice, often figuring out what I was trying to say before I did. I love you and am thankful for your partnership. Last, but certainly not least, I'd like to thank and acknowledge my entire family and especially my parents, Clem and Kathy DeCoste, and my sister, Nicole Spurrell, for encouraging me to chase my dreams even when it meant I was not always as present as I'd like to be. I love you and owe who I am today to all of you. This book is the product of a huge communal effort, and I am so thankful to everyone who played any part in bringing it to print. To anyone I may have missed, charge it to my head and not my heart.

CAN'T BE
FADED

Wind It Up!

Walter puts down his horn and picks up the mic. "The name of this song, y'all, is called 'Wind It Up (Like Michael Buck).' We have a real simple dance step: two steps in the front, two steps in the back, and then you wind it up like that!"[1] Over a groove of keyboards, guitar, congas, and drum kit, the horn players of the Stooges Brass Band demonstrate the dance moves in sync, raising and spinning their right fists behind them to "wind it up" while verbalizing the dance steps in real-time instructions ("Left, right, left, right / wind it up, wind it up!").[2] Following the band's instruction, the audience slowly trades their reticence for spinning fists, the familiar one-two step, and an occasional pelvic thrust.

"The party people are definitely on this side of the building!" bandleader Walter Ramsey yells into the mic. Half the audience responds with a chorus of hollers and whistles, attempting to stake their claim as the good-time side of the club. Not wanting to be outdone, tuba player Javan Carter and trombonist Al Growe, huddled at the other side of the stage, work their side of the club in a semiscripted routine befitting the band's namesake, the Three Stooges. "Say, Al," Javan half recites, "I think the party people is on our left side." He raises his hands above his head, and the audience in front of him responds accordingly, their raised arms appearing as silhouettes against the stage's blue and tie-dye backdrop. "I tell you what," Walter intones in his characteristically raspy voice, "I bet y'all the party people over here can wind it up better than everybody over here." "You said 'bet'?" Javan asks, as if happily stirring up a hornet's nest. Walter fires back: "I tell you what, we gonna put some wages up. It's gonna

The stage band version of the Stooges playing the Blue Nile on March 17, 2018. *Left to right:* Elliot Slater, Al Growe, Walter Ramsey, Virgil Tiller, and Javan Carter. Photo by Kyle DeCoste.

go like this: if the party people on our side wind it up better than the people over here, we need y'all both to do twenty push-ups—twenty-five push-ups!"[3] A member of the audience at the foot of the stage yells out increasingly high push-up numbers, and Al jokingly scolds the push-up zealot, pointing and yelling, "Hey, hey, *hey*! Be cool."

Despite being labeled a "brass band," their instrumentation on this day isn't typical of the genre. A staged performance with keyboards, guitar, percussion, drum kit, and horns is a far cry from the street parades where many of the Stooges grew up playing music. Every Sunday from late August to late June, there's a second line parade in New Orleans organized by social aid and pleasure clubs composed primarily of the city's Black working class.[4] Bands lead a sea of people through the city streets in participatory processions that build community and mark places of importance—homes, watering holes, churches, and cemeteries—along parade routes. Club members burst through doorways, dressed to the nines, floating on footwork and dropping low to chest-rumbling blasts of the tuba before parading through the streets of the city en masse. The term *second line* refers to the entire parade, though it was once used to refer only to onlookers in jazz funerals who formed a second line behind the first line of the family and band. As anthropologist Helen Regis notes, the term

Walter Ramsey and his tuba stick out of the crowd at the Original N.O. Lady and Men Buckjumpers second line, November 29, 2009. To his left is Garfield Bogan and to his right are Eric Gordon (trumpet) and Antione "Ace Free" Coleman (snare). Photo by Pableaux Johnson.

now simultaneously refers to dance steps, a characteristic syncopated rhythm, the participants who follow behind the club and band, and the entire event.[5]

The Stooges began playing at second lines not long after their founding in 1996, but the tradition has roots that reach back over a century earlier. In the mid to late nineteenth century, the bands that paraded through the city resembled those elsewhere in the United States; they consisted of around fifteen members who dressed in military garb. Their music included marches, European dances, and popular songs.[6] From their inception, brass bands were fixtures at outdoor events (baseball games, picnics, etc.), and with the increased hiring of brass bands, musicians began paring down the instrumentation in the name of cost-effectiveness.[7] Bands eventually came to consist of the eight- to ten-piece configuration that has, with few alterations, continued into the twentieth and twenty-first centuries: trumpets, trombones, tenor sax, snare drum, bass drum, and tuba. While there were originally many bands whose membership was circumscribed by ethnicity—Yugoslavian, Irish, and Portuguese, for example—Black brass bands are the ones that have remained vital and relevant in the city's music scene well into the twenty-first century, sustained over the years through their employment by benevolent societies, social aid and pleasure clubs, bars, and individuals who hire the bands for thirty-minute wedding, funeral, and party gigs.

The brass band idiom has always been highly adaptable, and today's brass band music owes much to musicians who looked to 1970s funk to introduce repetitive tuba riffs that became the foundation of contemporary brass band music.[8] Under the leadership and vision of banjoist Danny Barker, the Fairview Baptist Church Brass Band was founded in 1970 and became an institution for continuing a tradition of experimentation within the brass band idiom.[9] Coming from the Fairview band, the Dirty Dozen Brass Band maintained a repertory of traditional hymns, brought in their penchant for bebop and funk, and expanded the instrumentation to include guitar and drum kit on staged gigs.

In the 1980s and '90s, a new generation of musicians brought hip-hop into the brass band genre. The Rebirth Brass Band was founded in 1983, the Soul Rebels and the Pinettes in 1991, and the Hot 8 in 1995. They made sampling a prominent part of their compositional practice, incorporating riffs and bass lines from artists like Donny Hathaway, OutKast, Frankie Beverly and Maze, and the O'Jays in their original songs. The Soul Rebels were among the first brass bands to move away from the streets, officially announcing their departure with the release of their album *No More Parades* in 1998. They broke away from second lines, and they did so with gusto.

It's within this context that the Stooges began their careers in 1996. They were interested in expanding the reach of brass band music and developed a keen business sense to capitalize on developments within the tradition. Coming of age in the late 1990s and early 2000s, they were surrounded by the booming hip-hop industry of Cash Money and No Limit Records. They watched as local musicians exported their musical products to the world and built a substantial music empire. Today, they still have the same conversations they were having when they were younger: Why don't hip-hop stations pick up brass band music? They've struggled to access a larger market for their music and have made adjustments to try to take brass band music mainstream.

Al, Garfield, and Walter playing at Garfield's 35th birthday party at the Regency Reception Hall. Photo by Karen Lozinski.

Coming from an impressive musical pedigree, the band members take their musicianship seriously. They've received top-notch musical educations in some of the city's most prestigious high school band programs as well as training in university bands. They're world-class musicians who make the choice to play brass band music, which is seen by many as a working-class Black music— something played more in the streets than in concert halls or arenas.

Despite their serious ambition and ability, they're sure to never take themselves too seriously, incorporating performance antics that befit the band's namesake. They choreograph dance moves on the stage and in the streets, crowd surf, and always do something extra to help audiences enjoy the music. At one of their regular Thursday night gigs, they would host themed nights like the "Pajama Jam" or "Back-to-School" parties, much to the amusement of showgoers, who weren't accustomed to that level of silliness at brass band gigs. Indeed, a line of humor and playfulness runs through the Stooges doctrine, which is evident not only in performance, but also in band practices and in the interviews and meetings for this book, which were often punctuated with bursts of laughter as musicians poked fun at one another while remembering past escapades and controversies stirred up in the brass band community. When you get the Stooges in a room together, your cheeks will hurt from laughing. They roast each other with side-splitting irreverence.

The band has their own comedic trio in Walter, Al, and Garfield. "You look at Curly, Larry, and Mo, you got me, Walter, and Al," Garfield told me. After

Hurricane Katrina when the band went on hiatus, they re-formed around this trio. Walter is the strategist. He's the determined bandleader, the diplomat, the franchise quarterback, an Energizer Bunny type with a steady handshake. Unlike many musicians, he neither smokes nor drinks, and he keeps a firm grip on the band's operations. Early in the book's process, he welcomed me into the Stooges family after only our first two hours of interviews. As the bandleader and holder of the LLC, Walter and the band name are indelibly linked. Uncle Al is the old soul. He's careful and considerate, sometimes putting a lid on the band's rasher decisions. He's sure to always put his wife and kids first, and pays respects to the elders of the brass band scene. He took me under his wing throughout the book-writing process and became something of a big brother, giving me relationship advice and teaching me when to assert myself and take control of our final meeting for the book. Garfield is the troublemaker of the group. Whereas Al would earnestly suggest I take control of a meeting, Garfield would poke fun at me for not doing it. His willingness to poke fun at anything and anyone often lands the band in hot water ("I'm the Ninth Ward, I'm the guy that begets the controversy," he told me), but he firmly believes in the band's brotherhood and acts out of loyalty. This is the core of the Stooges family. Like any other family, they're complicated, but they each play their role in making the outfit function. When you get a group of past and present Stooges in a room, you can be sure you're going to laugh.

Behind all the laughter, the roasting, the unabashed ability to be honest with one another, is loss and a justified fear of further loss. I awoke one morning to a text message from Al that summed up the drive of *Can't Be Faded*: "Man, we have to finish this book before someone else die. It's going to be a dedication book in a minute. Ersel suppose to have some pics, I'm going to go by him this week to see what he has. Time to close this project boss. Lol." Days earlier, we had lost Mookie Square, a photographer who had been photographing the band since they were the Lil Stooges and who had promised to provide us with pictures for the book. Loss hung over the whole book-writing process and provided the motivation to finish—especially after we lost tuba player Arian Macklin in the fall of 2017. Over the years, the Stooges have seen their brothers killed by the police or swallowed up by the prison-industrial complex. They've had to appear before the court for publicly playing music, and they've seen their city destroyed by Hurricane Katrina only to return to it in the throes of gentrification. The city has endured wage stagnation and rising housing costs because of short-term rentals. As hard as those trials may have been, they were always addressed with laughter. When we talked about the dedication for the book, for example, we hit a point of disagreement. Al wanted a dedication, John Cannon didn't want one, Garfield wanted more

The Stooges trading stories before playing a memorial for Walter's mother, Demetrie Harris (a.k.a. Nanna), in front of Walter's childhood home at 2024 N. Villere on November 6, 2018. *Left to right:* Drew, Virgil, Garfield, Walt, Al, and Thaddeaus "Peanut" Ramsey. Photo by Karen Lozinski.

people added, and Walter was just trying to explain to everyone why books have dedications. "You ain't gotta put all those fucking dead people in that book, man!" John Cannon said, baffled. "What about *in memory of*?" Al suggested. "Dedicate it to She She's," John joked back, in reference to an adult entertainment store.

Despite controversies within and without the band, the Stooges are still here twenty years later, even as other brass bands come and go. As the title of one of their first originals declares, they "Can't Be Faded." The song was written by Walter while still in high school. It's a flex on his composition chops, and he used it to put a technical flourish on the brass band genre. It has elaborate melodies that don't fall easily under the fingers, and the older members of the band use the song to teach young brass band musicians how to work with chord changes. To me, the song succinctly conveys the spirit of the band and our book. On the phone one day, Walter told me what the phrase "can't be faded" means to him. "*Can't be faded* is when you working hard on whatever it is in life that's your goals and somebody hate on you for no reason—no matter who you are in life. You're working on your goals and somebody block you or just be mad at you, or just tell you you can't do something. That's saying we can't be faded. No matter how bad you want to erase us or shadow our color, we cannot be faded. That's what *can't be faded* means to me."

PART I

The First Generation

CHAPTER 1

School Days

"*Hey*-oh, oh! *Hey*-oh, oh!" The front line of the Stooges marches down the street, instruments nestled into their right arms and bottles of beer held tightly in the other. John Perkins, one of the younger members of the band, marches in front. Wearing a tall busby hat like a drum major, he playfully wields his trumpet like a mace. In the back of the band, Walter and Spug work in tandem, ping-ponging the tuba line off each other like a street-oriented experimentation in Dolby surround sound. The song "AP Touro" has an instantly identifiable tuba line written by Kerwin James of the New Birth Brass Band.[1] Left, right, left, right, left, right, left, right. "*Hey*-oh, oh! *Hey*-oh, oh!" The band lifts their knees high into the air, their toes pointed downward, as they do a loose parallel knee bend.[2] Seeing a brass band take on the mannerisms of a marching band is certainly an oddity at second lines, but the sidewalk follows suit, trading their usually individualistic footwork for high stepping.[3] Many in the second line crowd embody the same learned marching techniques, signifying their common marching band pedigree. Those directly behind the band create a rhythmic clatter, striking tambourines, wine bottles, and cowbells. Amid this joyful commotion, Al's son, eleven-year-old Que'Dyn Growe, plays snare drum while sixteen-year-old Dorian Jones follows alongside the bass drummer, carefully observing the musical interplay of the tuba, bass drum, and snare that make up the band's back row. The streets offer an invaluable training ground for young brass band musicians, but, as the Stooges' tribute to high school march-

The Lil Stooges in 1999 on A. P. Tureaud Avenue near St. Aug. Seated (*left to right*): Walter Ramsey, Garfield Bogan. Standing (*left to right*): Drew Baham, Ellis Joseph, J'mar "Buzz" Westley, Devin Phillips, John Cannon, and Yorel "Yogi" Gardener. Photo courtesy of Garfield Bogan.

ing band performance suggests, training happens not only in the streets but in classrooms as well. This chapter is about those formative schooling experiences.

The story of the Stooges, like so many brass bands before and after them, begins in a high school music program—well, two of them. When they first got together as the Lil Stooges Brass Band in 1996, their members primarily hailed from John F. Kennedy Senior High School and St. Augustine High School. The story of their combination was unusual at a time when brass band membership was typically constrained by school affiliation and school rivalries were rarely transgressed.

The Stooges' membership was split evenly between Kennedy and St. Aug. At Kennedy, Walter Ramsey, Drew Baham, Ersel "Garfield" Bogan, Brian Gerdes, and "Big Sam" Williams made up the front line of trumpets and trombones.[4] Kennedy was a public high school located within the confines of City Park, near Lake Pontchartrain.[5] There, they studied under the directorship of Mr. Walter Harris, better known to most of his students as "Doc." With the exception of Drew (who got a ride to school with Doc every morning), they woke up every morning at five o'clock, caught two or three buses to school, got to band practice at seven, and did field drills before school started at eight. Their musical training continued in the afternoons thanks to the school's partnership with the New Orleans Center for the Creative Arts (NOCCA), a tuition-free, preprofessional training program in the arts that admits students by audition. Leaving their classmates, they would be bused from the lakefront to the NOCCA campus Uptown at 6048 Perrier Street (NOCCA moved to the Marigny neighborhood in 2000).[6] Since its founding in 1973, NOCCA has provided many hardworking young musicians with the necessary training to become professional musicians, expanding their training beyond marching band and other musical styles typical of high school band programs. It was here that the Stooges learned from some of the city's most accomplished musicians, including Clyde Kerr Jr. and Kidd Jordan.[7] They experimented with genres of music beyond marching band, learning, in Walter's words, "what happens in the blues, or what happens in gospel, or what happens in rock 'n' roll—how to put these chord structures together." While their training at Kennedy gave them fundamental lessons on their instruments, NOCCA exposed them to a wide array of genres that eased their entrée into musical careers.

The other half of the band received a similarly robust musical training despite not partnering with NOCCA. John Cannon, Ellis Joseph, J'mar Westley, and Wayne Lewis all got their stripes in a rigorous and disciplinary band program that remains the pride of St. Augustine High School.[8] A Black, all-boy parochial school in the Seventh Ward, St. Aug was founded by Josephite priests from the Archdiocese of New Orleans in 1951. The band program, which was set up the following year by Mr. Edwin "Hamp" Hampton, was eventually dubbed the Marching 100.[9] Mr. Carl Blouin Sr. was brought into the fold in 1959 as both a math teacher and the assistant band director. When the Stooges joined the St. Aug marching band in the 1990s, it was still run by Hampton, who had by then cemented his place as one of the city's most respected music teachers. Virgil Tiller, who joined the Stooges shortly before Katrina and eventually became the St. Aug band director after Hurricane Katrina, told me that "all the bands were based around discipline, and your band director was like your second father." Band directors like Doc and Hamp assumed a secondary parental role to young musicians, some of whom, like the Stooges, went on to play professionally.[10]

The Stooges' transcending the school rivalry between St. Aug and Kennedy happened organically. Prior to the band's founding, John Cannon and Drew Baham were both members of the Blue Jay Brass Band while attending F. W. Gregory Junior High School. Even though Al Growe wasn't yet playing with the rest of the Stooges, he was still known to the rest of the band members as the drum major at McDonogh 35 Senior High School. Virgil was the drum major at St. Aug and also led the Ace of Spades Brass Band, of which John and Ellis were members. Though there was serious competition among their schools, they crossed paths at each school's talent show, where bands would face off. "All high schools and cliques had their own little brass band," as Walter put it. Kennedy, St. Aug, McDonogh 35, Alcée Fortier, Alfred Lawless, Eleanor McMain, and St. Mary's each had brass bands, and their school talent shows were where the seeds of spirited rivalries were planted.

In high-stepping fashion, the Stooges still pay tribute to the marching band schooling that laid the groundwork for their careers in music, even though many of them are twenty years removed from high school. Though up-and-coming musicians receive essential training at second lines and other musical and social events throughout the city, formal school training is important in their development. These formal educational environments are all too often overlooked in writings on New Orleans music, where "talent" is too often understood as innate rather than as the product of dedication, hard work, and rigorous formal and informal training from the city's streets to its classrooms.

✦ ✦ ✦

WALTER: Back in those days, the brass band playing the talent shows, that's how we would do. And we would go to all the talent shows. You would play Kennedy, St. Aug, McMain, McDonogh 35, St. Mary's.

AL: It's a talent show. It start at seven o'clock and whoever win, win!

VIRGIL: And you had to audition for it! You have to come a certain day, you have to audition for the talent show, they say if you're good and get in or not. Look, how I met Al, his band—

AL: So my band, we come to the talent show and St. Aug, you go through a door and they got a stairwell that leads to another area. We come in the stairwell—we hear them finish playing—and the only way they can get out is that stairwell. Marcus "Red" Hubbard that play with the Soul Rebels right now, he grew up with me. We got our band and one of the band members was like, "Say, brother, go blow at them. In the stairwell." I said, "Huh?" He said, "Come on." So as they coming out the stairwell, we coming in the stairwell. We start cranking. I don't know what we played. After we finish, they play a song. Now it's a war.

VIRGIL: The talent show's going on. We in the bottom challenging.

AL: Song for song. And we did it for about thirty minutes, back and forth, song for song.

WALTER: The rivalries and the culture, it was just like that.

VIRGIL: We were scared to go to a Kennedy talent show, man. I was scared. I wasn't a punk, though. I went. I was scared, though. It's just what it was. We used to have this discussion: "Look, anybody do something, you better hit them and we all going; we gonna all jump in." We all St. Aug people that sit in the Kennedy talent show or McDonogh 35 talent show. They just looking at us, like, "Please, no nothing. Please. We just want to play this music and get out of here." Some of the time, we would just play and everybody looking, "I ain't waiting till the end. We just gonna go and leave right now because I ain't got time for this."

WALTER: We'll find out later who won!

VIRGIL: Yeah! That's what I'm saying!

AL: Ain't nobody really went to a Fortier talent show.

ALL: No!

WALTER: I ain't gonna lie. We was going to NOCCA and Fortier Uptown. And I remember one time, we had to catch the Magazine bus home, and Andrew used to teach the band at Xavier Prep. He in school *teaching* their band—fucking motherfucker here! So anyway, we going to teach the band at Prep with Andrew one day and we on the bus and they got Fortier dudes on the bus.

DREW: Because they're just getting out of practice.

WALTER: Yeah, they getting out of practice. I remember Sam getting on the bus, and I can remember Sam straight sit down on the first seat in the front. Then Brian get on the bus. We always called Brian "Cool Cat." *That* guy in high school. You know, him. Smoking cigarettes, he a cool cat. I know him and I'm saying to myself, "Lord, please let Brian sit on the front of the bus." Sam already sat down! Not Brian. Brian goes to the back of the bus because he ain't scared of shit. I know if Brian go back there and one of them dudes tell Brian something, it's over with; we got a fight. So we got to go to the back of the bus because Brian went back. Nothing happened but it's just the point of it, like, it's fucking Brian, boy.

AL: Yeah, that Fortier shit was dangerous.

DREW: They hard.

AL: They used to march in Mardi Gras parades with forties. Your people be passing out water, they passing out forties!

WALTER: And they had the whole school with them! Like, the band, then the whole school was to the side.

VIRGIL: I remember having a St. Aug jacket on standing in the parade—one of the few times we had a parade—I had my jacket on. "Hey, who's that coming down the street?" And I see the blue and white things moving like this and I see the shakers moving. I see a whole crowd of people.

WALTER: The whole school walks with them.

VIRGIL: Just walking down. All of the sudden, I just took my jacket off like this.

DREW: "Not tonight!"

WALTER: Yeah, because they would just jump you or sneak you or whatever they did. That was the culture of that.

AL: They used to say—how'd they say?

ALL: "Not one 'tier, not two 'tier, not three 'tier, but Fortier!"

AL: That was they thing. And Lord, them dudes, they was rough.

WALTER: They was grown men! Bennie Pete from the Hot 8 was marching in the band. Bennie Pete was like, what? Twenty! Yeah, like, they were grown men.

VIRGIL: And Mr. Brimmer was more like their father figure. I was a band director, so when I became a band director, he was one of the cats I talked to. My band director was Mr. Hampton, so I already talked to him a lot. I talked to Brimmer, I talked to Lloyd Harris, I talked to their band director, Walter Harris. I got a lot of things from them. What Brimmer's whole thing was, he taught them music, but it was so much where the music was secondary with him. With those children, it was almost like, "Let me get them in the band so they won't be in the street."

WALTER: So they won't get killed.

VIRGIL: Or so they won't get killed, or something like this. It was more of a "I'ma use this music thing that they like—because that's part of the culture of that area—to get them out of where they are." And for the most part, he did a lot for a lot of students, all the students that he had. And they love him to death up there. They would tell me stuff like, he would go to their classes, sit in the class, "Why you ain't doing it?" And for us, I think we were privileged to have band directors who were like that. *All* of us. It wasn't like your band director at St. Aug is good, the band director here is good, and everybody else. No. When we were coming up all the band directors were good and all of them taught music. All of them cared about you in a sick kind of way. You know, like, they cared about you, but they would do stuff to you.

DREW: Curse you out. They'll do you right.

VIRGIL: Yeah, they'll do you some real harsh stuff.

WALTER: Yeah, they weren't scared to discipline you and they weren't scared to tell you about yourself.

VIRGIL: And then they'd tell you, "You can tell your mama and daddy, but tell them the same thing."

DREW: "And tell them 'come here.' Let me tell them."

VIRGIL: Yeah, "I'll tell them, too."

✦ ✦ ✦

J'MAR: Coming under Mr. Hampton, learning from him was one of the greatest advantages around, man. I always heard about Mr. Hampton before I got there. Very strict, very strict. You have to be on everything. The purple and gold—St. Aug colors—meant a whole lot to him and us, and it wasn't a game. He took it real seriously, man. But we learned a lot from him. You have fun at the same time, but it was a serious thing with him. It was a great opportunity working with him and learning from him.

KYLE: And did that kind of provide you with the fundamentals for brass band? I mean, obviously marching band and brass band are quite a bit different.

J'MAR: Yeah. Actually I've been playing the drums since elementary school and middle school, high school. I used to play with the Junior Buck-jumpers Brass Band. I was always around that culture. My auntie started the Lady Buckjumpers, so it was natural for me, especially second lining and playing the drums. So I always was kind of into it before I even joined the band.

KYLE: What did the second line environment provide for you in contrast to the marching band environment at St. Aug? Do you think both of those things are necessary to kind of start in a brass band?

J'MAR: No, I don't think that both of them are necessary, because if you playing music, man, having the soul and the feeling of it, I don't think you necessarily have to march and be around both of them because it's a natural feeling. Even coming from the city, even if you don't march in both of them or be a part of them, I think that it's not pretty hard to pick up. You'll be surrounded by it somewhere. I don't think that you have to be a part of them, it was just fortunate that I was.

✦ ✦ ✦

JOHN C.: When I came along, it was like, this is the perfect fit. The guys I was playing with at St. Aug, they knew brass band—well, let's say the Ace of Spades knew brass band, but it was what they heard. The Stooges knew brass band based on what they felt. It was just a different feeling. When I stopped playing with Ace of Spades, Virgil was like, "I wanna play with y'all." So that's how Virgil got introduced to the Stooges. Andrew and I met in '91 at Gregory. We were thirteen or fourteen, something like that. Me and Andrew played in Blue Jay Brass Band back at Gregory. So when he left and went to Kennedy and when I left and went to St. Aug, we went in different directions, but the music still brought us back together.

The Lil Stooges playing an event on N. Rampart Street for the Corinthian First Baptist Church in the mid-to-late nineties. The church was advertising their church suppers, and this photo was taken down the block from Walter's grandparents' house. Photo courtesy of Ashton Ramsey.

But I didn't get in the Stooges till '97, and from there on, it was just every-thing was the Stooges. I would say six days a week practice. We were a real close group. When we started driving, we were inseparable. We would go bowling, we would shoot pool. We really hung out. We was really a broth-erhood and then we did stuff with the band. All of the creation, all of the music that came about over the years, all the original songs that came out of the first band, that was all because we really spent a lot of time with each other. My mom had a pool in the yard at the house, so my house was the summer house to hang by. It kind of all came together just from us all know-ing somebody. And like I said, we were all in the same homeroom. I had no idea that two people in my homeroom were working on a brass band some-where else. Some of the things that I was dealing with in the band that I was in, they could have fulfilled that. But things happen for a reason.

ELLIS: But we wind up getting Ace of Spades.

JOHN C.: Yeah, but what happened with Ace of Spades and Stooges, I would say in the first two years, probably was one band. Because what hap-pened is a lot of times the people from one band couldn't make it so we had a group of replacements in another band. And then eventually Ace of Spades just kind of faded out and just Stooges is still here.

KYLE: Stooges is still standing twenty years—*over* twenty years—later.

JOHN C.: Yeah, over twenty.

KYLE: It was pretty rare at the time to have a band cross schools. Because St. Aug and Kennedy were rivals, right?

JOHN C.: Rivals to the *death*. Even when we were in marching band, we all marched in high school bands. When we had our school uniforms on, it was, "You're my enemy." And then we came together. Being friends with everybody, we kind of knew some of the things they were doing, some of the inside scoop. They kind of knew some of the inside scoop of what we were doing.

KYLE: Like, in marching band?

JOHN C.: In marching band. Not that we would sit down and give each other secrets, but just because we was so close, we could feel the energy from them. And Andrew was writing some of the music for Kennedy at the time.

KYLE: Yeah, he was arranging all that stuff.

JOHN C.: Yeah, so it just was crazy. And then being on the opposite side of the field, and your opponent is playing a song, one feeling is like, "Damn, they sound good," and then the other feeling is like, "Man, my friend wrote that song!" It put you between a rock and a hard place. But it was all fun and games. I wouldn't change my high school days for nothing. If I could relive it, I probably could relive those four years over and over for the rest of my life.

✦ ✦ ✦

DREW: Every Tuesday Kermit Ruffins would barbecue on the lot and just have somebody play. The thing is, Walter was already known through his grandpa, Big Ashton. And Big Ashton was one of those people that everybody knew because he would do unique things. For the last fifteen, twenty years, he would be riding this tricycle that he has. He's been riding it for the past twenty years.

KYLE: That's the kind of thing that's gonna get you noticed, I guess.

DREW: Exactly, exactly. Riding the big-wheeled tricycle or whatever. And then from Kermit hearing us play and everything else, Phil Frazier, bandleader of the Rebirth Brass Band, heard us and was like, "Y'all got some little things going on. I like what y'all doing." And of course everybody was taking notice because what we were doing was the same, but it was different. Our approach was a little different. We took some of those marching band tunes and we'd do our own little arrangement of the marching band tunes that we been doing because they're pop tunes anyway. And most brass bands throughout history covered a number of the popular tunes of the day, so we

Walter grew up in the culture. Here he is dressed to the nines as king of the Lady Rulers Social Aid and Pleasure Club second line in the early 1980s. Photo courtesy of Ashton Ramsey.

thought the same thing. We were just taking those marching band arrangements and making them a little jazzier and not so marching band-ish. It still sounded like marching band because the chords were heavy-handed and we were blasting melodies. We sounded pretty bad, but people saw potential. But after a while we started to work and get gigs. On-the-job training is the best development that you'll ever have because you can actually listen to what the people are saying, you can actually listen to what they're listening to, you can check out what they're dancing to. You can check out how they respond to certain things. For a while people didn't respond to things because we didn't have *the* sound. There's a certain sound that comes with the brass band, especially in New Orleans culture. And so we didn't necessarily have that sound. So we kind of learned through the various things and people were giving us chances because we were cheap. It's cheap and you get what you pay for sometimes. So we were able to get in by doing second lines where we were doing all the kids' divisions. If they had a kid division, they would call us. And we didn't mind.

KYLE: I mean, you got to go through the paces, right?

DREW: Right. You got to pay your dues. And that's what we got, and that's what happened. And eventually, slowly but surely, people were starting to notice what we were doing. And suddenly, the kids' divisions had a crowd.

✦ ✦ ✦

WALTER: Andrew live in the same luxury apartments with Doc, the band director. He lives in the same place. And so his house down the street. He could catch a ride with Doc every day. Cool. And we ain't have cell phones then, we had house phones. So Doc called my house in the morning at five because he know I'm up because I have to get to band practice. And he would tell me, "You need to call Baham because he's not answering the phone"—like he's going to answer the phone from me! Now, mind you, they can walk to each other house, he can knock on his door. I *still* have to catch two buses. So he catched a ride every day. I guess one time he missed a ride so he had to catch the bus, so he get to practice late. The band director don't tell him shit. Let me get to band practice late, I have to run from the Franklin bus to the Cartier to make sure we get on. So then he come another day late—like, back to back. I'm in the band room, like, "Yes, he gon' get his ass today!" Now, I'm praying on this—me and all the rest of the band members—because he teaching the band so he kind of like lenient towards him. So it's like, "Alright, Andrew. Get up there and go right back to teaching the band late." One more day he missed a ride and he come in there late. The band director holler at him, say something about it, we all clap. Yes!

DREW: And I got the same speech that I got when I first got there: "See this picture on the wall? See, that's Terence Blanchard! He was here *every* morning!" "Fuck. Now I got to deal with this bullshit."

WALTER: I was so happy he bust that out!

DREW: Well, you see, the thing is he never realized how it felt to have to get up in the morning. It got so bad that my daddy was like, "Son, that man said you have fifteen minutes to get to his car." "I'm just waking up!" "Son, you got fifteen minutes to get to the car." So I had to ride with him every morning. And he had a little pastime where he would go to the barroom and have drinks, and go hang with Hamp. He'd go hang with Mr. Hampton. And every morning, he would kind of reek of—

AL: What he was doing last night.

DREW: Yeah. You know, he would start pouring. It's hard to just get rid of that if you came in at one in the morning.

AL: It's like, six.

DREW: Yeah, you got to get up for six. It's hard to shake that loose. So every morning I would get in the car and he'd have his plastic cup still in the car because he couldn't bring it inside, and I got to sit here and listen to him talk to me about everything that's going on and he still smell like breath. You know, the alcohol breath. You know what I'm talking about, man. He smelled like dehydration and I had to deal with this every morning! Every morning! And if I missed, I would get called, called, and called again. And I didn't want to deal with that shit. I'm just being real. I didn't want to put up with that shit. Fuck that. I don't care.

WALTER: I remember he used to get in the band room in the morning and he'd go in and say, "Alright, what is affirmative action?" Every fucking morning! And none of us was smart enough to say, "Let's go look this shit up."

DREW: No. He would find the dumbest motherfucker to answer. That was his problem.

WALTER: And we had some dummies. Boy . . .

DREW: But at the end of the day, that was an era where the teachers taught. The band directors cared so much about their students that not only would they sit there and teach them music, they would sit there and do everything, be everything.

AL: And it was serious, too.

WALTER: Yeah, Hamp would throw keys.

DREW: But that's why I believe that every school had their own brass band. Why? They all encouraged it. They wanted you to go a little further. And so they encouraged you and they supported you doing it.

AL: Back in that time, music was the way out for kids in New Orleans. It wasn't how everybody was playing sports and everything. Music was the thing. And band directors knew all of us, too—I mean, from different schools. I was the drum major, and Dave Harris and my band director Lloyd Harris was first cousins, and he used to come to the school sometimes. I'm walking around in the school. I got my shirt out my pants, we talking and whatnot. He pulled me over. He said, "Hey, man. Put your shirt in your pants." And I'm looking. They got a whole bunch of people around here with their shirt out. He pulled *me*. He said, "Put your shirt in your pants." I looked at him—I knew who he was—but I'm looking like, "Man, what you talking about? You ain't even the band director here." He looked at me, he said, "Look, I know who you are. You need me to ask you this again? Put your

Ellis Joseph playing in front of First Emanuel Baptist Church in the late 1990s. Photo courtesy of John Cannon.

shirt in your pants." "Alright, Mr. Harris." But they knew the drum majors. They knew who was who and they made sure they took care. I think that's what really built us to do all the things we did with the Stooges. We had that foundation to know what was organized and what was chaos.

VIRGIL: They gave us our first gigs. My band director Mr. Hampton was crazy. We would go to a convention. Part of the convention was the marching band would march the convention, and then you had a brass band. He'd say, "Guess what? I got a marching band and a brass band." And he would get paid off of both of them! I remember we had St. Aug uniforms, brass band going through. Then the band come through. He said, "Look, we got to go around two more times. Y'all go get out of the brass band, come march in the band, and then play this." Or there'd be some certain situation where he gave us our first gigs. And that really taught me how to be professional and really deal with it. Because sometimes he would deal with it and he would send us out there by ourselves and tell us, "Don't mess this up." And I'm like, "alright," because I know I got to come back to school the next day, so I'm not gonna mess it up. That taught us how to go get the gigs, how to show up at a gig, how to do what the people tell you at the gig—just to be professional. Part of us being like how we are now is because of our band directors. That's kind of crazy. That's my first time really realizing. All of the stuff that we've done, it's because of the band directors we had that taught us how—they gave us the music foundation and they taught us how—

DREW:—to conduct ourselves.

VIRGIL: Yeah. To be men, more than anything.

WALTER: And sometimes I feel like our band director, he was a psychic. He could look into the future. I remember one day he used to talk about that affirmative action shit and I was like, "Man, I'm tired of this, man." And he was like, "Mr. Ramsey, what's wrong?" I was like, "I'm bored." That was the worst shit I could have ever said. He was like, "So you're bored are you, God dammit? I remember when you couldn't play 'Mary Had a Little Lamb' on that horn and now since you going to NOCCA *parochial* school. You go to NOCCA. Pop your collar. Just wait till your band members turn on your ass!"

DREW: And he messed up the whole thing and I was like, "You got to be kidding me." All they had to do was one thing to set it off. Somebody would say something and somebody would do something and Doc, for the rest of the morning rehearsal, would talk. A lecture—he gave a lecture. If he started talking, it would be like, "Shit." You have to think about it. You get up at five in the morning, you have to catch two buses. You want to play your horn now. You don't want to just come here for a lecture. Like, I could have stayed at home and caught the bus—I could have been on the bus with all the girls and the regular kids and all the others I want to see. Now I'm here and this motherfucker talking.

AL: Yeah, but I think it that really helped us especially with us being the Stooges and teaching other band members how to do music. And it gave us structure to be able to teach. Because if you look at our history and look at how many people we actually had in the band, it's crazy.

WALTER: We probably had over forty band members.

AL: You can go to anybody band right now and we can pick two people who played with the Stooges before they played with that band. We got to a point where it's like, "You know what? We good at that. We good at showing people how to do this shit, so let's keep going."

✦ ✦ ✦

VIRGIL: Our best times was going into other people's schools; "I'm about to take your house." We loved it. But that whole marching band thing, the rivalry with different marching bands, with the different band directors, they had rivalries amongst each other. Even with Doc at Kennedy and Mr. Hampton at St. Aug and Lloyd Harris at McDonogh 35, even Brimmer and them that was at Fortier, they all had their rivalries, but they were all friends. We saw that. I don't think we consciously saw that. Looking back, we were all friends, but there was time you had to perform. I'm trying to do you something at that time. That was the thing that we took from that. They really taught you the value of being accountable for yourself, being accountable for the things that you do, owning up to your mistakes, and being responsible. Because all of us were in positions of leadership inside the band.

KYLE: You were a drum major right?

VIRGIL: I was a drum major for two years. And all the rest of the cats that played, they were section leaders. And so they had their section leaders. Alfred was a drum major, too. It's not like how it is now. When we would get to a performance—he would say, "Okay, I need you to do x, y, and z." And I would have to take one hundred and fifty of my peers at that age and get them to do that. And so we didn't question it. That kind of set me up for what I'm doing now as far as being a teacher and being a leader. And just leading the kids to do the right thing. Even if I make a mistake, I tell the kids, "I made a mistake and I'm gonna do this." And that shows them that even though you are in a position of leadership, that you can be wrong, but you have to own up to it and correct it and not just hang out there. That was the thing: just being a man, being accountable for yourself. You know, accountable for things that you do. And that's just it.

CHAPTER 2

Where Ya From?

The band, engulfed by throngs of second liners, passes by the old Dryades Library.[1] Way Uptown on the edge of the Tenth Ward, the library is sandwiched between the old Magnolia and Melpomene projects and is just a few blocks lakeside of the former site of the St. Thomas Project.[2] More recently, developers and realtors have rebranded the neighborhood "historic" (as if it could be anything else), calling it "Faubourg Livaudais" after slave owner Jacques François Enoul Livaudais. The way it feels today, that name either has little significance to us or just sweetens the joy of a Sunday afternoon well spent despite it. The music names a proudly Black geography. This is the Tenth Ward.

At the recognition of a tuba line, people throw their sets up: an open five-fingered hand and a middle finger or downward thumb for the Sixth Ward, four and five fingers held aloft for the Ninth Ward, and two wide open hands for the Tenth. New Orleans is divided into many neighborhoods and wards, all of which harbor distinct local identities that are a point of pride for residents. Even among these neighborhood rivalries, there's at least some solidarity in being from either side of the Downtown-Uptown split. The Stooges play a revamped cover of "Life" by R&B duo K-Ci and JoJo (of Jodeci fame), a throwback to 1999, a time when the projects still stood. The Stooges replace the refrain of "Life, life" with "Downtown" and "Uptown" interchangeably, strategically breaking the second line's unity so neighborhood affiliation fuels involvement. The second line follows a social script, and everyone in attendance knows how to participate. The crowd falls in line and fractures almost evenly with one side representing Downtown and the other representing Uptown.

The Stooges' cover of "Life" is just one of many in the brass band catalog that uses neighborhood identity as a launchpad for audience participation. Another is the Stooges original "Where Ya From," in which the city's predominately Black neighborhoods all receive shout-outs. Joining the ranks of bounce songs and barroom hits like Gregory D and Mannie Fresh's "Buck Jump Time" (1989), Ricky B's "Shake It Fo Ya Hood" (1995), or Juvenile's "Nolia Clap" (2004), "Where Ya From" is a ward roll-call song, an ode to the city's neighborhoods that stirs up spirited divisions at any second line and gives everyone a way of belonging.[3] It's a celebration of difference within unity.

> *Where ya from, where ya from, where ya from?*
> *Where ya from, where ya from, where ya from?*
> *Is it Uptown or Downtown?*
> *Where ya from, where ya from, where ya from?*
>
> *Sixth Ward, Seventh Ward, Eighth Ward, Ninth Ward!*
> *That's Downtown!*
> *Third Ward, Tenth Ward, Twelfth Ward, Seventeenth!*
> *That's Uptown!*

The song cycles through a number of chants that mark the Black neighborhoods in the city, including one with shout-outs to the projects and neighborhoods of Uptown:

> *From the Mag to the Melph to the Callio*
> *UPT!*
> *Gert Town, Pigeon Town, Hollygrove!*
> *UPT![4]*
>
> *What goes up, must come down*
> *Way Downtown!*
> *What goes up, must come down*
> *That's gravity, baby!*
>
> *Five plus four and what do ya get?*
> *You get a Ninth Ward, running in your shit![5]*

Few brass bands can get the crowd involved at a second line quite like the Stooges, and they call themselves "the people's band" for a reason. Songs like "Where Ya From" are composed in conjunction with the "sidewalk," the people

An early group photo near the truck stop on Elysian Fields Ave. *Left to right:* Garfield Bogan, Dwayne Williams, Shamarr Allen, Sammy Cyrus, Walter Ramsey, Al Growe, and Ronald Stokes (a.k.a. Uncle Ronnie). Photo courtesy of Garfield Bogan.

that follow alongside the band during neighborhood parades. The sidewalk generates improvised chants and melodies that become the scaffolding for songs built during rehearsals. As Al remembers it, "I think Troy ["Trombone Shorty" Andrews] made this up in the Sixth Ward: 'That Sixth Ward, Seventh Ward, Eighth Ward, Ninth Ward . . .' We heard that, it was like, 'Did anybody wrote something on that?'" From there, the Stooges got together and composed a hit from and *for* the sidewalk.

But the same neighborhood belonging that launched "Where Ya From" and generates belonging at second lines once held the Stooges at arm's length from the brass band tradition. For the Stooges, participation in the brass band community was less a matter of where they *were* from and more of where they *weren't* from.

The Stooges weren't from the Sixth Ward. Also known as the Treme, the Sixth Ward is widely regarded as the musical capital of the city, particularly in regard to the brass band scene. As one of the country's oldest African American neighborhoods, with a deep and rich musical history, few neighborhood affiliations carry a greater sense of pride for residents. The Rebirth, Dirty Dozen,

New Birth, Lil Rascals, Treme, and Soul Rebels brass bands are all from the Sixth Ward, the offspring of a brass band history including longstanding bands the Olympia, Eureka, Tuxedo, and Onward, to name a few.[6]

The members of Rebirth, in their typical fashion, were supportive of the Stooges. They gave Walter the inspiration to start the band in the first place and offered them their first gigs. But there were many other musicians in the Sixth Ward who weren't so welcoming. When the Hot 8 Brass Band and the Stooges entered the game in the mid-1990s, they were met with resistance from many of the older Sixth Ward musicians, who denied them learning opportunities. The original Stooges lineup came mostly from the Ninth Ward, and their encroachment on Sixth Ward cultural turf wasn't always welcome—ditto for the Hot 8, who hailed from various Uptown neighborhoods. To make inroads in the Sixth Ward, the Stooges snatched up some of the Treme's youngest talents, bringing in Troy Andrews (a.k.a. Trombone Shorty), Dwayne Williams (a.k.a. Big D), and Sammy Cyrus (a.k.a. Lil Sammy), all of whom would have otherwise joined Sixth Ward bands. Years later, they would also bring in Sixth Ward trumpet player Chad Honore, who now plays with Rebirth. Bringing young Sixth Ward musicians into the band was mutually beneficial. Though the Sixth Ward was rich in community, it was far from rich in any material sense. Years of governmental disinvestment and redlining had negatively affected the material conditions of its residents. The predictable products of structural violence—drug abuse, interpersonal violence, crime—took their toll on residents. "Musician cats at the time, they would die," Walter bemoaned. "And I was like, 'Man, I have to set an example.' I got the *young* Sixth Ward cats in my band, and even though they see this every day, I want to show them a different life." Walter focused on developing his business acumen as one avenue to material wealth for him and the kids coming under him. "They parents saw what was going on in the Sixth Ward and they didn't want them to be a part of that, but they knew their kids wanted to play music. So they was like, 'They need to play with y'all.'" The Stooges' maxim was less *if you can't beat 'em, join 'em*, and more *if you can't beat 'em, have 'em join you.*

✦ ✦ ✦

CHAD: Let me explain it to you right here. Sixth Ward, they call it like that because everybody in the Sixth Ward is family. No matter where you from— and I come from cousins fucking cousins and aunties fucking uncles. I'm telling you, I'ma be real with you. But it's like a *family*. Everybody's cousins. We got Walter here from the Seventh Ward wants to come to the Sixth Ward. Know you're not easily accepted because you ain't family. You didn't grow up around here. Well, we show that. We show that we family. All I got to do is be like, "Yeah, I'm from the Sixth Ward." "You're from the Sixth Ward? I'm from the Sixth Ward, too!" And it's all love. It's not that we look down at nobody else, it's just that that's a family thing over there and a lot of people want to be involved in that family.

KYLE: And there's like some cultural capital to it.

CHAD: And it's the cultural capital because we got the best musicians! Simple. Straightforward. We got the best musicians coming out the Sixth Ward. I'm not saying that we're better than everybody else; it's just that as a family, we push everybody. Trombone Shorty, Travis "Trumpet Black" Hill, they pushed me. Because we all family, you dig? It's different if you from Uptown or you from the Ninth Ward or Seventh Ward or Eighth Ward and you want to come and be down. You can come and hang and be in the club, but if anything going down, you roll with your family. *That's* love. And that's law still to this day. That's my boys, but that's my *family*. You dig? Like I told the Stooges a lot of times, "I cleared a lot of ways for y'all to even come and perform in the Sixth Ward because I was in the band." The Sixth Ward already got they band: it's the New Birth and the Rebirth, done.

KYLE: Yeah, there's no one else coming in—

CHAD: And if it wasn't for certain motherfuckers like me and Troy coming to play with y'all, some of that shit wouldn't even have happened for y'all. It's another thing when you have to humble themselves. It's okay to feel like you're the street kings. But at the same time, you ain't breaking barriers. Rebirth broke *barriers* for brass band, period. And that's what I be trying to explain to them. It's not that we better than them or they better than us, it's all in the work and the effort that you put into making brass band itself bigger than what it is.

✦   ✦   ✦

WALTER: The uniqueness of my life is my mom from Downtown New Orleans and my dad from Uptown New Orleans, so I grew up being a *New Orleans* kid. I didn't represent a ward. Most of the guys was like, "Man, I'm from the Ninth Ward." Man, I'm from the Ninth Ward. I'm from the Seventh Ward, the Eighth Ward. I *know* I'm not from the Sixth Ward because obviously they make sure I'm not from the Sixth Ward—which is nothing wrong with that. When I used to try to play when I was young, they used to have the band on the street and they used to tell me to go play on the sidewalk with my horn. I used to be feeling like, "Aww, man. Why do me that?" And they meant you got to be from the Sixth Ward, those musicians.

KYLE: They were serious.

WALTER: Yeah, they were serious. And part of me look at them and it was like, "This is the craziest shit ever. And when we get popular, we not gonna do people that." That's probably why we became a institute, because we allow people to come in. They wasn't allowing people to play music, and I understand now. They was trying to protect it, and they had their reasons. But I'm not like that. Like, "Man, you want to come play music? Come join us. Yeah, just come." It's crazy.

And that's what started our growing up controversy. I remember our first year ever playing Krewe du Vieux. We were so excited to be in a brass band parade. "Oh my God, we in the Krewe du Vieux!" This is huge for us as a band. We played, we not that good, we trying. But we get to the end of the parade and I can remember this. It was like, "Man, we tired of y'all coming around here trying to learn how to play our music!" And they just swamped us. Now, we teenagers. We eighteen, nineteen years old, we just fresh probably out of high school. We not thinking we doing them wrong. "We feel like y'all undercutting, y'all underbidding our gigs!" Man! They attacked us so hard, it was like the Sixth Ward against the Stooges. And I was kind of looking at the Hot 8—because you know, they're a little older than us—I was looking at them like, "Man, help us! Tell them something!" I swear to God, they had them Hot 8 black hoodies with they little Hot 8 logo on them. They had just got that new logo. They was looking super cool and not getting into our controversy.

KYLE: You're just there left to fend for yourselves—and you also look up to these guys, too, right?

WALTER: Yes! These are the people who inspired us to play. We was just like, "Wow!" And they was just talking down to us, cursing at us, and I remember Ellis Joseph, he took his drum off and shook his head. He was like, "Man, they right. We got to bow down to them." And I was like, "Man, no! I ain't bowing down to no one! You don't have the right to come tell us nothing!" So I jumped on top of a car, and I don't even know who car it was. I was like, "Look, I ain't got time for this. If y'all don't like us, then go to the street right here. I'll beat all y'all up! I ain't got time for none of this, fussing at us telling us what we ain't doing." I stood on top of the car and they was lined up across the wall. They getting all hyped, a person pushing them back. It was like the beginning of the first controversy. We about to fight. I was like, "Look, I promise all y'all, I'm gonna put *all y'all* out of business. I promise." I pointed at them, too. And I was a little short kid with this big old lion roar like, "I'ma put all y'all out of business. Y'all gonna all have to come see me for gigs. I promise y'all that. And if you say anything else, you can step in the street, we can fight, but I promise all y'all, y'all gonna need me for gigs." So they just looked at me like, "Whatever. Y'all just need to go back and do some other stuff. Don't play our music." So we walked off. It was just a walk-off type thing, but I knew. You know, that was my goal to put all y'all out of business. And I ate, slept, studied that, and breathed that—my words. From that day forward, my grandfather used to bring VHS tapes of brass bands playing at parades. I studied everything they did. I studied every last one of them as a musician. I knew what they was good at, I knew what they was bad at. I studied this so hard, they don't even know. I took on this like it was a game and I had to win. And then we was trained because we went to NOCCA. So our musicianship is already better than yours.

✦ ✦ ✦

GARFIELD: It wasn't that we was from the Ninth Ward, it's just that we wasn't from the Sixth Ward, and they feel like in order to play music—*this* music—you have to pay some type of dues. You have to either go through the French Quarters or you have to be part of the Andrews family or something. And it wasn't hard. You just had to know certain people, be in certain areas. We were taken as a joke, first. So we put that chip on our shoulder, like, "Hold up. This what we want and ain't nobody gonna stop us, so ready or not, here we come." We dressing alike, we having practice every day. We became the people's band. It started to be like, "Y'all worrying about us when we worrying about the people. We know once we have the people, y'all wouldn't be able to stand. So it came Rebirth, Rascals, New Birth—the only people that liked us from a distance—almost—was the Soul Rebels. When we were coming up at the time, you didn't have forty brass bands. You had maybe no more than twenty. Half of them were traditional brass bands. The rest of them, like street bands, were Dirty Dozen, Rascals, the Hot 8, the Stooges, the Rebirth, the New Birth. You can name them. Now, you'd really be looking into space and trying to pull them down. Like, okay, you have "the Most This" and "the Little That."

✦ ✦ ✦

J'MAR: You have guys from the Sixth Ward that feel that everything actually started in the Sixth Ward. Then you have a group of guys that's from different parts of the city that's just as good as y'all. So that was a problem with some of the guys back then. But I was cool with some of the guys from the Hot 8 when they started. I been knowing them all my life. It was always kind

Garfield playing snare outside Walter's childhood home at 2024 N. Villere. Photo courtesy of Garfield Bogan.

of like a challenge. And we had our problems with some of the guys from the Sixth Ward. They didn't like the fact that we was an upcoming band at the time. And Rebirth was our mentor and a lot of the guys didn't like that. And we had some problems with that in the beginning, but eventually they got over and realized that, "Alright, these guys are kind of like the real deal."

KYLE: Right. And Phil and Kermit and those guys kind of gave you some opportunities early on, too, right?

J'MAR: Yeah, Kermit. Rebirth actually gave us—especially the Stooges—they really opened up the platform for us, man. They gave us gigs that they couldn't play at the time. And people were still looking for Rebirth. They gave us a chance to play for their anniversary, so they kept us around and they really opened the door as far as letting people know about us. So I have to give props to the Rebirth because they was always pushing us more than we were pushing ourselves.

✦   ✦   ✦

ELLIS: They always thought that we was too much. That's what everybody was saying: "Y'all think y'all too much." They wouldn't use the word conceited. They'd say, "Y'all think y'all too much."

JOHN C.: "Y'all just got here. We been doing this." So what? What does that mean? We don't give a shit about that. We gonna show y'all better than we can tell y'all. And that is what we got from everybody. So many people thought we were arrogant back in the days. We would be the band that get up on a Saturday morning to go to the French Quarter, everybody would run us. "Y'all can't play out here! I been out here!" "What the fuck you mean, 'We too loud'? I got to lower my levels so you can be heard over there?"

KYLE: "You play louder."

JOHN C.: Yeah. "Bring *your* volume up!" It was just a group of kids from all over New Orleans. And that's the other side of it: I don't think nobody was out the Sixth Ward.

KYLE: Right. But then they got Lil Sam and Big D and Troy.

JOHN C.: Yeah, well that's after Ellis and them left out the band. Sam and Wayne was at the end of my days. Sam and Wayne used to be at my house every day. And I really pulled them under my wing because I had played with them so long and hung out with Ellis and J'mar that I *had* to get with them so we could rehearse and practice and become cohesive for what the music needed outside of just gigging. So they was hanging with me. "Man, we coming with you." And then their parents—I was married—their moms was like, "They can go by you because you married and you doing the right thing." "Alright, well come on. I'm gonna smoke a bunch of weed when I get home, but if you think I'm doing the right thing, come on. I'm gonna make sure they eat and they gonna take a bath and clean up and all that." But it was really just giving a thousand percent. I think that's what really made the Stooges push and push and push and push. And just not really caring what people thought. We were ridiculed about everything. Every move you make, "Oh, you're playing that song wrong. Oh, you got to tie your shoes like this." Come on, man, what are you talking about?

ELLIS: And some of those things still follow us today. People know us from being in the Stooges and they'll try and critique you and watch your every move, and just basically be on your ass about stuff. Everybody used to mess with Walter about his playing style and how he played. They still look at Walter and be like, "Boy, you sad, bitch." Or say something like that. And I just know that that's buried hate that people have for us from way back then because they followed it.

Garfield with Sammy Cyrus (snare drum) on a gig. Sammy wears a "6th Ward" dog tag. Walter is in the background with his trombone. Photo courtesy of Garfield Bogan.

KYLE: And does that have to do with them seeing your success or branching out into other areas where other brass bands haven't?

ELLIS: I would think so—and also because we were so young at the time. We were fearless. And that's the aura we have about ourselves even now to this day. The hate is like confused admiration. They like us and they see us and they used to want to be basically like us. I don't care if they were older than us or not. I still think they used to want to do the things we did, and they were upset because they weren't doing it.

✦ ✦ ✦

AL: Another thing that we did was we infiltrated. One time we had Ellis, they let Ellis go. And then they had J'mar and let J'mar go. Like, "Man, we need a drum set. We need to figure out where we can get a drum set from." These two little fucking boys in the Sixth Ward—the baddest two motherfuckers in the Sixth Ward. Little bitty boys going to play gigs. It was like, "You know what, let's go meet their mamas and shit, get cool with them, bring them under our wings."

WALTER: But it was smart because that's the next group of cats that was supposed to join the Sixth Ward bands and we took them all. And we went for Troy. Bam, we got Troy, too. We would have got Travis "Trumpet Black"

Hill, too, but he was a gangster at that time and he winded up going to jail.
So we was smart.

✦ ✦ ✦

WALTER: Some of the younger kids gravitated toward us because some
of them didn't have fathers. Man, it was like a big-brother type situation. I
remember we got Chad Honore, we got Dwayne Williams and Sam Cyrus,
we got them when they was like twelve or thirteen. Now don't get me wrong,
they had they parents, but they was—I ain't gonna say struggling, we all was
struggling!—but they parents looked at us like, "If I had to choose my kid
going to play with y'all or play with these other people, I choose y'all."

DREW: Same thing with Big Sam Williams. Big Sam was already six feet
tall at fifteen years old. He had no problem getting into the clubs to play the
gigs. He looked like a grown-ass man back then. But the thing was his mom
was very, very protective of him, so she literally would tell us, "My son is not
going to play with nobody else but y'all because I don't want my son anywhere other than"—you know?

AL: And Dwayne mama used to always call us up—me, John, all us. "He
acting up, come get him."

WALTER: Yeah, even when we was in school, I had guardianship and I'm
nineteen years old, but I'm going to his schools and making sure they principals know to go discipline him. His Dad and his Mom are living! He'd be
in trouble, the principal stop calling they parents and they would call the
phone, "Look, such-and-such is cutting up in school, I need you to come in."

AL: It was for Dwayne and Sammy.

WALTER: And the same thing with Troy, but what's great about Troy's
situation is that he had this lady take him in that was able to give him a different environment, because when he was playing with us, they parents saw
what was going on in the Sixth Ward and they didn't want them to be a part
of that, but they knew their kids wanted to play music. So they was like,
"They need to play with y'all."

AL: Right. And what people liked about us the most was we wasn't on
drugs. That's the main thing. None of us was on drugs.

✦ ✦ ✦

WALTER: I'm maybe six, seven years older than Troy. I think six alto-
gether. But he's like my little brother. Like, when I say my little brother, him,
a guy named Big D, and a kid named Lil Sam. They all men now.

Garfield Bogan, Sammy Cyrus, and Wendell "Cumberbund" Stewart wearing their
Lil Stooges shirts in front of a stretch limo. Photo courtesy of Garfield Bogan.

KYLE: Who does Big D play with?

WALTER: Big D, he play the bass drum, but he don't play no more. He play,
but sometimes he play with the Rebels, he still out here, but he live in Houston. And he played percussion in Troy band. But he and Lil Sam and Troy
and Trumpet Black, those guys grew up together on the block. Like, when
we was—

KYLE: But they're all Sixth Ward guys.

WALTER: Yeah, yeah, they all Sixth Ward guys. So they grew up together
listening to their older cousins and their brothers playing music. And when
we started playing music at the time, they was playing music, too. Now, mind
you, we was in high school—they was like in elementary school, but they
could play! Like, what the fuck, they could really play! I looked at it like,
"Man, these guys gonna be great one day." But the older cats that we look up
to, they was great musicians, they wasn't *business* musicians. But they had

great music. The Lil Rascals was one of my favorite bands and they had all killing musicians and they could do some stuff together.

KYLE: Yeah, their album is awesome.

WALTER: Right. And all these bands—they was doing good, they was getting gigs and making money. Not knocking none of them, but it was like, no business sense to this. And so I was like, "Man, when we do this, we gonna *do* this." The Stooges sound alright, but we was missing stuff. And what we were missing was the soul, because that soul come out the Sixth Ward. We was like, "The older guys ain't gonna come play with us." So then we picked up the younger kids and now they're like twelve, thirteen at the time. They in junior high school.

KYLE: And you were like, sixteen, seventeen?

WALTER: Yeah, so we like sixteen, seventeen years old at that time. We picking them up and they have the soul because this all they do is listen to their older brothers and cousin play. Like, *all* they do. And then they take and go beat on boxes in the French Quarters or go around the block. But now they at the age when they got drums and instruments now, so they really could play. So our bass drummers and snare drummers started going to college now. We at eighteen now. So they're going to college or whatever. We pick up on these kids to keep the gigs going. And so they come join the Stooges and become like our little bitty brothers. They parents saw that I was a little educated and smart about business and stuff like that and saw that I had the best interest of their kids because I used to make their parents sign a contract just for them to play. Like, "Hey, you gonna sign a contract for your son to be in the band for this amount of time and I'ma make sure I pay your son this amount of money." And everything would be good. So now these kids at thirteen, fourteen years old making money. Like, they really making money where they can really pay they parents, take care of they parents' household because they're making more money. I'm raising them as little brothers so I'm teaching them about everything—life, cars, women, everything. So each one of them—Trombone Shorty, Big D—I bought them their first cars, made sure they got to school. And Troy was blessed to get picked up by a lady named Susan Scott, which started managing them at a young age, got him into Gregory Junior High, and took him out of that neighborhood—like, the Sixth Ward neighborhood—and all of the poverty neighborhoods we grew up in.

KYLE: I mean, it's a hell of a lot different now.

WALTER: Yeah, it is. It totally is gentrified. It's totally changed. So she took him out of that environment and put him in really a rich environment. Her dad was a Black journalist who sat in four president cabinets. You

A weathered photograph shows the Stooges playing at a 9 Times second line in the late 1990s. Photo courtesy of Garfield Bogan.

see what I'm saying? So he went from seeing the life of, "Cool, this is what I grew up in," and to now, "Oh, I have my own room, I have a flat-screen TV, I can learn, I can go to a better school." And so she put him in a better environment.

KYLE: Okay, so how did that happen?

WALTER: Well, I'm not sure. She talked to his parents about it and they just—

KYLE: And they saw him play or something?

WALTER: Well yeah, she saw that he had talent, and she wanted to develop his talent. And so she took him out that environment, got him in good schools. He went from Gregory to Warren Easton. He living in a mansion, got his own room. And so it was cool. And then they looked at me like, "Well, you the beginning stage of a young man and you look like you got your business sense together and you taking care of your responsibility." I used to come over there, they gave me my own room. Man, it was like a door like this. It look like it's a part of a wall, you open the door, it's a room with a bathroom, everything. But when you shut the door, it's got pictures on it, you'd never know it was a room. It was like a hidden room. They gave me my own room there. And that's how I look at life. I grew up with Troy and all those guys like brothers, not knowing that we building a brotherhood.

KYLE: Not at the time.

WALTER: Yeah. We just like, "Alright, cool. So this my little brother, I'ma make sure you get this car, I'ma help you with the money for this car, or whatever. And then I'ma buy Dwayne this car." You know, and different things like that. And make sure you go to high school and all y'all in high school, sixteen years old. And I might be twenty-one or something like that, but y'all have y'all cars and y'all have this, and I'm teaching responsibility, insurance, everything. I developed them into men, and they looked at me as a big brother who does the business. I remember when Troy first got into NOCCA and he was having a hard time reading the music or whatever. Now, this his first month in NOCCA or whatever. I went there to help him do this. Shit, I come back the second month, he teaching me! I'm like, "Oh my God!" He caught on so fast and he teaching me stuff! "Oh, no. You got to do this." And I went to NOCCA, so I'm like, "Yeah, I know this. But, hold up, what they teaching *you*?"

KYLE: And so was there a different teacher by the time he got there?

WALTER: Yeah, yeah. It was different teachers.

KYLE: Oh, okay. Who was the teacher?

WALTER: My teacher was Clyde Kerr Jr., and by the time Troy got there, I think he had one year with Clyde Kerr and then they went to switching teachers and then they went to a new location.

KYLE: And where was NOCCA located when you went there?

WALTER: It was Uptown, Perrier Street, off of State. Down the street from Tulane. And so me watching him grow and to develop into this great genius trombone player today, it's like, "Wow." He always had the street skills in him, but when he took the street skills and got with NOCCA and got like the music structure of it, he exploded. He took that and ran with it and developed those guys that was going to NOCCA with him and he started Orleans Avenue. And I'm proud to say I watched him do this as a little brother. Seeing him grow up into the artist he is today, man, like, I'm so proud of Troy. And the humbleness that he have today with all his success: his humbleness is unbelievable. And even today! Even when he was calling and dealing with all his business and all the structures—even though he got managers and he got all that now—he still called me and be like, "Alright, what I should do with this? Think about this, or let me show you this." So I've been a mentor to him and a big brother to him and vice versa. He helped me on certain things I needed to know about, too.

CHAPTER 3

The Process

At the end of Tulane Avenue—a busy thoroughfare dotted with hourly motels, a couple of hipster bars, and a major development—the Fontainebleau apartment building rises eight stories into the air. A motorized gate at the rear of the building allows entry with the pressing of a five-digit code. Past a parking lot filled with vehicles, boats, and tour vans, an elevator in a cigarette-scented entryway takes you up to the eighth floor. The code-locked door to Livin Swell Recording Studios opens up to a reception desk and framed gold and platinum records by artists on No Limit Records, including Silkk the Shocker, Master P, Fiend, Mia X, and Young Bleed. The interior is red and black with hardwood-framed windows and doors, a large mixing console with a couple of screens, and all the bells and whistles you'd expect in a professional studio.

The Stooges own much of the eighth-floor space and most of the first floor as well. Downstairs, they have a rec room complete with pool table, flat-screen, fridge, couches, and Walter's 2014 Mardi Gras Indian suit. Adjacent to it, the "stage hall" is a large rehearsal space with drum risers and an isolated sound booth. Several rooms act as rehearsal spaces and offices for other bands. Another room houses a screen-printing press and all the supplies needed for bands to print their own shirts. Two other massive rooms currently store heaps of damaged instruments, which were purchased in bulk. These rooms will eventually become a photography studio and instrument repair shop and retail store. Long in the making, the Livin Swell compound is part of the band's vision of creating a self-sustaining communal enterprise.

From the beginning, the Stooges sought economic empowerment through their love of music and ambitiously worked within the wildly uneven economic terrain of capitalism to offer their families comfort and build generational wealth. Whereas Drew was tasked with learning the musical ins and outs, Walter, a self-professed "*48 Laws of Power* guy," ambitiously learned about contracts, licensing, investing, and various facets of the music business.[1] They wanted to build up a community of skilled and professional musicians

To better understand the Stooges' capitalistic ambitions, it's useful to contextualize their coming of age in the political landscape of mid-nineties New Orleans. Racist rhetorics about the crack epidemic, cultures of poverty, and Black criminality pervaded the national media. The period was characterized by an eroding social safety net, disinvestment in communities of color, racially disparate drug laws, police violence, and political corruption. As John Cannon related to me, "When you start talking about the streets of New Orleans back when I grew up in the nineties, the crack epidemic was horrible. And, I mean, it's not any better now, but 90 percent of the police department was the drug dealers back then." In 1996, the same year the Stooges were founded, Bill Clinton signed into law the Personal Responsibility and Work Opportunity Reconciliation Act (PRWORA), the policy decision that best exemplified the United States' insistence on a bootstrapping narrative for the poor and working class. With the swipe of a pen, the law effectively ended welfare and placed the blame of poverty on a conservative narrative of a culture of laziness, which was linked in the white imagination to the failure of the Black family rather than policy decisions that sought to further inequality and prevent social mobility.[2] The 1990s saw the war on poverty transition fully into a war on the poor. As Walter put it, "We was *all* struggling."

The myth of a welfare crisis took aim at the nuclear Black family and demonized single, low-income mothers of color.[3] Put forth most prominently by Reagan in the preceding decade, the harmful and overdetermining stereotype of the single "welfare queen" was applied to Black women across the country in dominant media narratives.[4] As a report by New Orleans's Institute for Women and Ethnic Studies notes, the stereotype depicts Black women as "lazy, having multiple children and draining the economic system by utilizing resources generated by working people."[5] This stereotype didn't exist in isolation, extending to the Black family more generally and the idea of the absentee father, a controlling image that was only further exacerbated by the unjust incarceration of Black men in New Orleans and around the country.[6] In our first group interview, Al summarized one of the predominate stereotypes of Black men most succinctly: "We're not *supposed* to take care of our kids."

The stereotype of the absentee Black father links race, class, and gender. Being not only a musician, but a *brass band* musician, implies working-class status,

The Lil Stooges playing an event on N. Rampart Street for the Corinthian First Baptist Church, of which Walter's grandmother, Mrs. Ruby Ramsey, is a member. *Left to right:* Andrew Baham, Brian Gerdes, and Walter Ramsey. Photo courtesy of Ashton Ramsey.

and with it, stereotypes the Stooges have attempted to combat. As the Stooges entered into adulthood and began starting their own families, the weight of these stereotypes hung heavy. Nancy E. Dowd notes that "the most critical way of proving one's masculinity is by being an economic provider, and it is precisely in that respect that Black men are denied the means to be men in traditional terms."[7] By honing their business chops, the Stooges sought to provide for their loved ones and combat those stereotypes, which were (and continue to be) held by many white New Orleanians and some in the Black middle class. They aimed to produce generational wealth, acquire residual income for their families, and build a community of musicians that could do the same.

I don't, however, want to boil down the Stooges' motivations to some kind of economic determinism: every band member loves what they do and, while they're capable of playing music in many genres, they proudly choose to play brass band music. "I think a majority of us just had a true love for the music," John Cannon reflectively told me. "I watch some of the comments on some of the social media now, and some of the brass bands having arguments about finance. And when we look back to what we got paid back then, it was *never* about the money. . . . That was a labor of love." The question facing the Stooges in the early days was how to transform a love of music into a viable career. The answer to that question came largely by way of Walter, whose ambition was expansive enough to include everyone in his orbit. In a job market that was increasingly defined by low-wage service work, a job you love provides a step up and the possibility of socioeconomic mobility.[8]

As the band has grown, they've expanded their influence well beyond the streets of New Orleans. They've been featured in *XXL*, hip-hop's premiere magazine, and they've extended their reach to produce music for major television networks, including CBS, ESPN, and BET.[9] Their music has also been licensed to a number of television shows and films, and they've appeared in more than a few music videos.[10] But these diverse musical credentials and the modicum of economic security they afford required the endurance of years of toil and hard work playing for as little as fifteen dollars a day. As the Stooges note, even with the sacrifices they've made, an escape from the hustle is anything but guaranteed, requiring constant work and perhaps a few lucky breaks. In the brass band game, sometimes you just have to trust the process.[11]

✦ ✦ ✦

WALTER: One thing I think the Stooges brought to the game was business. Before there was Stooges, this was just a hustle. Most of them guys had jobs, and it worked like that; it was a hustle. I remember when I came and I was like, "Man, look, we going to pay out in a check." Man, those dudes laughed at us for months. No band ever did that. No band was ever incorporated until 2000. You go look at Rebirth orders of incorporation, they got incorporated in 2002 or something like that. They didn't have no sense of business—not knocking them. They was good, but we brought that to the game, too. And I guess that's what made younger cats gravitate towards us. We had role models to look at because, at that time, we started looking up to like the Soul Rebels. It was like, "Damn, they playing some good music." And they was like, "Fuck the streets, fuck the Sixth Ward." They was the first band kicked out the Sixth Ward.

Andrew was always like, "Man, I'm gonna take care of music." And then he handed me a music business book and he was like, "You learn the business." Even with doing our first recording when we was still in high school, people would be out to get you and we ain't know nothing. They give us a bogus contract for $4,000, and so Andrew was always like, "Man, I can always take care of the music, you just start getting into the music business, but here. Read it and give it to me. We'll discuss certain things about the book." We started reading these books, so we was very educated on music business just as well as music, because NOCCA don't teach us music business.¹² We knew that. When you joined the Stooges, you had to sign a contract to get in the band.

AL: That stupid contract. I don't know whatever happened to my contract. It was a year contract.

WALTER: Yeah, every year you got to renew it!

AL: That stupid-ass shit. I look at that right there, that stupid-ass contract. I signed that stupid shit. Why the fuck I got to sign a contract to get a fucking thirty-minute gig? And then we wouldn't get paid with twenty dollars! So I'm about to sign a contract to play for a twenty-dollar gig. What the fuck, man?

WALTER: Oh boy! You talking about funny!

AL: What the fuck am I doing, man?

DREW: Those were some hard times, man, where we would just play—

AL: Can you imagine that? Twenty dollars! We would play thirty minutes, drove all across the river, and got paid twenty fucking dollars.

DREW: Any given Saturday, our day would start around 10:00 a.m. Every Saturday, I can guarantee it. We'd do a funeral, followed by a repast, followed by a early birthday party, and then a early wedding is done and then we do another party.

AL: All throughout the night.

DREW: Yeah. And then next thing you know, you done ten gigs in one night and you just fucking pooped. You done ten sets.

WALTER: It used to be crazy because we was about music business so we had these contracts and then we wind up incorporated and stuff like that and then, the checks, it was like, "Man, you paying us in checks. It's not even enough money!"

AL: No, no. Before the checks we decided, "Man, we can't get in touch with all these band members at one time." Man, that was the time that Nextel came out with the chirp phones. We were like, "Man, that'd be nice if all of us can have one of them chirp phones." We decided as a band to go get the Nextel phones. And look, the Nextel thing was going to be a good thing until Walter's cousin decide he want to call Tokyo.

WALTER: And then once we did it, the Hot 8 got onto it. So now we got turf with the Hot 8, too, because now they got a contract for they band. We always was the innovators of doing stuff. We like the first iPhone. We gonna get criticized. "Y'all not supposed to be doing this. Y'all ain't that. Who told y'all y'all could do that?" We never asked permission for nothing. Nobody don't tell us what to do, we just do it. And that's what made us. And then we was just brothers because we always be around each other. And then once we started really becoming family, we *really* family now. Because now my kid's his godchild, he married my cousin, his kid's his godchild, Trombone

Shorty's son is my godchild, which is my cousin baby. So now we in this motherfucker. If we didn't like each other, we still gonna see each other because we family! And it grew to this big brotherhood thing. Like, even the cats that's not playing with us right now, they still alumnis, or brothers, or they part of us.

✦ ✦ ✦

WALTER: I realized the other brass bands wasn't very good at business, and that's why I was like, "Man, that's why we losing as a whole. We're not smart at business, and I have to make us smart at business." I took on that challenge and I just went for it. That's how it was. And then tragic things started happening for some of the bands. The Rascals were going through so much tragedy from losing band members, so they wasn't no more competition for us. And then the New Birth, they was alright. They had some songs. We would take they songs and probably help make them hits.

But then the Sixth Ward bands started dying. And then at one point, it was like 2002, 2003. And now it's just three of us bands. They was musicians and they lived that life. They did the women, the sex, the drugs. They lived the rockstar life. And I don't knock them, because I learned a lot from them, but it was just that I wanted a clean-cut band and I used to be hard on my musicians about that. I mean, the most they were doing was smoking weed until Arian and Joe, they wanted to be accepted into that Sixth Ward and that's how they got into heroin and all that shit. Because they wanted to be accepted. I didn't give a damn about being accepted into the Sixth Ward musicians.

KYLE: Well they're not going to accept you anyway.

WALTER: Right. I don't really care. But I wanted my band to be clean-cut. And that's where it started going bad for Joe and them. The musicians would be like, "Man, you could play better if you took some of this." And it was like, "Fuck." So with Joe and Arian, we wind up putting Arian out of the band. And we fired Joe, too. And then Joe went and started playing with the Hot 8 and shit like that. I didn't want nobody using drugs in the band. I was strong about that. I didn't care. I was like, "Man, I want us to try to become millionaires off of this." I used to always preach that to them. And some of them older than me!

Some of those guys was dying from OD'ing. A few of the Rascals players, they checked out from OD'ing. All them Sixth Ward musician cats. And I'm not just gonna say Sixth Ward, but it was just musician cats at the time, they would die. I was like, "Man, I have to set an example." I got the *young*

Sixth Ward cats in my band and even though they see this every day, I want
to show them a different life, so even though I'm not that much older than
them, I still want to show them something different. So that was my goal
to not be on drugs. So we started having a clean band, we started getting
more musicians. I ain't gonna lie, I looked up to the Sixth Ward musicians,
but I also saw that, as a brass band, we wasn't taking care of business. And
that's what I wanted: an infrastructure in all the bands. Let's learn how to
do music business, rather than just let everybody else speak on our behalf.
That's something that I fought with for years. They looked at me like, "Would
you *please* stop it with the checks every week? Can you *please* stop trying
to bring contracts around this? Oh my God, little Ramsey, just go sit down
somewhere." That's how they used to be. They would be frustrated with me,
but I was steady trying to push the issue. Even today, now everything's looking more business-orientated. I'd like to say I'm one of the pioneers of that.
I'm not the only person that did it, but I know that I'm probably *the* person
that kind of pushed the envelope.

✦ ✦ ✦

VIRGIL: Unfortunately, some musicians, or some street musicians, or
some musicians that play brass band, they may do some things in the street
that may be perceived as being incorrigible—some bad behavior. It kind
of like demeans the value of a musician. Even, pretty much the brass band
players. They look at us like we're not really trained musicians. And so if
you look at all of us that's here, when I say trained musicians, I'm twofold:
trained musicians and upstanding citizens.

KYLE: Okay, so these things go hand in hand. Like, the genre of music and
how you're perceived to be as a human—just as a person.

VIRGIL: Yes, a person. And so we try to break those myths that they have
about us, but every time, it rears that ugly head. Sometimes people look at
those street performers—when they're on the street and they're playing—as
being panhandlers, like they're just playing music for money, they can't read
music, they haven't been trained, they just picked up a horn, they play by
ear, they don't know anything about theory, they don't know anything about
music in general, or history—anything. That's so far from the truth with our
band. And then even on the citizenship side of our band, a majority of us
are straight-up family-oriented men. We have families, we have wives, we do
things outside of music. And we're good people to people. Sometimes that's
not how they look. I have all of these degrees, teach in school. I used to teach
music, and now I teach science. I'm certified in the sciences. Guess what?

If I say I play in a brass band, some people will stand and look at you like, "What?" Or they'll say, "Well why you do that?" I'm like, "'Cause. Why not? That's what I can do." But they'll start saying "those people."

KYLE: And "those people" is racist.

VIRGIL: And sometimes musicians do propagate the things that they may say. It might be the drug usage, or the drinking, or it might be profanity or something like that. They're *people* and they still play music. And what they don't understand is how this music came about, which is very important to this city's culture, is that you had to learn in the street. You had to go to Jackson Square and learn how to play this music. You had to go listen. You're not going to get it on a CD, you're not going to get it reading a sheet of paper. You *have* to do it.

KYLE: It's that feel. It's that street sort of feel.

VIRGIL: Yeah. I can write every head or every chord that goes for any traditional brass band song, but if you don't have a feel for it, those notes don't mean nothing. You can play them, but if they don't have that feel that you need to have that comes from New Orleans, that comes from those people that played in the street, those older musicians that taught you how to play traditions and taught you how to play the music, then it means nothing.

✦ ✦ ✦

VIRGIL: We was like the cleanest-cut version of a brass band that you could get at that time.

AL: Right. You know what I'm saying. I'm not trying to knock none of the cats, but a lot of the bands had drug addicts in them.

DREW: I mean, it's almost the stereotypical—

VIRGIL: For a musician, period.

WALTER: That what we used to tell the street musicians, like, "Man, look. We can play this, but you have no clue. You don't know how to play this. We can play this, too." You see what I'm saying? So, like, we can play jazz and we understand it, and that's why we was able to take it and put a structure to the street music. They didn't know what they was doing. They just playing it because they hearing it. You know? They hearing it, they feeling it. We was able to tell them—even the older cats—"Oh, this is what you playing. That's a F-minor 7." "That's—what the fuck? What?" You know? We able to say that. Us and maybe the Soul Rebels are probably the only brass bands that was able to do that. And then we started teaching all the younger kids, like, "Alright, learn music theory, too." Like, "What you playing? Why you playing this like that?"

John Cannon (tuba) playing with the Stooges. Judging by the Larry Bagneris election sign in the background, this was likely circa 1998. Photo courtesy of John Cannon.

VIRGIL: Even with the stereotypes, the biggest problem I have is being a teacher and playing in a brass band. That's like the—people just they feel like I'm not supposed to do that. That's a big thing I have to fight with my profession—that they feel like I shouldn't be doing that. And so in some respects they're correct for assuming that because of what they've seen outside of us. But that's the biggest stereotype, that I shouldn't be doing this. "You're around the wrong type people." Who is to judge who we are around, who we friends of? There's a lot of stereotypical things about them that I try to tell the young cats that's out there, "This is what they think of you, so don't give them that perception of who you are as a musician." There's a band out there that plays black and white gigs and they're not good, but they're respected and they are drug addicts.[13] Partly because they present themselves in a certain way, they will look at the little young cats that's on the corner playing for tips as if they are hoodlums when a lot of them are not. But the one's that's playing, before they even hear you, their perception of you as if you don't know music, you're not educated, you have no sense of what's going on in the world. "You're on drugs. You're not going to really amount to being anything." You know, because their biggest thing with me is that, "How do you have a degree and you still play brass band music?" Like, "Yeah, that's what I choose to do." "Well you must not know how to play music that much." "No." And then when I start playing, "Oh, you really do know how to play." "Yeah. I just *choose* to do this." And so I think that a lot of us—a lot of the perception that you have of musicians in New Orleans, we're the complete antithesis of what people think of us as being musicians, even down to us having families that we deal with.

AL: Yeah, we're not supposed to take care of our kids.

VIRGIL: Like, I take care of my family. I have a wife and we go off and chat. We go places and they see us and we do things together. They don't believe that. That's not supposed to happen. We are not those people.

WALTER: It was like that for me, I can say. Because most of the brass band musicians never had shit. They don't have houses. I ain't gonna lie, the first time Andrew started playing with the Soul Rebels—and "Let Your Mind Be Free," I could have sworn Rebirth made that because that's all I know. Andrew started playing with the Soul Rebels and I'm like, "Aw, fuck it. I'm gonna go check them out. Andrew and I got to go there anyway; that's my friend." And they go pulling up with motor bikes and shit and I'm like, "Whoa. Who the fuck y'all? Y'all can have these things?" It's like, "Yeah, what makes you think we can't have this stuff?" "Brass band musicians don't have shit. Rebirth—I'm basing it off of them. I ain't trying to say nothing bad about them, but I'm like, "You got *two* cars?"

VIRGIL: And so they see us like that.

WALTER: But it was inspiring to me! I was like, "Oh my god! You can have shit doing this! And my mama told me it was a hobby. 'Nobody gets money from this.' You know?" It inspired me. When we built the Stooges up, all of us were respectable men and, except for Andrew, we all got four kids. He about to break the rule, he about to have five. But we work hard and we raise our families and stuff. And it's like we the role models. I remember fussing with someone about why I put rims on my car. I told him it was like for the neighborhood. Kids can not just see the neighborhood drug dealer with the big rims, he could see me with this. So when I hand him that horn, he can feel like now you got two choices. You got the horn and this pound of weed. But that horn can get you this same outcome. And that's what we started doing with the Stooges. Saving people, you know?

VIRGIL: And we didn't start that. My grandfather played with the Olympia. He had money. That's what attracted me to doing it. I was like, "I want to do what you do, man." The man used to come home with *money*. I used to remember him bringing money to my mama house so she could put it in his safe so his wife wouldn't steal it from him. It was my grandmother. He used to be like, "I need you to hold my money because, shit, when I leave and go out of town, I know she going in and go and get it." He would bring big old stacks of money from when he would travel and stuff like that. And he was a carpenter, too. It was like, "This man really has money." I associated him with that job with having money, not all the negative stuff, not all the stuff that you hear now. I think they place themselves in that environment. See there's one thing it's about. You either hustle or you can make a living for yourself. Hustling, well, hustling never changes. Making a living for yourself, you're gonna start off hustling and then you're gonna gradually get to a certain point. It's like, if I'm a massage therapist, when I come out of school and I get a job, I'm not going to have clients. I got to have to hustle in the beginning and I build up my clientele and then I start making a living for myself. Then maybe I can make my own business with this, then I won't have to do any more massages. Hustling people, they keep hustling. And when you make a living, you start hustling and then you wind up building something greater than from where you started. And I think that's what's going on right now. These kids right now, it's a hustle game.

DREW: My dad always had a saying when it came to dealing with the system, the cycle. He was like, "Look, if the system keeps beating you, you have to learn the system." And I think that's the most important part of it when we're talking about why *we* have become who we are as opposed to the stereotypical musician. I've been playing music, you know, as a professional since I was about sixteen. I've never held down any other gig except playing my horn—or playing my horn or something that's dealing with music. I'm one of the fortunate ones. Why? Because I was able to sit down and deal with all of the aspects of it and learn the system and learn how people make money and those types of things and *then* get my hustle. And then you get the hustle. Fortunately, I had a group of like-minded people.

AL: And you were good! [*laughter*]

DREW: Fortunately, I had a group of like-minded people who were on that same plane. Not everyone gets that same privilege. And that's the reality.

WALTER: And another thing that people don't know about the Stooges. They'll be like, "Man, Walter made this decision" or "Walter did that." The Stooges are ran like a business. We board of operations! I might be the leader, but I don't make them decisions. We always made these decisions based on a core group of people. And it'd be like, "Okay, cool. We got this, this. How we gonna do this? What we should do about that?" And that's this circle along with Ersel. It's like we always based our decisions off of that.

✦ ✦ ✦

WALTER: The beginning: it was fun, but it was hard. You know, because it's like, you playing, and I remember we played a Friday night gig and it

John Cannon and Walter Ramsey playing a second line. Photo
courtesy of John Cannon.

was Uptown in New Orleans. And we'd just play every Friday trying to get
people to come out. We wasn't making no money. And then we got paid fifteen bucks per person. My tuba player at the time, his name was John Cannon. Him and his wife, Tonya Boyd Cannon, the singer, they was just started
going together. And I remember he was like, "Man, I can't take no more of
this shit. This is not enough money." And he left the gig and he was like,
"Man, look. I quit." I was like, "Quit? Man, we got to do this *next* Friday." He
was like, "Man, for fifteen dollars? Twelve dollars? Come on, Walt, bruh!" But
I was like, "Man, come get your money." I'm counting the money to separate
the fifteen dollars. He was like, "Man, fuck that money! Keep that money!"
And he drove off. So I was like, "Alright, cool. He's a little upset, I don't know."

But I still had to pay him. And I decided to drive to the East where he was living at in his apartments at the time and knock on his door. He was like, "Man, fuck that money! Fuck these gigs! Fuck all that little money. I'ma go cook. I'ma be a chef or some shit." I was like, "Alright, that sounds good, big brother, but we got gigs tomorrow. We got like four weddings." "Fuck them weddings!" I was like, "Who gonna play the tuba?" "I don't know who gonna play the tuba! I ain't playing!" So I slid the money underneath the door, the little fifteen dollars under his door.

KYLE: Was he yelling this to you from the other side of the door?

WALTER: Yeah, through the door! It was crazy. I slid the money underneath the door and I try to go pull off and hear somebody slam my hood of the top of my car. Bam! He put the fifteen dollars back on there. "I ain't want no money! I don't want this!" I was like, "Damn, he really upset." I was like, "How—we got gigs tomorrow—who gonna play the tuba?" He come back out with the tuba and stow it in the car. Bam! "Take the tuba, too. Play the tuba." So I was like, "I don't know how to play the tuba." I went home. I was like, "Damn, he really upset. We got to do something." So I got up the next morning and the gigs wasn't until the evening, so I was like, "If I just learn five songs on the tuba, I could probably carry us for these gigs tonight until he'd be back to play next week." He ain't never came back. I was like, "God damn!"

KYLE: And had you never played tuba before then?

WALTER: Nope.

KYLE: Oh wow!

WALTER: Yeah. And then I became the tuba player in the band, but it was just like—

KYLE: Necessity.

WALTER: Yeah. I had to keep the band moving. The low points for me is when band members leave the band. Because it will be like, you're losing your band member—you're not losing your brother, because they gonna be around for life. But it's just that you go through the awkward stage of readjusting, redoing this, or redoing that. And today, where we got these many Stooges players can play, you can just, "Alright, you can't play. Cool. Sub in, sub out," stuff like that. Back then, it felt like you was losing a family member. Like, "Damn. He going cook now." I thought we were going to play for the rest of our life. I thought we were going to do this. So it be like that. But I can say that my low point is really just going through different band members, losing your core ones that you put all into everything with it. Because after a while, you get new band members. They come and they not making fifteen dollars. Like, "You don't know that we blew all night and just got paid fifteen dollars. You have no clue about that struggle." But they got their own struggle, too. The ones that travel on the road, they see how it is. Some days might be good, some road trips might not be good. But it's a equal balance. For me, one day, this is probably going to turn into millions of dollars. So I stay optimistic and just stay pushing.

✦ ✦ ✦

AL: Listen, it wasn't all pretty with us. We clashed, we had issues. I don't know if they ever told you about the twenty dollars a gig.
KYLE: With John Cannon?
AL: All that!
KYLE: "Take your fucking twenty dollars!" Yeah, Walt told me all about that.
AL: We was playing gigs, man. At one time when we was young, we would get all the gigs. We would play thirteen gigs on a Saturday from the day all the way to the night. I'm talking about we might take a lunch break or a dinner break and then we playing gigs the rest of the night. And then we look at the money, thirteen gigs, top twenty dollars. You might have got 300-something dollars, $340, $360, something like that.
KYLE: Wait—$360 each person?
AL: All of us! For the night!
KYLE: $360 for thirteen gigs?
AL: Thirteen gigs, something like that! That's how that was going. It wind up being cats was starting to get agitated. Twenty dollars a gig, you playing thirty minutes, you get twenty dollars a gig. Just imagine. Now we're young, we're like, "Twenty dollars, we do seven gigs, three to four hundred, that's cool. We ain't worried about it or whatever." But then after you start getting a little older . . .

✦ ✦ ✦

CHAD: Everybody always think that Walter takes the Stooges money. But I'm trying to explain to the guys in the band at the time—and even to today, I still take Walter's back when I hear them say that shit. It makes me angry because I was there with him. I was there with him before he bought his first house. I was there when he only had the Expedition, the Expedition truck. He only had that. After a while, once he started learning the formula and making his money, he started buying property. And then at one point in time, when the Stooges really got good and started taking over the street, Walter went *all out*.

KYLE: In terms of his investments?

CHAD: No, in terms of material, you dig?

KYLE: Oh, okay, is that when he got the Hummer?

CHAD: No, this is before the Hummer. The Hummer is small change. No, no. This dude had a car every day of the week—a different car! It was his cars, though! He had a Jag, a Benz, a Tahoe, a Silverado, two F-150s—a white one and a black one—and then he had an Infinity car. Every car—the Benz—it was top of the line.

KYLE: Who needs two F-150s?

CHAD: Man, that was his thing! At that time, that was his thing. He loved F-150 trucks. And then he didn't have the regular F-150 trucks, he had to have the Harley Davidson F-150 trucks. On top of that, he had six, seven houses! People were starting to hate on him like, "Man, you got all of this?" And he used to wear his diamond chains and shit. I'm like, "Man, he worked for that!" Everybody thinking that they only see him with the Stooges that we making this type of money for him. Nah! This nigga *owns* six or seven houses, seven cars. We can't possibly make enough money in a year to afford his one-month bill, you dig?

KYLE: And what does that say about the audience that they think that brass bands can make that much money just off of playing?

CHAD: They do. I mean, they think that. They think that now—I don't think they think that about the Stooges—but if I come around, it's a total different thing. "Hey man, here come the money, here come the man. This the man with all the big gigs here." They say certain things. And it is true! I used to tell Walter, "You think you got it like this with the women and all this stuff, imagine how *Phil* got it, our tuba player. Our bandleader?" Man, it's crazy. Now that my band is getting smarter with their money, everybody got some type of luxury car now, so to people, automatically, we rich. Automatically. Plus, we got a Grammy.

KYLE: And does that come with any money or anything?

CHAD: It doesn't come with no money. It's just a fucking trophy.

KYLE: See, I didn't think so.

CHAD: It don't come with no money. It's just a trophy. To this day, that's exactly what it is. A trophy, a nomination, and you might get a few extra fans. But like I told them, on our Facebook page, when we won the Grammy [February 12, 2012], we had fifty-five thousand followers. We won the Grammy and right now to this day [March 22, 2016], we only got sixty-five thousand followers. It didn't double this shit. It didn't help us out too much. It's the same shit. With the Stooges, I probably had a Grand Am. Now I got a BMW and a fucking Range Rover, and I got a Jeep. So it's like you got to be rich—that's what people in brass bands think. But then my band member, Stafford, he drive a Lexus. My saxophone player Vince, he drives a Benz. My other trumpet player—we just got him in the band—he's only been in the band four months—

KYLE: Is that Glenn Hall?

CHAD: Glenn Hall. He just got in the band, he just bought a new Mercedes. So people see this and they think that we're rich. Our snare drummer, he got an Audi *and* a Benz. My bass drummer got two BMWs. Phil just got a Lexus. My other trombone player, he got two F-150 trucks. So people see these types of things and automatically categorize our pay. No, I just think that we reaping the benefits of what they worked so hard for. They worked thirty-three years to drive these fucking cars.

KYLE: And the other thing is you're standing on their shoulders.

CHAD: Yeah, pretty much. It's not that we balling. These people worked thirty-three years for this band to be in the position that it's in. What you gonna do? Your band could be doing the same thing. There was a point in time where, right when the 350Zs came out, the new Nissan 350Zs. When I was in the Stooges band, Walter had it so good—we can call him on the phone right now—we had nine band members at the time and Walter went to the Nissan dealership, had them pull out nine 350Zs ready to put the money down and we were gonna use them as company cars. At the time, he had already put down money. The band had Nextel phones. Everybody had they own home. Everybody was gonna have they own car. That's the moves that the Stooges then was making. So we was making money, too, at the time. If we had kept it together man, no telling where the Stooges would be at right now.

PART II
The Second Generation

CHAPTER 4

It's About Time

In a taxi blocks five blocks away from the Hi-Ho Lounge in the St. Claude corridor, I could see the beams of four searchlights roam the night sky. On my way to the release of the Stooges' second full-length studio album, I wondered what might be happening in the vicinity of the bar. Sure enough, as the driver dropped me off at the Hi-Ho, I chuckled at the realization that Walter and the guys had spared no expense for the release of their new album, *Thursday Night House Party* (2016). In the middle of the neutral ground, a truck with rotating searchlights announced the venue's location to anyone even remotely close by. Their tour bus, a tri-axle coach that sleeps twelve, was parked outside the bar, the silver and black design on its sides glistening in the streetlights. Laid out in front of the club, a red carpet and well-lit backdrop bearing the Stooges Music Group logo and the logo for the band's production company, Livin Swell Entertainment, provided the perfect space for red-carpet-style photos, many of which circulated on Facebook in the weeks following. Adding to the flashiness of the night's festivities, hip-hop producer Mannie Fresh soon pulled up in his silver Porsche Panamera, parking it in front of the tour bus. The Stooges had spared no expense. They were doing it big.

It had been over a decade since their first full studio album, *It's About Time* (2003), was released. In the interim, they put out a six-track vinyl-only release, *Street Music* (2013), a project led by Brice "Brice Nice" White and Scott Borne of Sinking City Records.[1] Back in 2003, after more than a few long and expensive studio sessions, they finally cobbled together the tracks needed for their first full-length album. Over the past decade, the Stooges have attempted to release new music, but their plans were hampered by a few factors. Firstly, the Stooges are perfectionists. Walter has a large catalog of unreleased music that won't see the light of day until the band is completely happy with the product. An even larger obstacle to releasing new music was that one of their albums, tentatively titled *Stooges Reunion*, was allegedly leaked by an incoming band member. This became apparent when some members first heard the recordings blaring from car stereos around town.

Though the Stooges' hopes with the *Stooges Reunion* album (now nicknamed "the leak") were dashed locally, there's a possibility that today, with better access to wide distribution through the internet, such a recording would find a market outside of New Orleans. Recordings are often the first means through which brass band fandom is cultivated abroad. Digitally available albums are able to extend the reach of the music and have the possibility of eventually providing touring gigs and other significant and unpredictable returns on investment. Take my experience, for instance. In 2012, By way of a smattering of primordial online streaming services and YouTube, my friends and I were able to access music that, to small-town Canadians raised on fiddle music, would have seemed inaccessible only a few years prior. For an increasingly broad international market, brass band music isn't encountered through parading traditions or even through touring bands, but through recorded music. This book, an unexpected return on investment, was ultimately made possible by my introduction to brass band music through recordings. Unlike the performance of live brass band music (whether in the streets or onstage), recordings can be enjoyed privately or publicly and circulate with greater ease than live music.

The Stooges' first album, *It's About Time*, wasn't their first trace in recorded music. Prior to its release, the band's arrival on the scene was announced on several other brass band albums. The Stooges are name-checked in each of the most iconic hip-hop-infused brass band albums—and on the songs that have become classics in the repertory. As John Cannon told it, "It was to a point to where the Stooges name starting to be wrote in the songs of other brass bands. And when we saw that, it was like, 'Okay, we doing something.'" Most notably, the Lil Stooges are named in Rebirth's "Casanova" from their 2001 release, *Hot Venom* ("Lil Stooges hate me, hate me, hate me!"), and the Lil Rascals' "Knock with Me—Rock with Me" from 2001's *Buck It Like a Horse* ("I said the Lil Stooges tried to get me!"). *It's About Time* jumped headfirst into a brass band discography in which the Stooges were already enmeshed.

With its high-quality production, the album provides a distinctive entrée into brass band music. It opens with a spoken introduction referencing the Stooges' namesake, the Three Stooges. The band sings a major 7th chord built up on the word *hello*, followed by Drew's fourth-wall-breaking declaration that "you've been waiting five long, long years." The band then thanks everyone in the second line community for their support, and Walter makes sure to pay his dues to all the bands that paved the way for them: "the Dirty Dozen, the Rebirth, the New Birth, the Hot 8, the Lil Rascals, the Treme." Summing up the band's approach to the album, Al simply states, "This is us. This is the way *we* do it. This is *our* music. You can close your eyes and picture you're at the second line, y'all." And with that, the album launches into fifteen tracks of party music.

The studio-produced intro aside, the album is manufactured to sound live, placing the listener in the auditory environment of a second line. The first song on the album, "Stooges Party," serves as an example of this. Originally written by Al for the Mahogany Brass Band before being altered for the Stooges, it includes all kinds of wonderfully excessive chatter added atop the standard brass band instrumentation. Exclamatory shouts by individual members ("All aboard!" "Come on!") paired with what almost sounds like bird calls ("Oooo-*oooo!*") pepper the track for a bit of manufactured authenticity. The suggestion that a studio album be able to place the listener in a second line is a tall order if nothing else, but the sounds of chatter, cheers, cowbells, woodblocks, and tambourines provide some semblance of a street-like ambience.[2] These first two tracks demonstrate the dual aims of the recording. On the one hand, as Al says, the album should place you squarely in the sonic space of the streets. On the other hand, the dialogue in the intro is clearly studio-produced. The interspersed ad-libs that the Stooges sow throughout the album give it a feeling of liveness that is then exported globally, providing an auditory approximation of a second line for people who may never even have been to New Orleans.[3]

It's About Time carries with it a double meaning. It most obviously references the long waiting period leading up to its release, but, as Walter told music writer Geraldine Wyckoff about the album's release, it's also "about the time it takes as far as learning and about gaining progress in the music."[4] The album signaled the transformation of the Lil Stooges into the Stooges, a maturation that required trust in the process. The process not only *takes* time, it's also *about* time.

✦ ✦ ✦

KYLE: What about the recording of the first album, *It's About Time*? That took a long time to come out with that, right? And you've got that track on there with Buzz, "The Chosen II."

ELLIS: So in my mind, that wasn't our first album.

JOHN C.: No, we had about two or three more albums. That was the first album that was *released*. We went to Milton Batiste's studio for about six months straight.

ELLIS: I'm still looking for that album.

JOHN C.: We sacrificed a bunch of gigs for that album. We went to Noise-Lab Studios Uptown. That was the second project. So *It's About Time* would have been about the third or fourth project.

ELLIS: Carl Marsh.

JOHN C.: Well, we didn't really lay that down by Carl Marsh. We played that one or two songs in little meetings, but we didn't record anything. I'm talking about actually physical recording—physically recording by Milton's, we did that for six months straight.

ELLIS: And NoiseLab, we sacrificed gigs for that, too.

JOHN C.: And then we went to NoiseLab, we spent a bunch of money in NoiseLab recording music. And then *It's About Time* came out. I would say that, on paper, that would be about the third or fourth album.

KYLE: Okay, what happened to all the rest of them?

JOHN C.: We didn't like them. We were perfectionists. "That shit sound horrible, we not doing nothing with that." We spent twelve hundred dollars on this recording session.

KYLE: Twelve hundred dollars when you're making like fifteen bucks a gig!

JOHN C.: Yes! Yes!

ELLIS: Imagine how much we were working in order to save that kind of money.

JOHN C.: Yeah, that shit sound bad. At least we were honest with ourself, though. And that was the biggest part of it. I think because we were perfectionists, a lot of the time we found ourselves in the studio rehearsing. We're paying for rehearsal time!

KYLE: You'd think if you were a perfectionist, you'd want to perfect it before you get to the studio.

JOHN C.: It didn't go that way! No, no!

ELLIS: We would change our minds once we got in the studio.

JOHN C.: Listen, we'd put a list down, we're gonna record x, y, and z, we're gonna get it done in this amount of time, it's gonna leave this gap for them to mix it down and do whatever. You pay for a twelve-hour block, you can record in four hours, they can mix in eight hours. That shit didn't go like that.

ELLIS: We had it all mapped out. It never went like that. Never. And NoiseLab, then, that was a high-end kind of studio. It was a big deal to be recording in there, so you know we had to work our way from Milton Batiste's house studio to NoiseLab.

Al "Big Al" Huntley, Walter Ramsey, and Garfield Bogan at a gig. Photo courtesy of Garfield Bogan.

JOHN C.: And NoiseLab was a house, but nobody lived there. It was a big mansion Uptown off of St. Charles and Green. And the entire basement was gutted out and made into a music studio. You go in and you say, "Oh, yeah. We gonna go in and record." We laid four or five songs down and, fuck, we'd order pizza and sit around and have a good time and nobody doing nothing! I think the biggest part of it was because we hung together so much, it didn't bother us.

KYLE: You're spending time to rent out a house to eat some pizza.

ELLIS: In a different environment.

JOHN C.: You'd play the music back one time. "No, we don't like the way that shit sound. Let's do it again." And, fuck, by the time you know it, your whole session's gone. You didn't have time to mix nothing. And then they went to Tim Stambaugh at Word of Mouth. Before that, they ever did that, they had another one that they did by Tim. So, like I said, that would be about the fourth project. And I actually sung on that project, too. I sung on the reggae song on that. Buzz and them did the "Chosen II."

✦ ✦ ✦

KYLE: On that album, of course, is the "Chosen II" track with you and Ejo, right?

J'MAR: Ejo, yeah. We the Chosen II.

KYLE: So how did you guys come to call yourselves the Chosen II? And can you tell me a bit about that track, maybe? Because it's not like the other tracks on the album.

J'MAR: Well, at that time, me and Ejo, we was going to St. Aug. We was rapping. We actually thought we was going to be some rappers at the time. So maybe in '95, we named ourselves the Chosen II. We made a couple songs in the studios and we was always rapping around. We at the time thought that maybe we was gonna get signed to No Limit during that time frame because we had some connections with some people. We would actually go into the studio and make some songs. And we made some songs a long time ago that a lot of people may not believe, but it was a song called "We Gonna Make It." I think it was '96, '97. And later on, Jadakiss came out with a song, and it was kind of curious to us because we was trying to figure out if the guy that we paid the studio time for actually gave our song away, because it was similar to our song. I was always asking Ejo, "Can you find that tape, man?" Because people don't believe the song that we made that this guy, this aspiring rapper, made. But we was always rapping around, man, come up with the name. We'd open up talent shows. And we'd rap at some of the gigs that we used to play with the Stooges. And Chosen II is just me and Ellis, man. You know, at the time, we thought we was going to be big rappers, but, you know, things happen.

✦ ✦ ✦

WALTER: Fresh out of high school, we started doing events at clubs. But then at that time, me and Andrew sit down. Andrew was like, "Man, I want to do my own record, my own jazz record." Sam was like, "Alright, cool. I think I got my band together. I want to record a record." And then I was like, "Yeah, I still need to do a Stooges record. We almost five years in the game and we don't have a record." So it was like, "Man, we gonna start something called the Gruve Label and we each gonna help pay for each other's records to come out." So we did that with me, Andrew, and Big Sam. And then we produced Andrew record first and it was cool. And then it was time to produce the Stooges or Big Sam record. We brought in another partner to help us pay for it, and then we was able to produce Big Sam and the Stooges' *It's About Time* record. It was like a whole 'nother generation of musicians on there. So it was like, "Alright, we in the second generation of the Stooges now."

KYLE: Okay, and that was 2003?

WALTER: Yeah, 2003. But then, also everybody who played with the Stooges up until then got a chance to be part of the record, too, which wasn't

Left to right: Garfield Bogan, Wendell "Cliff" Stewart, Dwayne Williams, Nicholas Ramsey (Walter's eldest son), and Walter Ramsey. Photo courtesy of Garfield Bogan.

planned. But now we understand it's a collective of these musicians coming together. We're like, "Whoa, we're not just a band, we're a *brand*," because there's about twelve to fifteen musicians that recorded *It's About Time*. Some first-generation, some second-generation Stooges. Some old, new, but they all came in. Even J'mar and Ellis came for the recordings even though we have a drum section now. They came in and they played on some of the record and then they put down a track called "Chosen II," because that's what they was calling theyself. And they had that rap song, so even in the rap, "Ain't no L.S.—which is Lil Stooges—without Ellis." But it was still a group effort and project and it came out and it was pretty cool. It was like our first record that ever came out. We had recorded records before, but we never pushed them out due to the record label that we was dealing with or us not being comfortable with the sound. That's why it was named *It's About Time*. It took time to develop that sound.

KYLE: Like, eight years.

WALTER: Yeah, and then it took time to really craft it and put it out, so that was the thing. But we was building a brotherhood back then and we ain't even realize it. It was just like, wow.

KYLE: I mean, there're really deep ties between you guys.

WALTER: Right. Right. Because, after a while, being around each other for so long, we started marrying into each other's family, because this is all we do, this is all we know. We wake up, we practice on Tuesdays, we play on Thursdays, Friday, Saturday, Sunday, and we do it again on Tuesday. We was just learning to build a brand together. And it wasn't a walk in the park. We have our difficulties with anything—especially me being a leader. Back then, I probably wasn't a pleasant guy to be around. I used to be hard on them. They called me Otis from the Temptations. That's how I was. Like, "We got to rehearse, we got to do this." So when the Temptations movie came out, my mom looked at it, she was like, "Yeah, you definitely was Otis."

KYLE: Yeah. Have you mellowed out now?

WALTER: Yeah, as I got older, Whoadie sort of died and then Walter started becoming—you know.

✦ ✦ ✦

AL: Up until that time, we was doing a recording session over, and over, and over, and over. We have so many people that recorded different songs, they got so many songs that didn't make the CD, that just sat on a hard drive, because we was trying to figure out which ones we were gonna do. I actually made a song up for Brice Miller, for his band, but Brice had done already made up a song that was close to what my song was, so it really didn't gel in this band. I was like, "Alright, I'll bring it to the Stooges." We was just sitting on Villere Street, practicing and going over original songs, and I said, "Man, I think I got a song." I went to humming the song out and showing them the song. And we clown around with the song and whatnot. We ain't really get through the whole song, so I was like, "Alright, I ain't gonna worry about it." I think we practiced on a Thursday. That Friday night, we played gigs. One of the first gigs, John Cannon start playing my song. I was like, "John, the song is nowhere finished." Like, "Man, let's go for it, man."

KYLE: And what song was that?

AL: "Stooges Party."

KYLE: Oh, okay, right. It's kind of funny that you wrote that for another band and it kind of ended up being "Stooges Party."

AL: It was supposed to be "Mahogany Party."

KYLE: I mean, "Mahogany Party" has a nice ring to it, too.

AL: That what it was! And then it transformed to "Stooges Party." I mean, it's cool, man. I met my wife on it. Once again, we had a gig. Walt said, "Man, we got to play a gig, man, for my cousin baby. We just hooking up a couple people to go out and play, but I want you to meet my cousin." And he was like, "You know, if you're doing it for her baby, her baby's making three." We hooked the band up, we go in Gentilly, and a woman came out. She had on a Lakers jersey. And I looked, I'm like, "Is that your cousin?" He was like, "Yeah, that's my cousin." So she started organizing and getting the gig together and whatnot. I'm looking. She had three sisters and they was all there, but she caught my eye. We played a little gig and he introduced us. Like, "This is my cousin." I called him on the phone after the gig. I said, "Bro, I'ma get your cousin, dog. That's straight up, bruh. I'ma get your cousin, man." He was like, "Alright." I courted her, I went along with it. And she had a boyfriend at the time. And I got to know the mama and the daddy and got cool with the mama and the daddy.

✦ ✦ ✦

DREW: One of the main reasons I went to Berklee was to dabble in production work and learn the main things that producers do.

KYLE: Yeah. Those main things being . . .

DREW: The whole job of the producer is not the way we see it in hip-hop or like that type of thing. Producing is saying, "Okay, I like these lyrics to this song. I like this song. Okay, I'ma set it up to get it arranged or whatever. I'm gonna oversee this whole thing from start to finish. I'm gonna be in the studio from start to finish. I'ma sit with the engineer as they set up the mics because I need these mics set up a certain way to get this certain sound." And that's what a producer does. You produce the product. It's not as much the intellectual property; it's the actual tangible product. It's kind of like I didn't come up with the blueprints to the product, but I put up the blueprint to manufacture it, to mass produce it.

KYLE: And so that it's one final product that will sell well and sound good.

DREW: Yeah, it's kind of like the producer's the one that sets up the machines perfectly right so when this piece comes in, the machine can put in this piece and then put in that piece and make it a total assembly line.

KYLE: You're like a plant—you're setting up all this stuff that needs to be put into place to turn it into a widget or a CD.

DREW: Exactly. And so that's what a producer does. And if you're not that type of person who sees it from start to finish, then you're not producing the record. I tell people that all the time. Man, you need to oversee the whole process. They trusted me enough to oversee the whole project. I would go in there, and I'm always asking questions out of the artist, out of the cats in the band. It's like, "Okay, now y'all need to be together. I need y'all two together. I need you to come back in and redo your trombone part. I need you to come back in and do this, that, and the other." It's not like I'm coming to crack the whip, but it is something like that. It's like, "No, I need you to come in *now* to make this happen. We need to make this happen. And every project—every album—needs that person who's going to whip it into shape and shape it and form it. You have the modeling clay. Your hands have to sit in and model the whole thing. So I cut my teeth with that because I had to go through the whole process of recording an album telling cats, "No, bro. Look, I need you to come play this tambourine part. Nobody plays a tambourine part like you. I need you to come play this tambourine part." And when cats tired, you the one that still has to be like, "No, we got to keep going." The *It's About Time* record was three days of recording and like two more days of mixing, which is fairly a short amount of time for that type of record. But the good thing about brass band records is that there is no need for this extra glitter.

KYLE: Yeah, I mean you get some group singing over something and get a few yells and hollers in there maybe.

DREW: Yeah, exactly. And what makes this music great like that is those little raw elements.

KYLE: Yeah, it's the liveness to it. It feels immediate. You can be put in that space where a brass band would be playing.

DREW: That was the whole gist of it. And once I finished that record— once we finished that record—that's when I left for Berklee. I loved it there because I was able to pick so many brains.

KYLE: And who did you study with at Berklee? What brains did you pick?

DREW: The main brain that I picked, actually, his name was Willy Weeks, a bass player. He used to play in Donny Hathaway's band. I used to pick his brain, like, "Why did you write it like this way instead of that way?" And usually the answers would be like, "Because that's the way I was hearing it." Or, "That's because I wanted to."

KYLE: Fair enough.

DREW: But he would always share techniques with me and that type of thing. And I would sit in that arranging class, and there was another cat, his name way Billy Pierce, a saxophone player that played in the Blakey bands— one of the last couple Art Blakey bands. And he noticed me because I was shedding in the room, and he's like, "You from New Orleans, ain't you?" I was like, "Damn! Was it *that* obvious?" But I would just rap with him and they would always come to share knowledge with me because they felt that somebody like me needed it. They would always entertain my inquisitive nature.

✦ ✦ ✦

VIRGIL: Like, stuff that you might hear us playing, we'll make up stuff on—like, I ain't gonna lie to you, me and Al, almost every picture of the band, I'm standing next to him. So just me and him playing together, we get to a certain point where we start making up parts. It's like we doing it together. So you might hear the recording when you get in the street or you get on the stage, you're like, whoa. Same thing with Soul Rebels. You get on the stage with Soul Rebels, you're like, "Man, I'm about to do this." And they do something and they laughing at you, they like, "Yeah, yeah, you don't know this."

WALTER: "Got him!"

VIRGIL: "Yeah, you don't know this." You know what I'm saying? Part of that is going out to hear it. I think music is more of a living entity rather than just, "We gonna play this and that's what it is." What we do is we grow with the music. We might play the same song all the time, but it's going to add something new every time till you get to a point where you're like, "Hold up. This is too much. Let's stop. Or let's change it."

AL: And another thing we used to do back in the day. We didn't care if we got to a gig and we messed it up. So we'd learn a song in practice and then be like, "Let's play."

WALTER: And then we used to practice on Thursday before the gig and then go play.

AL: When I wrote "Stooges Party," we practiced it one Thursday and we had gigs that week, so I was like, "Alright, we ain't gonna do it this weekend because we ain't really got it together. We gonna wait till next week." We get to the first gig that Friday. I think it was in Kenner—that little Kenner place. John Cannon started playing the bass line. I'm like, "What are you playing?" John Cannon looked at me and said, "Fuck it!" There it is. And you know how he would say, "Fuck it, bro! Bro, just do it, bro!"

✦ ✦ ✦

CHRIS: You can play "Do Whatcha Wanna," everybody know that song, and it will be recognized everywhere, but until the Stooges gets recognized everywhere like "Do Whatcha Wanna"—I mean, that's my dream. I'd like to see the Stooges, everybody wants to play the Stooges songs or, at the end of

A promotional flyer for the Stooges Music Group. Image courtesy of
Ashton Ramsey.

the party, "Put on that Stooges!" instead of "Do Whatcha Wanna." And the
way that that happens is you have to promote that.

KYLE: You need to build up that familiarity with audience.

CHRIS: Yeah. People know the Stooges right now and people know some
of the Stooges' music, but I think *we*, the Stooges, or whoever the Stooges is
in the future, needs to work on putting out more music.

KYLE: Like, in terms of CDs and stuff?

CHRIS: Yeah, yeah, yeah, yeah. Yeah.

The cover of the Stooges' 2003 album, *It's About Time,* complete with the bling aesthetic that dominated hip-hop in the early 2000s.

KYLE: Like, albums?

CHRIS: Yeah, albums. Putting out albums. Because it's only one CD that we have out right now.

KYLE: And the vinyl, too, right?

CHRIS: Yeah, the one CD and the vinyl. The vinyl came out in 2012, something like that. The Stooges, we've been traveling for four years, man. We should have an album for every year—or maybe two albums—from that time period to showcase the growth of the group. Rebirth can go like, "Hey, man. This is Rebirth from when Kermit Ruffins started the band, this is Rebirth right before Kermit Ruffins left, this is Rebirth right after he left, this is Rebirth five years after he left, this is Rebirth ten years after he left!"

KYLE: They've got five-year intervals. It's an anniversary album every five years.

CHRIS: Yeah, and I don't want to compare or sound like I'm trying to bash the Stooges, but I'm just saying that I'd like to see the Stooges for the thirtieth anniversary with more albums than three albums, though.

KYLE: Right. That is a very fair criticism, I think. I would like hear more than that.

CHRIS: It's possible, because right now with the people who are on the Stooges side—you told me you interviewed ten years' worth of trumpet players with the Stooges.

✦ ✦ ✦

AL: That first CD when they pressed it, we called everybody up and we went by Walt house. We opened up the box and we saw how the CD looked. What happened was, we took the picture and the person that got the picture that was going to do the cover said, "Man, I can make this look real good." Because, at the time, bling bling was the thing.

KYLE: Right. It's totally that aesthetic, too. It's very 2001.

AL: Yeah! So they took the CD and put it with gold and with silver and platinum chains at a second line. And when we got that CD, we opened it up and looked at it and saw we was there on our first CD, that was like our high. We was giving it to everybody, selling it. We did a CD release party at Tipitina's and that was beautiful.

KYLE: Was the whole place packed?

AL: Fucking right, yeah. Fucking right. Every time we played at Tipitina's the place was packed.

CHAPTER 5

Why They Had to Kill Him?

The second line winds its way through the streets of Central City past the former site of the Calliope Projects to its destination at the Foxx Bar just a few blocks from my house. It's a chilly day, and the clouds have receded, throwing sunlight that warms our faces and refracts off the band's instruments. Turning onto South Dorgenois Street, the tuba signals the start of one of the Stooges' most popular tunes, "Why They Had to Kill Him."[1] The band thinks of the second line as a football game, dividing it into quarters with the stops at neighborhood barrooms acting as dividers. They usually play "Why They Had to Kill Him," (or, as it's abbreviated, "Why") near the end of the parade. If the football comparison is upheld, "Why They Had to Kill Him" is like the final play that sends the ball soaring through the goalposts, eliciting cheers and a heightened emotional response from the crowd. With our bodies tightly packed and the sun in our eyes, sound overtakes our senses. The chorus rises above the enduring thump of the bass drum and clattering of cowbells:

Why they had to kill him?
They had the nerve, to say they protect and serve.
Oh why?
Why they had to kill him?
They need to change they logo, 'cause we like, "fuck the po-po."
Oh why?

Al raises his trombone into the air, its slide pointing to the heavens. The congregation of second liners sings in unison, "We all gon' miss Joseph," in tribute to the life of trombonist Joseph Williams.[2] Also known as "Shotgun Joe" or "Lil Joe," Joe was a first-generation member of the Stooges. A skilled trombonist, he played in the band alongside his half brother, Arian. They subbed in and out when John or J'mar couldn't make it to gigs. He grew up in the Lastie family, one of New Orleans's musical dynasties, and was immersed in music from birth. An otherwise joyful upbringing was disrupted by the presence of Joe's father, an army vet who, on an April evening in 1989, shot Joe's mother dead within earshot of Joe, Arian, and their sisters, Unetra and Unell. As Matt Sakakeeny writes, "Joe's life from this point forward was defined by a tug-of-war between expression through music and suppression through more damaging means."[3] He found both community and escape in the streets.

Joe and Arian both played with the Stooges, but their ties with the band became tenuous after they fell into well-worn patterns of drug abuse and addiction. In the interest of keeping the band clean, the Stooges fired Joe, and Arian followed suit a few years later. Joe soon began playing with the Hot 8, but spent time in and out of prison, at times pawning his horn, which Walter would buy back for him.

Despite the ups and downs of his addiction, things seemed to be getting better when, on August 3, 2004, Joe borrowed a truck known to many as a "rock runner," which passed hands among drug dealers and users. Joe had borrowed the truck before, but the owners were unaware of its whereabouts and reported it stolen. While on his way to play a funeral gig, he was stopped by the NOPD outside the Food Store in the Sixth Ward, directly across the street from the lot (now Tuba Fats Square) where the Stooges first gigged as kids. As Joe motioned to grab his trombone from the passenger-side seat, officers Jonathan Carroll, Kevin Scruggs, and Bruce Little littered him and his truck with twenty-one bullets. His body hung out the driver's-side door, his life taken at just twenty-two.

The next day in the newspaper, Joe's history of arrests was published alongside the police story, which justified his killing by claiming he used the truck as a weapon. That claim was refuted by his family and friends. Mixed in with the published narrative was a quote from Walter. "I just want answers," he said. "I'm trying to calm my family down because that ignorance is not going to get you anywhere. I just need answers."[4] But the NOPD could offer none. The officers who killed Joe were assigned desk duty, and the police department feigned an investigation. Where was the NOPD's accountability to themselves and to the community?

Arian and the Stooges were given no time to mourn or process their loss because they had gigs in Japan the following day. In a small Japanese hotel room,

Suspected truck thief shot and killed by N.O. officers

*Driver hit cop, aimed
for 2nd one, police say*

By Tara Young
Staff writer

In the second police shooting in three days in New Orleans, a 22-year-old man was shot and killed by three police officers after authorities said the man hit

one officer and attempted to run over another with a stolen pickup truck in Treme on Tuesday afternoon.

Relatives said Joseph "Shotgun Joe" Williams, a trombone player, was on his way to play in a funeral second-line when he was shot and killed. Though relatives acknowledged Williams was in a stolen

See **SHOOTING**, A-6

▶ **Police officer shot, seriously wounded in eastern New Orleans, A-6**

STAFF PHOTO BY ELLIS LUCIA

The article about Joe's death, which appeared on the front page of the *Times-Picayune* on August 4, 2004, identified him as a "suspected truck thief."

Arian picked up his tuba and cathartically emptied his feelings into the bass line of Frankie Beverley's "We Are One," a tune Joe had recently introduced to the Hot 8's repertory.[5] Within minutes, Garfield echoed Walter's sentiments from the newspaper, singing, "Oh why?" in a smooth tenor lament. If they wanted answers for a senseless tragedy, asking "Why?" demanded justice and pointed to the senselessness of injustice. That night for sound check, they played a rough version of the song that became "Why They Had to Kill Him." Returning to New Orleans, the song became a galvanizing force at second lines, highlighting the injustice of violent police practices in Black communities.

More than fifteen years after Joe's death, "Why They Had to Kill Him" still resonates with purpose and urgency. Black Americans killed by police officers are still eulogized in newspaper headlines and now in hashtags. The tools with which to fight systemic racial violence have changed. The Nextel phones the band used in 2004 have been replaced by smartphones with cameras that can document acts of police brutality—documentation that has proved effective in mobilizing people in the Movement for Black Lives. Through this documentation and its dissemination on social media platforms, activists, witnesses, and survivors have brought the police killings of Alton Sterling, Sandra Bland, Philando Castile, Eric Garner, Tamir Rice, and many others into the national conversation.

Although "Why They Had to Kill Him?" rose from a tragedy in the band that is deeply personal, it has broader relevance as a song that criticizes a system that sanctions the killing of Black people. "There was a message behind it," Virgil told me somberly. "Not just even for Joe—I mean, it's for Joe—but other kids who have been shot by the police unjustly, everybody across America where all that stuff has happened." Joe's life and death are part of a larger systemic problem that, years later, still gives relevance to the question: *Why They Had to Kill Him?*

✦ ✦ ✦

ARIAN: Yeah, so you know, my brother got killed.

KYLE: And that was 2004, was it?

ARIAN: Yeah, 2004. The same day he died, we was on our way to Japan that night to catch our flight early that morning. And we got more closer when he died.

KYLE: You and the rest of the Stooges?

ARIAN: Yeah, me and my cousin Walter, we got more closer. And Ersel and them, they came to me and were like, "Man, don't ever forget that we your brothers." We all cried together. To this day, I love them guys like my brothers. Nothing will ever change that. Nothing will ever change. But that's how that really started. But I traveled—I was already going overseas because Trombone Shorty's my cousin.

KYLE: Right, because that's the Lastie side.

ARIAN: Yeah, yeah, yeah. I started out traveling with him, going overseas. And then I went to Japan with Walter and them. And when I left the Stooges, I was on tour with the Youngblood Brass Band. I started traveling with Youngblood for four or five years, so I was all over the world doing all kinds of stuff.

KYLE: Okay, so do you want to tell me—I mean, if it's okay with you— maybe tell me a little about Joe's death and how—it's okay if you don't want to talk.

ARIAN: Come on, man. It's just a book, man. What happened was one of the neighbors had a stolen truck—well, the truck wasn't stolen. Down here, it's a rock runner. You know what rocks are?

KYLE: Yeah.

ARIAN: Yeah, crack. It was a rock runner and they had the keys to the truck. The guy who the truck was for, he was on drugs and so he let him use the truck for the drugs.

KYLE: Okay, is it just kind of a truck that's passed around?

ARIAN: Yeah. My brother, he was trying to get to the gig. What happened was this gig was for somebody that died in the courthouse. The guy caught a heart attack in the courthouse and died and we had to play for him.

And so my brother, he called me that morning, like, "Fat Boy"—they called me Fat Boy—"I need you to come play." And I'm like, "Where?" And he said, "Around the corner." So I said, "Okay, I'm going by my uncle Jeffrey"—Jeffrey Hill, the tuba player. "Uncle Jeffrey want me to come over there instead of me being all the way in the Ninth Ward. I can just chill right there for everybody to get together to get on the plane." This is around

The Stooges at a second line shortly after the storm. *Left to right:* Arian Macklin, Drew Baham, Dwayne Williams, Sammy Cyrus, Garfield Bogan, Walter Ramsey, Virgil Tiller, and Al Growe. Photo courtesy of Garfield Bogan.

twelve, early that morning. And he was like, "Fat Boy, I got a truck." I said, "What kind of truck?" He said, "Man, I got a truck from Darren." And I told my brother, I said, "Joseph, don't drive that truck, bro. Somebody will wind up hurting you for being in that truck." And I regret that to this day that I told my little brother that because now my little brother's dead. And he was in the Sixth Ward on St. Philip and Robertson and we was waiting on him to come. We were waiting on him, telling him, "Come on, Joseph, we got to play." We waited for him to come so we could play.

What happened was by the time I got to the gig, I just caught a bad headache and then I was catching bad chest pains. I never felt that before. But I caught the chest pains and all that. I'm like, "Damn, what's wrong? I never felt this before." My brother then was in the Hot 8, so they had the Nextel walkie-talkie phone when Nextel came out with the walkie-talkie. So Terrell "Burger" Batiste that play trumpet in the Hot 8 kept hitting him up. The first time he hit him up he was like, "Man, I'm around the corner. I'm on St. Philip around the corner. I'm on the way." It happened so fast, in the next fifteen, twenty minutes, we called him back, no answer. Called him back, no answer.

And somebody called and said, "Say, man, the police just killed somebody around the corner." Like, "Damn. Man, who that is?" And they said, "Man, we don't know." In about two minutes, they called Terrell on the phone and said, "Man, that's Joseph!" And Terrell looked up at me. He said, "Fat Boy!" and I broke out running. I ran at least seven blocks. I ran all the way to around there and I see my mom's name tattooed on my brother and I knew it was my little brother in that truck.

Now, they say that my brother was trying to run over the police. That's a lie. They was talking about he was trying to hit the police and all that. That was a lie. My brother had his hands up and he had his horn case in his hand. Now, that horn case, how could you think that's a gun if it look like that? Well, he had the case in his hand, he had his hands up. And they shot my little brother twenty-one times.

KYLE: Twenty-one times?

ARIAN: Yes.

KYLE: That's murder.

ARIAN: Yeah, that's straight murder. After they shot him twenty-one times, the people in the neighborhood, they had protests. Like, "They wrong." Back then at that time, the police was so crooked and they threatened the community and said, "If y'all go to court for that family, we gonna fuck with y'all." They were gonna deal with the community. That threatened the people and they didn't testify. They didn't come to court for us, so we lost the case.

KYLE: Yeah, that's real crooked. And so I guess the next day you're in Japan, right?

ARIAN: Yeah, the next day I'm in Japan with the Stooges and we had small little rooms in Japan and I was just playing with my horn. I was playing with my horn and I went into Ersel's room. You remember the song by Frankie Beverly and Maze, "We Are One"? The Hot 8 was playing it already and my brother came up with the song for the Hot 8. And I was playing the bass line to it and I took some of the parts out the bass line and I was like, "Man, look, I got a bass line. Let's see what we can do with it." And the saxophone player Cliff was like, "Man, let's do something with that." Cliff came with the little horn parts and then Ersel came in the room and Ersel heard it and he came with the chorus. And Ersel started singing, "Why, oh why?" And we did it like that. So Ersel was singing the song: "Oh why?" He kept repeating it. "Oh why?" And I'm like, "Okay, oh why. What else?" After that, he was like, "Why they had to kill him? / They had the nerve / To say they protect and serve / Oh why?" I said, "Alright, yeah, yeah, I like that! I like that!"

After that, Walter came in the room. He was helping us, too. He came with some parts and we did it onstage for sound check in Japan and just to collaborate everything together and see how the song would come out. When it came out, they had to take my horn off me. I just broke down because it came out so good. It was so beautiful and the sound check was so good, I never had a sound check that was so good since then. And that sound check, it really touched me because we were doing it about things that happened.

My cousin, I love him to death. We had our difference and stuff—Walter—but he stood by me the whole while and was like, "Cuz, I got you." I said, "Okay." And we came with the song. We came back to New Orleans after two and a half weeks and they was having a second line every night for my brother till the funeral, so I was telling them, like, "Y'all ready?" And they be like, "Yeah, come on, Fat Boy. Come with it." I came with the bass line and everybody like, "What the hell they playing?" When they start singing the song, the crowd was like, "Yeah! Yeah!" Everybody loved the song and they be like, "Damn, they come back with a fire song! They made a song." So, that's how "Why" was started.

✦ ✦ ✦

GARFIELD: One day we was at Family Ties and Joseph Williams, "Shotgun Joe," came to Family Ties and he tore a hole in me and Al's ass, boy. Man, we were playing something and we had the whole crowd rocking. He came in there with his horn and, God bless the day, he was loaded. And on his best day, he came in there and I'm talking about *went to playing.* We was trading fours, so I'd play and then he'd play, and then Al would play, and then he would play, and he was tearing our ass up! Then Walter got the horn. Now, out of the three of the trombone players, Walter is more technical and have the theory. But once he got the horn, it was like, "Dang, he messed over Al and Garfield, now Walter getting on the horn!" And he tore Walter ass up. I'm like, "God damn, we gonna take a break and then we gonna talk about this and come back and play again later." That was big beef, like, "We gonna catch y'all, boy. Ooooh, Joseph came up in there and got us, but boy, we gonna lay it all on y'all."

✦ ✦ ✦

CHAD: It was a hard experience because you never expect for the *police* to do that to you. And it could have been some dudes on the street that had killed him, and we could understand that better. But these are the same people that protect us at the parade. It's the same people that protect us when we go out and do our job. "Y'all done killed one of us." So now, after that happened, a lot of shit happens now. They start shutting the brass bands down in the French Quarters, start shutting them down and they can't play past certain times and now they only can play at this certain time because the noise ordinance and shit. It never was like that.

KYLE: Right, with the TBC at the Foot Locker.

CHAD: But it never was like that until that shit happened. After that happened, that sparked wildfire. For a minute, police couldn't even trail a second line closely like they do now. They would be two blocks up or two blocks behind the second line. The cars would ride along the inside while they're second lining. Because when the Stooges bring "Why They Had to Kill Him," it's pandemonium. And if you a police officer, you better get the fuck out the way because we feel for our people.

KYLE: I mean, the emotions run really high.

CHAD: The emotions, yeah!

KYLE: I mean, when they play that on the streets today, people—

CHAD: People still cry when that song come on, man. Yeah, man, people still cry. That's a truly dramatic song because it got so many meanings to it, bro. Like, it's not even just for Joe, you dig? It's for a lot of motherfuckers around the country, a lot of people around the country.

✦ ✦ ✦

DREW: Basically, there had been a systemic running problem with us. The reality was I wasn't much of a confrontational person, but I didn't have to worry about it because I was in the band. The local dope boy—even the local contract killer—would look at me and if there was an instance where there would be a confrontation, they would look at me and go, "Man, you playing the second set? Man, look, we ain't gonna worry about it. Leave that man alone, he in the band." It's like I always had this little pass—especially when it came to that culture. But on the other hand, when it came to the police, we didn't. I remember one time we were playing in the Fischer Project across the river. Things were getting good and we were playing for somebody who died. Somebody died and I think he was either a dope boy or the cousin of a dope boy or whatever. We go into his apartment to deal with this money and he gives us a stack of fives, so we're like, "Alright, we know what you do. We know what your profession is." It's getting good, so somebody's like, "We'll pay you extra to bring us down the street to such and such." Running without a permit can be a little tricky. And there's five or six hundred people, literally, that's running with us at that time.

KYLE: And it's even a problem across the river without a permit?

DREW: Well, any project, we always had a problem. Every housing development had their own police substation. We're going and as long as we were in the courtyard, we were alright, and they let us do what we need to do. As soon as we turn the corner to go into the street, the police car comes around. "Hold up, y'all, you got to go back." It made the people rowdy.

KYLE: I mean, you're there for a specific reason; it's there to commemorate the life of someone.

DREW: Right, exactly. But the police was like, "No. Y'all need to go back. Just go back to the courtyard," and so many of the people was pissed. It wasn't even the people who paid us, but it was just the other people that was around, the random people who come in and they start acting a fool. The next thing you know, some of them start jumping on the back of the police car and everything else, so the police skirts off. It was like, "Alright, let's get this over with because I have a feeling it's about to get real." We're going and all of a sudden just about twelve police cars just come and circle everybody. And one of the policemen gets out, "Take your fucking asses back to that fucking court!"

KYLE: I mean, you're just playing a gig, too, you know?

DREW: We were just playing a gig. And they were going to give us the summons because, at the end of the day, we get arrested for inciting a riot, so we're like, "Shut down. Uh-huh. We don't want that type of situation." And it's interesting because we just look like a herd of cows just walking.

KYLE: Without any music.

DREW: Without any music at all, we just look like a herd of cows going back to the courtyard. And there was one of them I remember in the St. Bernard Projects. It was the same thing. It was in the courtyard. We leave out to go just around the block. The police come around and they didn't even bother to try and stop and use the intercom. They jumped out of the car: "All you motherfuckers, go on, get on the car!" We're trying to sit there like, "No, the hood is hot as a motherfucker on your car, man." "No, fuck that. Put your hands on the car." They was starting to draw guns. We was like, "Nope. Nuh-uh." We all put our hands on the car. And it's like, "Who told y'all you could do this?" It was like, "Man, look. We were paid to do this. We were paid to do this."

KYLE: You were working.

DREW: And so after the interrogation, I remember they made Brian get on his knees with his hands behind his head and that type of thing after the whole ordeal. Brian was being kind of flippant with him. My daddy always told me, "You're not going to win that situation. Shut the fuck up. Take your paperwork and then you file a complaint."

The Stooges with some fans on their 2004 trip to Japan. *Left to right:* Garfield, Sammy Cyrus (*front*), Cliff Stewart, Arian Macklin (*back*), Dwayne Williams, and Walter. Photo courtesy of Garfield Bogan.

KYLE: It's good to be idealistic and fight for what's right, but at the same time, there's a pragmatic—

DREW: Right. This situation, you will not win. After all of the song and dance, they write a citation for public nuisance or something like that. It just so happened that the judge that we went before is like, "What y'all got cuffed and tied in for? You Ashton's grandson, huh?" Walter was like, "Yes, we were playing a gig and they came and we was trying to take them around the block." He was like, "Man, get the hell out of here." But we've had those encounters all the time.

When Joe got killed, everybody—literally, everybody—was running in and asking, "Why? Why did this happen? Why did you do this?" And one of the things that I distinctly remember is Dinerral Shavers.[6] He was working at the sheriff's office then and playing with the Hot 8. And he's trying to ask the police officers, "What happened, why did y'all do this? Why was he a threat?" They told him, "We don't have to answer any of your questions. You need to go sit on over there." He took his uniform and threw it down and was like, "Man, I don't want to be associated with you, you motherfuckers! This is bullshit!"

For me, I think the worst part about it was his brother Arian. They were all leaving for Japan the next day and they were going to be gone for two weeks, so they had to wait to bury him because they wanted him to go. All Arian did was stay in the hotel room the entire time he was in Japan. And then they came up with "Why They Had to Kill Him." At the end of the day, you, as the police, you gave no explanation. While I understand that you thought his trombone was a weapon, you still could diffuse the situation because it wasn't like he was trying to point the thing at you. Somebody yelled "gun" and everybody started shooting. That's just what it is. While I understand, I think two of the officers weren't even put on leave at all while the investigation was going through. They were still working their post, so there was no sort of remorse on the police officers' part. And even some police officers didn't like that. The blue wall wasn't as strong.

KYLE: What do you mean by the blue wall?

DREW: I mean the code of silence, the code that stays amongst police officers. Even that wasn't as strong in this case because everyone knew who this cat was. And the circumstances of the case is what blew it out of the water. Joe borrowed a vehicle—well, he took it without these people knowing, but they always let him borrow that vehicle. At that point, he took it without them noticing and they reported it stolen. I get it; stolen vehicle, you find out where it is, you surround it. He's coming out, he has his hands up, he went in to pick his trombone up, and somebody yells "gun." But just for the police to say, "You know what? We don't owe you an explanation." It's kind of like you're already realizing that the tension is already there between—*especially*—the Black community and the police.

KYLE: It says so much about the value that is systemically given to Black life that a stolen vehicle is somehow worth more than a human. And then also what you're talking about before: like the policing of Black spaces, too. That would never happen in a white community, and everyone knows.

DREW: And here's the thing that I tell people all the time. It's not like this neighborhood doesn't need policing, but the thing that I admired about police officers of the older generation is that they understood that. When they were policing these neighborhoods, they knew how to talk to people, they knew who was who in their district. They knew the criminals in their district. A lot of times, they just couldn't find a way to prosecute them because they would arrest them and then they would come right back out. So now you have this war going on at this point. But there was this whole thing where it's just like the police *knew* exactly who was who and doing what. The younger generation—my generation and actually beyond—they didn't have the same sort of rapport, the ability to talk to people. And the older generations were able to get information from people without outing them. And that was before this "no snitching" phenomenon. So just for the police to tell us, like, "We don't even owe you an explanation other than what's on the facts of this case," it infuriated a lot of people.

KYLE: And rightfully so.

DREW: Right. And there were a lot of people who were just kind of like, "Now, you know what? It's open season. We getting ready to go in." And it's like, "No, you don't have to do that. Just keep asking the question 'Why?'" That's the whole premise of it. "Why? Why did you have to kill him?"

KYLE: And even that points to a more systemic thing because if you think about the whole "tough on crime" stance and all that stuff that happened in the nineties. That seems to be something that really fuels this tension or this chasm between community members and police officers in some sense.

DREW: Yes, it does. Actually, I just got finished reading a book that kind of really touches on that. It's called *The New Jim Crow*.[7]

KYLE: Oh, that's Michelle Alexander.

DREW: Yeah, exactly. And she touches on how thirty years ago how the police became this paramilitary power.[8]

KYLE: The arming of the police forces and stuff . . .

DREW: And the incentives that they got from the government to be paramilitant, that type of thing. You have that sort of dichotomy and we just put it into song form.

✦ ✦ ✦

VIRGIL: As an African American male—and it's kind of sad to say this— I'm not a bad person, I'm not a criminal or anything; I'm a teacher. But when a police officer pulls up behind me, I'm scared. I am afraid. I have a fear. It's not a fear where I'ma start crying, but if they pass me up, I feel relieved. I shouldn't feel that way.

KYLE: And unfortunately, it's a rational fear. It is rational.

VIRGIL: It's rational. And I shouldn't feel that way. As a thirty-nine-year-old man, I shouldn't feel that way. That's a sentiment you can't get around because it's happened. I was a victim of police brutality on multiple occasions as I was growing up. And I wasn't a bad person. You're afraid and you hear the stories of what happened to people. I've had it happen to me, so I'm afraid. And do I have friends that are police officers? Some of my best friends, good friends. But when that police officer pulls behind my truck, I'm afraid. That song, "Why They Had to Kill Him," has meaning for me on various levels.

KYLE: It's also one of the only songs that's explicitly political in all of the brass band music that exists.

Walter takes to the mic for a rendition of "Why?" at the Stooges'
release of their sophomore album, *Thursday Night House Party*. Chris
Cotton and Eric Gordon sing along in the background. Photo by
Karen Lozinski.

VIRGIL: Controversial. We did that. We have police officers that like that
song.

KYLE: Oh, I'm sure!

VIRGIL: They love that song because it's the police officers that don't
do that. That has to be a wake-up call because we have police officers that
like that song. That must mean that they know some police officers that do
that type of stuff. And they know that it happens. But for the respect of the
shield, they may not divulge that. They may know some racist cops. I'm not
saying they have to be white and be racist. There are Black cops that are
prejudiced against people who make certain incomes. My worst experience

with the police has been Black cops because of their perception of who I was and where I was at the time.

KYLE: So is that kind of tied into playing on the streets? Just thinking about for Black people to be out on the streets making a claim on public space, and saying, "We are African *Americans*. This belongs to us as well." There's something that I feel white people perceive as threatening.

VIRGIL: As far as playing on the streets or Black second lines?

KYLE: Like, second lines. But I think it's something that's so far away from many people's purview.

VIRGIL: I would say it's a class thing. It is a racial thing, but it's a class thing.

KYLE: Those things are so bound together.

VIRGIL: I'm a teacher. All the teachers that I work with, all my colleagues, they are African American middle class. When they find out I play brass band music, they look at me like "Well, why?" "Well, why not? I love doing it." Their perception of it is that second lines are not a good thing. "That's not where you want to be. They're dangerous. You're gonna get shot. People are doing drugs, they're drinking in the street, all kind of stuff going on." Now, that *may* happen, but that happens all throughout Mardi Gras, so why you not looking at Mardi Gras? It's *worse* during Mardi Gras. There are more shootings during Mardi Gras.

KYLE: Drug use is way worse on the Tulane University campus.[9]

VIRGIL: There are more Mardi Gras shootings and incidents and fights and killings than they have at second lines. They won't tell you that because Mardi Gras is a big pull as far as money. That's just basically what it is.

CHAPTER 6

Made It through That Water

At the end of August 2005 the federal levees failed and New Orleans was submerged. The ties that bind the city were suddenly broken. In a matter of days, neighbors were moved to far ends of the country, families were dispersed, and homes were destroyed. In a city where music so often provides the impetus to create community, the silence of those spaces—neighborhood bars, schools, and churches—spoke loudest.

As much as Katrina may be a singular disaster, it brought into focus ongoing processes that long predate it. As Cedric Johnson puts it in his politically incisive book *The Neoliberal Deluge: Hurricane Katrina, Late Capitalism, and the Remaking of New Orleans*, "For many Americans, the floodwaters momentarily washed away the roseate democratic veneer of their republic, revealing vulnerability, corruption, indifference, and an unresponsive government."[1] For the Stooges, that rosy veneer had long been washed away to reveal the intertwined workings of capitalism and racism. Their tax dollars paid the salaries of the policemen who killed Joe, and the state rarely sought to serve Black and/or working-class New Orleanians in any substantive way.[2]

If the law fails to extend protections—and in fact becomes a danger—to you and your loved ones, Katrina comes as no surprise. Indeed, to bracket off Katrina as a *distinct* event would be to suppose that everything was fine beforehand and returned that way after.[3] For many of the city's low-income citizens, however, Katrina was simply par for the course. The failure of the levees showed how infrastructural disinvestment hurts all of us, however disproportionately.[4] The result of governmental neglect exposed by a natural disaster, Katrina was not only a "gap in the music," as John Cannon described it, but a personal and political tragedy made all the more tragic because it was (and is) preventable. The failure of inadequate infrastructure was only exacerbated by slow and inadequate governmental response.[5] The storm exposed ongoing political corruption and infrastructural failure. Arguments about whether the city should be rebuilt often hinged on the idea of New Orleans as exceptional—either as a special place to be preserved, or a morally bankrupt place not worth saving—but always an exception to the rule.[6]

In the storm's immediate aftermath, grassroots efforts to locate musicians began amid a hubbub of confusion, loss, and anxiety. On the Rebirth Brass Band's online forum, a list compiled by Mike Olander of the Twin Cities' Jack Brass Band tracked the locations and monitored the well-being of brass band musicians who had quickly become part of the city's diaspora.[7] Fans, friends, and family all posted to the forum in efforts to find musicians. By the end of September, the list tracking the Stooges read as follows:

Stooges:
Walter (Atlanta, GA)
Ersel (B.R.)
Airen (TX) [sic]
Al Growe
Andrew Baham (Houston)
Lil Sam (TX—heading to Atl)
Wayne (TX—heading to Atl)[8]

The Stooges' inseparability was disrupted when the storm hit, and the band dispersed to cities throughout the South. Despite this momentary break in their brotherhood, they grew closer to each other, navigating new and unfamiliar surroundings and eventually consolidating in Atlanta where Walter had set up base. His bandmates joined him with their families as soon as they could, many of them living under the same roof.

The circumstances surrounding the storm also saw the Stooges chart a new musical direction. Disaster necessitated invention. They were confronted with a different music scene in Atlanta that had little use for brass bands for all the bread-and-butter gigs: birthdays, funerals, weddings, and Sunday second lines. The community and network just weren't there. They navigated this new landscape accordingly, moving away from the brass band format to something more hip-hop oriented, with keyboards, percussion, drum kit, and horns. In order not to confuse the branding of this new musical venture with the brass band, they called themselves JumpShive.[9] This was among the first of the Stooges' many flirtations with a stage band format that had already proven successful for the Soul Rebels and Dirty Dozen.

While the Stooges saw an opportunity to move beyond the confines of brass band music, brass bands were quickly becoming symbols of the city's recovery. Despite a small audience and not nearly enough gigs to support a living, Al, Garfield, Ellis, and John Cannon moved home and founded the appropriately named Free Agents Brass Band, the first brass band back in the city. Their original song, "We Made It through That Water," became the soundtrack to the city's rebuilding efforts and a testament to the resiliency of its residents.[10]

Meanwhile, the Stooges Brass Band was waylaid. Aside from their brief but ill-fated efforts to get JumpShive off the ground, they had stepped out of the game. Walter went on musical hiatus for two years while he attempted to rebuild his properties back home. When contractors scammed him and his business partner out of huge sums of money, his business partner took his own life. The sudden loss put everything into perspective, and Walter eventually had to cut his losses. "They're just things, man," he told me, while we drove to a gig outside of Atlanta. "They're not worth a life." Facing a critical juncture, he moved back home and soon began receiving inquiries about the Stooges from those in the second line community who craved the playfulness they brought to the streets. When Walter moved home and word got around that the Stooges were regrouping, Al and Garfield were summarily dismissed from the Free Agents (they "ran home to daddy," as Ellis openly jokes), and the Stooges returned in full force.

A decade after the storm, when we began writing this book, the city was by my measure facing Katrina fatigue. An abundance of scholarship either attempted to understand the political processes undergirding the disaster or sought to capitalize on the spectacle of it. Many people who weathered the storm were drained and in no need of reliving the collective trauma. Nevertheless, it seems impossible to tell this story without it.

✦ ✦ ✦

WALTER: It was the Saturday before Katrina. By that time in my personal life, I already started buying real estate, so I was like "Black-person rich." I got more money than my mom and dad ever had. I'm in a financial situation where I'm doing dumb shit. I got cars.

KYLE: Right. You had like two F-150s.

WALTER: Yeah, that was my high. I ain't smoke, so I bought cars. So I'm in a financial situation where I'm telling my band members, "Man, we got to do something. What your family doing?" They was like, "Man, I don't know. Walt, bruh, we just gonna be here. Y'all always run from the storms. We'll see y'all when y'all get back." We wind up leaving: me, my wife, two kids. We leave. I took some of my family members. I took my little cousin, Thaddeaus Ramsey, who play in the Stooges now. He was ten at the time. I took my brother, my cousin, and we left.

After the band members started being displaced and people had to start leaving New Orleans, I started calling for band members. I remember Dwayne called me up and I had got cleared through him on the phone and he was like, "Man, I'm on the bridge. I don't know what we're gonna do, Walt." I think I started calling FEMA and then I was like, "Man, I need to call the National Guard. I need to find someone. I don't give a fuck how much it cost to get them off the bridge, I need a helicopter to go get them." And one day, we had spoke to some general or some shit with the army and he was like, "Yeah, we gonna send a helicopter to your people." And then they wind up getting rescued off the bridge.

After that, once they all got displaced, I started calling for them. I was in Atlanta. I was living in one of my aunties' houses at the time with a bunch of other family members. Thirty people in one house. I'm already in the business of buying. The first day, I stood there. The second day, I had a realtor come over. My auntie said, "We have a realtor here." I said, "Yeah, I'm about to buy a house. I got to get out of here." I wind up buying a house in Georgia and I got all my band members to come stay at the house. And then once it got full—it was too many in one house because you having arguments and shit. And now we living different because it's usually just men and now we living with wives and girlfriends in the house. It's complicated. We went and bought another house, so we started just getting our band members to Atlanta. Some of them who didn't want to stay with us, we started helping them get houses and stuff like that until all the Stooges was all in Atlanta. It was me, Chad, Andrew, and Dwayne in a house together. But Alfred, Ersel, and all them had they own spot. Arian had his own spot, but we was all moving to Atlanta. At that time, Virgil had been playing with us, too, so he was displaced, but he had came back. And then Ellis was able to come back home and start the Free Agents.

KYLE: And they were the first band back in the city, right?

WALTER: Yeah. He started just getting whoever come home on the weekend to play for the people. And then eventually, that's when we first started forming our stage band and we first got into a lot of production, and that's why we was making money. We toured, but we was doing production and getting our stage band started.

The Stooges front line sporting "Stooges R Back" shirts. *Left to right:* Garfield Bogan, Walter Ramsey, Drew Baham, Chad Honore, Virgil Tiller, and Al Growe. Photo courtesy of Garfield Bogan.

KYLE: And were you guys doing the JumpShive thing at that time?

WALTER: Yeah, JumpShive. We didn't want to call it Stooges because Stooges already known for something and we trying to do something different.

KYLE: You don't want to dilute the brand, you want to have an offshoot.

WALTER: Yeah, so we on our JumpShive shit and we started touring and getting that together. Eventually, I had to stop because I had responsibility as far as my real estate and I'm letting that go because I'm trying to stay with the band. So now I got to deal with real business shit: mortgage companies and insurance companies. And now I'm in Georgia and I got three houses I *bought* in Georgia, but I still am neglecting my houses in New Orleans, so I need to get them fixed. I got beat out by a contractor.

After a while, I was like, "Look fellas, I can't play music right now. I need to go." I spent July 2007 till almost 2009 rebuilding, so I wasn't even playing music. The Free Agents, all them back, they was doing good. So I was home and I used to go to the second lines every Sunday. I would just go watch them. And somewhere between 2007, 2008, I was like, "Man, the music not the same." The people kept coming up to me and was like, "Man, why you not playing? These bands don't sound right. You got to bring the Stooges back." I was like, "The Stooges all displaced. They play in other bands now.

I don't have no band members." Alfred and Ersel, they play with the Free
Agents, Andrew playing at the casino, Troy got Orleans Avenue. Big D
playing congas in Orleans Avenue. Lil Sam is playing with the Hot 8. Chad
is playing with the Hot 8 and then eventually he started playing with the
Rebirth. I don't have no one. Everybody is gone. No more Stooges. It's dead,
it's gone. So they was like, "Man, you good. You trained all these musicians
for years. Just go get new musicians and start training them." I was like, "I
don't even know if I can do that. Naw, man." And the people was like, "Come
on, man. Start one gig at a time."

I went and got some shirts made that said "The Reunion." And I started
calling all the musicians that played with the Stooges. I was like, "Look, man,
would you be willing to do a record with me?" We started having rehearsals
and putting together a reunion record. And then the word on the street came.
"The Stooges back, they doing this!" So then people started getting scared.

✦　✦　✦

ARIAN: I was in Texas and I called Walter and he was like, "Man, what you
doing?" I be like, "Nothing." He was like, "You want to get off your feet and
make money?" I'm like, "Yeah." He said, "Well, find a way to get to Atlanta."
I got me a plane ticket and I paid for my plane ticket and I went to Atlanta
and I lived in with them and we moved and went on tour for three weeks
and came back home. I was living with them till I got married out there
in Atlanta with my wife—well, my ex-wife—and that's how we wind up in
Georgia.

✦　✦　✦

ELLIS: For the most part, the Stooges were kind of dormant right after the
storm. We started Free Agents and we started putting that fire into everybody to get back into it.

KYLE: Right. You guys were the first brass band back. You guys were
founded right after the storm, right?

JOHN C.: Right. We were the brass band that was founded out of Katrina.
That's why the name hasn't changed from Free Agents, because it was everybody that was spread out that didn't really have a band or they weren't with
their band. I was in Jackson, Mississippi. I was close to no one with music;
they all went to Atlanta. Even before I knew what was going on with my
property in the Lower Ninth Ward, I ordered a horn. I *need* a horn. I don't
know what else to do, *knowing* that your entire neighborhood is not there.

I was in the Lower Ninth Ward. Twenty-five feet of water. My home sat in about fifteen feet of water for about four or five days. Now, I'm back in my house. Rebuilt, new house, something totally different. It's all paid for. The amount of stress and struggle that I've gone through, I wouldn't wish it on anybody.

KYLE: And so you guys turned to music? That was all you had, right?

JOHN C.: That was all I knew, yeah.

ELLIS: People started. The need for musicians and for music, people started calling us a lot; the Phils, the Bennie Petes. Matter of fact, Alfred and I had never been in the Stooges together, but we were in Free Agents together. That was like three of the first people: me, him, and Ersel in Atlanta. But the need was just there and we just made it happen.

✦ ✦ ✦

AL: The year before the storm, Walt had his ideas again. He said, "Man, the brass band is good, we doing different things, but we don't get respected all over the country and the world being a brass band. We need to switch it over with the set and this and that." I was like, "Man, look. The brass band is what got us hot right now."

KYLE: And it's working, too. You know, it's really working.

AL: Yeah, the brass band. And we hot—I'm talking about, we *super hot*— on the street at that time. I'm like, "Look, man. I don't think we need to change what we do." So we going back and forth, back and forth. Once the storm happened, they wanted to branch off, leave Stooges where it was, and move it off to something called JumpShive. It was gonna be a branch off of the Stooges with the stage band thing. So I'm like, "Man, I'm not feeling that. I'm not with it." I was like, "Walt, maybe after all these years of me being in the band, maybe this is the time that we break ways." There wasn't no argument about it, it's just I'm letting him know. I didn't totally agree on that way of doing it. I'm like, "Man, I been playing traditional brass band music my whole life. We all have. And we see the value." They went off to Atlanta during the storm and me and Ersel went to Baton Rouge, then we went to Atlanta.

While we was in Atlanta and Baton Rouge, we hooked up with Ellis Joseph. Ellis was like, "Man, I got a couple of gigs out in Atlanta. We can play a couple of gigs down here." So we start playing gigs there. After a while, all of us start migrating back to New Orleans at the same time, maybe about six, seven months after the storm. When we all got back to New Orleans, we like, "Man, we had a good thing out there. Let's add a couple of people, come up with a thing." We came up with the Free Agents. We start playing a gig

Walter at the Original N.O. Lady and Men Buckjumpers second line, November 29, 2009. Photo by Pableaux Johnson.

because they ain't have that many people back in New Orleans. They had really no bands back here. So we started playing gigs as the Free Agents and Ersel wind up leaving Atlanta and coming back down because they wasn't really getting too many gigs as JumpShive.

Walt bought a nice house, was chilling in Atlanta. So I don't know, he must have felt like he want to be back home and whatnot. So he come back, he was like, "Hey man. What's up?" So I was like, "Look, bro, I love this brass band stuff, but this JumpShive thing just don't fit well with me. I'm your dog, I'ma always do whatever you want to do, but that JumpShive stuff, it's just not what I want." He come back, he was like, "Man, I want to bring the brass band back. We got more work to do. We got more." Me and Ersel was like, "We'll help." We come with a shirt that say "Stooges R" and then it had "Back." So we come up and when we started the Stooges off the second time, it was just me, Walter, and Ersel. And what happened was Ellis from the Free Agents caught wind of it. We had an emergency meeting. It was like nine, ten o'clock one night he called me up. He was like, "Man, look. We need to talk." I said, "Alright. What's up Ellis?" He was like, "Bro, I'm hearing Walter coming back in the city and I'm hearing he trying to get his band back together. What y'all gonna do?" Like, "Bro, we *free agents*, we all play gigs with other people. We just gonna play gigs." "Nah, man. You either with us or you with them."

KYLE: But didn't Ellis play with the Stooges?

Walter, Garfield, and Al sharing a laugh at the Original N.O. Lady and Men Buckjumpers second line, November 29, 2009. Al's shirt shows pictures of his wife, Shawn, who was an honorary member of the parade, and their eldest daughter, Que'Shawn, who was grand marshal of the kids' division. Photo by Pableaux Johnson.

AL: Right.

KYLE: Okay. So there's some bad blood there?

AL: It wasn't bad blood. At the time, the streets was competitive. The streets is competitive for gigs. And it ain't like it is now when everybody was playing with everybody and all of that. You either play with one band or you play without us. Straight up. Who you rolling with? Who you going to put your loyalty to?

So we telling Ellis, "Man, it's all good." But at the same time, we were like, "We playing gigs with Walt." One day on Frenchmen Street, we had just got more copies of the CD *Made It through That Water*, but me and Ersel was figuring something was weird about the meeting. We had a whole lot of band members around—and they got trombone players at the gig! Ellis was like, "Say, man, we'd just like to let y'all know we appreciate everything y'all did with this band up until this point, but we feel or believe we've reached an impasse, so here's y'all group of CDs. We no longer need you to play with the Free Agents." Shake everybody hand, dapped everybody off, told them, "We appreciate playing." Business is business.

✦   ✦   ✦

CHAD: I left the Stooges in 2007. What led to that is my family wanted to move back to New Orleans and Walter wanted to live in Atlanta. He wanted to stay in Atlanta. And the Stooges band had already moved to Atlanta to keep the band going, but we wasn't gigging, we wasn't working.

KYLE: There kind of isn't the cultural thing to keep it going.

CHAD: There's no parties, no weddings and stuff. So that's how the music group started. That's why JumpShive started in Atlanta. We was working as JumpShive and we forgot about the Stooges. The Stooges ain't come back until 2008 or 2009 when Walter and them decided to come back home. I moved back home, but I didn't know exactly what I was going to do. When I got back home, the Hot 8 needed a trumpet player and they had this gig on a Sunday. They asked me to come play.

KYLE: Okay, so you started playing with the Hot 8 when you came back and that was a logistical decision: you were here and the Stooges were mostly in Atlanta.

CHAD: Yeah, so by the time the Stooges had moved back home, I was already a year in the Hot 8 band. Most of the Stooges had moved back, but now I'm playing with the Hot 8, so we just kept going with the Hot 8. I played with the Hot 8 for maybe two or three years and when things got sour with them, I moved up to the Rebirth.

✦ ✦ ✦

GARFIELD: The Free Agents really started in Atlanta doing a couple of gigs and then ended up being the only band back in New Orleans at the time. It was pretty much the musicians that was able to hit the gigs was the Free Agents. The Free Agents were real hot until all the bands started coming back and it turned into being what the name was: Free Agents Brass Band. If you ain't have a band, you go play with the Free Agents; you're a free agent.

KYLE: And then when the Stooges came back, I guess you and Al were let go from the Free Agents?

GARFIELD: Ellis actually felt some type of way when he found out the Stooges was coming back. He felt like we were automatically gonna just walk away and go with Walter. I don't know why, but he got some more trombone players and we had a meeting at Ray's Boom Boom Room at the time—now Vaso's. He was like, "Look, I know Walter's back and probably gonna start the Stooges, so y'all can go ahead and be with the Stooges. I'm gonna take Larry." And I'm like, "That's where you're at with it? That wasn't the plan, but now it is!" You can't take me off. No matter who, what, where, why, we gonna make something happen. That's pretty much what Free Agents was. We got together to make something happen.

So with the Most Wanted Brass Band, same thing. When we got pushed out of the Stooges and the Stooges Brass Band was organized and situated where they had people playing in it and me, Cotton, Virgil, Spug, all of us had to find a way, I came up, I'm like, "Bro, let's think about this. We was the Stooges. The Stooges is the most wanted brass band, but they don't have the musicians. Most wanted brass band, Stooges, we gonna be the Most Wanted Brass Band!"

KYLE: Yeah, because I don't know the Most Wanted story.

GARFIELD: We were the Stooges. I guess Walter wanted more leadership, so he felt, "If I break off some of the people that have assets, or if this not working, I'm not fussing, it's not clicking, so I'ma need some more musicians that's gonna listen to me," pretty much. So "All y'all can be replaced." He told us that: "I'm replacing all y'all." It was serious shit. He called us to a practice to go over music while the people he had replacing us sat in there. We made it hard for them. Oh, man. We know y'all can't do this, so get the party started. We went through the whole show and they was just looking like, "You want us to do that?" "Yeah, come on, y'all, let's go. Man, he tripping." A lot of hurt came from the Stooges, but it's a brotherhood. Nothing in life is just gonna be real easy. The reason I left Most Wanted alone: because it stopped being a band and it started being one of those, "This person gonna play, this person gonna play."

KYLE: It was like a pick-up band almost.

GARFIELD: I can't deal with that. I was brought up better than that.

KYLE: Okay, so you want a core group of people that you're playing with always.

GARFIELD: You know this the Most Wanted Band because that's who he play with. He don't play with Stooges, Most Wanted, Free Agents. You know, he's not a Free Agent and I just called him because I didn't have a trumpet player. It became that. So I was just like, "Nah. I'll call y'all when we have gigs. We gonna shut this down, and if something come up, I'll call the band and we'll do something." But other than that, nah. But anyway, this the Stooges story. But that's what happened—that's why we got to Most Wanted, because of the replacements. And that's what we started calling the Stooges Music Group, the ones on the road, we started calling them the replacements. All in fun. But from hurt, you build things. Sometimes good things come out of it, sometimes nothing come out of it. Most Wanted could have been a good thing, but it's really not much. I would call it a branch off the Stooges.

✦ ✦ ✦

VIRGIL: The fun that we have is through competition. And through the competition, we challenge each other on the stage. And it comes up to the friendly competition and that—even though this happens on the stage—the crowd sees that when we're on the stage, when we're doing stage gigs, the crowd depicts it as being, "Hey, they are really entertaining us," which, we are trying to entertain. One of the hardest things, you know Al never really wanted to do the stage band thing. Now, I was for it. I didn't really think it was gonna work, but I was like, "Let's try something different," because, at that time, I was getting tired of being on the streets.

KYLE: Okay, but that was around the time that you left, wasn't it? Or I guess it was an idea at that time, but it wasn't something that had materialized.

VIRGIL: It was an idea at the time. They had started it in Atlanta and they stopped because when they had—what is it called? I forget what the company is called.

KYLE: Oh, JumpShive.

VIRGIL: JumpShive. That's when they did the JumpShive and they were doing it in Atlanta. When they came back to New Orleans, that kind of like stopped. And so the brass band thing started back up. And then they said, "Man, we got tired of the streets." Man, when I'm telling you, we were in the streets every Sunday. *Every* Sunday for about two years. Every Sunday.

✦ ✦ ✦

KYLE: How long were you actively playing with the Stooges?

ARIAN: From '96 off and on till 2007 or something like that.

KYLE: Okay, so that's a long run. How did you kind of get out of the Stooges or how did that work? Because I guess it was right after the storm?

ARIAN: Yeah, right after the storm. You know how people go through their little problems and all that kind of stuff. And I was dealing with a problem—a drug problem. And my cousin like, "Man, I love you, but you know what I'm saying?" He changed the band to a different thing. They was wanting to do the bass and all that.

KYLE: Right, yeah. The stage band sort of thing.

ARIAN: Yeah, the stage band. But I had moved on because I was playing with the Youngblood Brass Band.

✦ ✦ ✦

VIRGIL: I actually left the band right before the storm. For me, it was a money issue. Not so much that I wanted money as just the fact that some things were going on at the time that I just didn't like. It's nothing against Walter or anybody, it's just some things. The good thing I like about the band is that if you have a problem, we'll talk about it. It was never bad blood between us, but I just said, "Look, I'm not going to do it." And then the storm hit and they went to Atlanta and I didn't have anybody to play with. I was living in Jeanerette, Louisiana, and then Baton Rouge, traveling back and forth at one point in time, and they were in Atlanta. So when they finally came back and said, "Let's put the band together," I was like, "Let's do it." I think the month before the storm hit, I got out the band and then the year of the storm because I just missed that music. I missed my friends. They were all scattered out. I missed playing music. That's a feeling that I couldn't get at that point in time. Especially during Katrina, that was something that I was really searching for just to get through that point.

PART III
The Street Kings Generation

CHAPTER 7

Stooges Party

Thursday, June 21, 2018. The Well is a long-running Black-owned club in the Sixth Ward. It's packed from front to back. "Shack! What you say?" Walter yells into the mic. Comedian Shack Brown, standing over six feet tall with a lively grin and a twinkle in his eye, takes the mic handoff, and the band members spill out from the stage onto the floor. Years ago, Shack helped compose "I Gotta Eat," a track on the Stooges' 2013 album, *Street Music*. While singing about struggle with a goofy grin ("My mama sold drugs [I gotta eat! I gotta eat!] / And my daddy was a ho! [He a ho! He a ho! He a ho!]"), he inexplicably begins chanting about nacho chips and dip. "Walk with a dip / then you dip your chip!" Later that night, he hands me some spinach dip and chips from his company, Dip Wit It. Shack sells his spinach dip; others come through with a rack of snacks and homemade pralines. Al's wife, Shawn, sets up her clothing pop-up, Boutique de'Elegance. I buy a T-shirt from their son Que'Dyn's One Groove Brass Band. Cole Chris tends to the grill outside. Neighborhood bars are communal spaces of trade with a vibrant economy.

Thursday, July 19, 2018. After dropping a couple books off to John Perkins's apartment, I throw my bike in the bed of his truck and we drive to see his bandmates play at the Well. John still plays with the Stooges with some frequency, but not on this weekly gig. I take my spot at a table next to Shawn, and John makes his rounds greeting many of the people in the bar. He messes around on the cowbell on the stage, and when the Stooges play the first notes of their set, he hams it up on the dance floor, working up a sweat as he's joined by Tyrone

A Stooges Pajama Jam at the Well, July 26, 2018. *Left to right:* Al, Shawn Goffner-Growe, Kyle, Matt Sakakeeny, and Lyndsey Moak. Photo courtesy of Shawn Goffner-Growe.

"Tuffy" Nelson, a second line regular, who is going live on Facebook, the light of his phone joining others illuminating the dance floor. Other dancers join in, dropping down to the ground and crawling under each other's legs. John gets a water and some food from outside. When I look up, his truck is gone—and he accidentally took my bicycle with him.

Thursday, July 26, 2018. The John F. Kennedy class of '78 is having their forty-year reunion, and the barroom is blue and gold. A few days before, Virgil posted an ad on Facebook that the night would be a Pajama Jam, a long-running Stooges tradition in which audience members are encouraged to wear pajamas. Few people get the memo (Virgil somehow included), but some of us nevertheless show up in evening attire. Eric Gordon and his best friend, Chris Cotton, now seven-year alumni of the Stooges, come by, and Chris soon dances in the center of the bar with his signature footwork. Shawn later proclaimed on Facebook that "it went down like four flats on a Cadillac."

Thursday, August 23, 2018. The members of the Big 6 Brass Band, all of whom played with the Stooges at some point, come by the Well after their 9:30 p.m. gig at E & C Lounge. Entering the rear door, they spill from the doorway at the side of the stage onto the sidewalk by BYOB Catering. Feeling the effects of some Crown Apple, Thaddeaus Ramsey (the Big 6 bass drummer and Walter's cousin) leans up against a car on the sidewalk. Listening intently, he sings through the chord changes and chats with his bandmates as they enjoy their return to a Stooges Thursday night.

Weekly gigs come to be defined not by the venues that host them but by the people who attend week in and week out. They are home bases for Mardi Gras Indian tribes, social aid and pleasure clubs, and bands—gathering spaces in a vibrant Black public sphere.[1] They tend to be the kinds of places where the cover charge (if there is one) comes with a plate of food. The city government's Comprehensive Zoning Ordinance (CZO) regulates these neighborhood bars, which are usually not zoned for liquor licenses but have been grandfathered in. If a neighborhood bar is assigned nonconforming status by the CZO, it will lose its liquor license, and no bar can replace it. Bars often change hands and names, and their locations take on memories that are shared across generations. Bands, which usually have weekly residencies at these neighborhood bars, often bounce around, sometimes leaving one bar only to come back to it years later with a different name and new ownership (as the Stooges did with the Well, which was once Club N'Finity). As Walter remembers it, the police would "find a way to shut us down," and they moved from bar to bar with their weekly gig for years.

Though they've tried numerous venues and days of the week, Thursday has long been considered the Stooges' night, and they've maintained a solid core of fans, friends, and family who regularly devote their Thursday nights to the band. In New Orleans, you can fill your schedule with brass band gigs every night of the week: Sundays are for the Hot 8 at the Howlin' Wolf, Mondays are for the Big 6 at Da Jump Off Lounge, Tuesdays are for Rebirth at the Maple Leaf, Wednesdays are for TBC at Celebration Hall, and Fridays are for the Original Pinettes at Bullet's Sports Bar. It's a long list of bread-and-butter gigs. Musicians in the city have long participated in what some call the "gig economy," in which work is short-term, contractual, and volatile.[2] Having a weekly residency provides some economic predictability and helps mitigate the risks of contractual music work. While weekly gigs provide predictable income, they're also so much more than that: they're a means of creating community. They also provide a space for commerce and exchange as patrons trade skills and products. If there's anything you need, being plugged into the social network of a neighborhood bar is one means of getting it done and keeping your money in the community.

The Stooges hosted numerous weekly residencies over the years.[3] Although the locations and day of the week have changed, their most famous residency was Thursday nights from 2009 to 2012 at the Hi-Ho Lounge, a venue anthropologist Marc Perry describes as "on the now hipster-esque St. Claude Avenue situated at the expanding fictive border between the highly gentrified neighborhoods of the Marigny and Bywater and the historically black 7th, 8th, and 9th Wards."[4] In their heyday at the Hi-Ho, the Stooges blurred geographic segregation, performing night after night for a packed house with an interracial audience of Black New Orleanians and white transplants. The Stooges' residency became so successful that they were tapped by the owners to take over management in the final year of their tenure there.[5] This chapter explores the Thursday night residencies the Stooges have held over the years with particular attention paid to their stint at the Hi-Ho.

✦ ✦ ✦

WALTER: Usually when you find your passion, you do it because you love it, and it's not about the money. But then, eventually, some other people start loving what you're doing and start paying you for it. And then you take it on, like, "I love what I'm doing, but I also need to study business—music business and business *period*—to see how I can market myself to become great." It took years of just trying to get people to come listen to us one night a week—like a Thursday night, which the Stooges is famous for.

KYLE: And that was Thursday night where at?

WALTER: Well, when they first started, they was on Seven and Dryades at a club called Baby's. It was just in the middle of a "bad neighborhood," I'ma say. Back in those days we was able to get eleven by seventeen little poster flyers from Kinko's, and we'd post them up around the whole city saying "this is where we play at."

KYLE: It's like your entrée into marketing.

WALTER: Right. And two people would show up every week. It would just be this white lady named Brandy, whatever Black friend she had, the owners of the club, and maybe the bartender. We'd just be playing in there with them, so we had to learn how to market ourselves. We would go and do different gigs and we'd pass out our flyers at our different parties, weddings, and funeral gigs saying, "Look, come see us on a Thursday night." Eventually, two turned into four, and four went to six, and then we started getting a group of people. We were popular with the ladies and so we'd get a group of women. It would be like one of the meter maids would come in and then she would go out and tell the rest of her meter maids and the next week, we got eight meter maids. And we got the white lady and her Black friend. We have them and eight meter maids and the bartenders. It was crazy because it just kept building up slowly but surely, but it was just all women. I was like, "Where the men at?" I guess one guy came in there—he was like trying to see what

A promotional card advertises the Stooges Music Group's weekly gigs at Club N'Finity and Club Good Ole' Days. Image courtesy of Ashton Ramsey.

was going on—and he was like, "Oh my God! Look at all the women in here!" It was just the band and all these women. Then the following week, we had like tons of guys come there, and it was the women, and then somehow, they shut us down, so we had to move to another location.

KYLE: Wait—why'd they shut you down?

WALTER: I have no clue.

KYLE: If there was a bunch of people there, that's not wise business.

WALTER: It had to be something with the business or the business owners or something with the liquor license—something out of our reach.

KYLE: Oh, did the whole place shut down?

WALTER: Yeah, the police came and shut it down. But then in a few months, it opened back up, but we had to keep moving. We need to find another spot, because if not, we just got to start from square one again. I believe if my memory stand correctly, we went from there to Downtown and we kept developing it. Thursday nights in New Orleans, we probably did five to six locations.

We moved to Downtown at a club called Family Ties, which was one of the clubs for one of the social aid and pleasure clubs. Then the police came around there and shut us down. I don't know why, but they find a way to shut us down, and then we moved to another club called Club N'Finity, which is on Basin and N. Robertson. And this is all before Katrina, and then Katrina came and shut that down. And so then for three or four years, we haven't played on Thursday nights. And then we come back after Katrina and we start back up at the Rock Bottom on Thursday nights. And so we went from the Rock Bottom and then something happened at the Rock Bottom. I don't know, something always happen. Garfield, he was able to get a club Downtown again. So we went from Uptown to Downtown again. He called it Goody's.

KYLE: And he bought the place?

WALTER: Yeah, he had the place. And he was the owner of the place—him and his two cousins. We played at Goody's for three months and then I started seeing some different things that he was going through with him and his cousins or whatever. I was like, "I'm not quite sure about their business." So then a guy named "Jazz Fest Johnny" [John Driver], that promotes a lot of things around the city, he came to me and he was like, "Hey, Whoadie, my partner got a club. It's not really popping, but I would like for you to meet the guy and see what you could do. You could really help him to get the club popping." And that's when I went and met with the owner, John. Him and his wife owned the Hi-Ho. I went in there and I was like, "This is a nice club." He put a lot of work and money into the club to make sure that everything was nice, but they just couldn't get a break. They couldn't get well-known bands in there. At that time, we well established.

KYLE: So that would have been around what year?

WALTER: I want to say we probably went to the Hi-Ho like '07, '08, something like that. So then we got in the Hi-Ho and we played there and we made the club popular, so they started getting popular bands to come through there so the club could make money.

✦ ✦ ✦

AL: Ersel wind up getting a bar on St. Claude Street called Goody's. We playing in there and a guy comes and was like, "Man, look, there's this barroom right up the street on St. Claude that the guy's looking for a band to play in, and they've got some nights." Now, we playing at Ersel's spot on a Thursday. Walt was like, "Bruh, they got a guy want to meet us to come check out another spot. I'm going to go talk to him, see what's going on." I said, "Well, Walt, what night? We free other than Thursday." He said, "Bruh, I think they want Thursday." "Okay, Walt."

KYLE: So moving from Ersel's bar to—

Walter at the mic on a Hi-Ho Thursday night, August 4, 2011. Photo by Conrad Wyre.

AL: Yeah! I'm like, "Okay, Walt. Ersel is our partner." He said, "Bruh, let's go
see what he talking about." We go over there. Me, Walter, the guy that told us
about it, and the guys that own the Hi-Ho. We walk into Hi-Ho, it looks like
a straight hippie spot. I mean, they got sperm cells coming from the ceiling.
It looks like a cultural design art of sperm frying and they got all kinds of
shit.

KYLE: What year was this?

AL: 2009, something like that. We looking around the bar and they got
a stage—a big stage! It kind of look like the Maple Leaf a little bit. We walk
around the building and talk to the guy and whatnot. The guy was like,
"Man, look. Y'all can do another night, but I really want y'all to do Thursday
night." So I'm sitting at the bar, I'm like, "Well . . ." Walt was like, "That's the
night you want? Thursday night? Done."

KYLE: Okay, but there must have been some money. What were they paying you per Thursday?

AL: The deal that we normally do when we start a club: Let us get our
door and let us get our tips. You make the bar, we gonna get our door, we
gonna get our tips.

KYLE: And what do you usually charge at the door?

AL: Well, that's up to us because we knew how our crowd would be. We
got to figure out how our crowd was gonna be. At the time, we got to build it

to make money. Now, once we build it to make money, then, yeah, we gonna come at the bar and say, "Well, look, hit us off because you made—"

KYLE: Right. Because you get started and then you say, "Hey, well this is working out well for you, right? Do you want to kick back a little more in this direction?"

AL: Right. So, we go outside after the meeting and I said, "Walt, bruh, we play Thursday night at Ersel's spot." He was like, "Bruh, we got to do this. Business is business. Ersel's spot is good, but it's not gonna attract a crowd. You want to get a crowd, you want to get a crowd that you want, you got to make moves."

KYLE: There was probably also way more room at Hi-Ho, right? That's a big space.

AL: Yeah, it was a bigger venue. So we break the news to Ersel and I don't think he really liked it too much. I saw it in his eyes. I was like, "Man, that's cold." Because it was his business!

KYLE: Yeah, of course! I mean, he's going to lose money.

AL: And his main thing was us playing. *And* he had to play!

KYLE: And run the bar at the same time, I guess.

AL: But the other thing was, we make the move to the Hi-Ho, he got to leave his spot and come play the gig!

KYLE: Walt is cold. He's a capitalist with a capital C.

AL: I'ma tell you the story what it really is! That's what we writing a book for: to tell you the story of what it really is.

✦ ✦ ✦

GARFIELD: At this point it was like, "Dude, right now you're stabbing me in the back. You know Thursday night at Goody's is *popping* because the Stooges is there." We got a full house. Me being the owner of Goody's, Walter felt like he needed to know how much we were making on the drinks and everything, and he felt like he needed to get a percentage. So I was like, "Walt, we been doing this shit for a long time. We have never went in a bar and asked them what they making." I said, "Why, because it's me and I know you, you want the details of it?" He was like, "Man, because we the ones making this bar on a Thursday night." I'm like, "Dude, my Wednesday Bike Night do good, too. I have good things going on at Goody's. If the Stooges leave, I have to put something else in that spot. I don't like that. You really gonna leave because I don't want to let you know how much?"

So then him and Al went to looking at different spots. "Man, we going to the Hi-Ho right down the street." I was like, "I'm running a business here,

bro. Y'all gonna go right down the street. I mean, *we* are gonna go right
down the street on the night I could be in my bar making stuff happen.
Alright, it's business, I understand. I'm gonna let my partners know what
we're deciding to do, and I guess that's what we're gonna do if y'all decide we
gonna go to the Hi-Ho." "Yeah, because they got the stage and they got their
own microphones. And he made it so much better. It's set up like Tipitina's."

KYLE: It's a bigger space, is it? Definitely the ceilings, I would imagine, are
higher.

GARFIELD: It was a bigger space. The ceilings were higher. For the band,
Hi-Ho could have probably been a better spot. But for friendship and business and the fact that he wanted to leave Goody's to go to the Hi-Ho was real
shady. So that right there, that was like "And you're supposed to be a friend?"
I wouldn't do no shit like that to you. If we're doing business together and
I'm helping you with your business, I'm helping you with your business. I'm
not gonna say, "Well, how much you making? You can't tell me how much
you making? Well I don't want to fuck with you no more." And I took that
like that. It took a while to really let that ease off.

KYLE: So, I guess you guys kind of fell off for a little bit?

GARFIELD: No, no. I'm not that type of person.

KYLE: It didn't become personal?

GARFIELD: It was personal, but I still know how to keep myself in all
type of situations. Any of them can tell you I'm a different brand. When my
daddy died, you can look at me and be like, "You know your daddy died,
right?" I'm like, "Yeah, I'm dealing with it."

✦ ✦ ✦

CHRIS: If I could say this one thing from the Hi-Ho Lounge, sitting on
the stage, I can remember some nights warming up before the gig. The gig
was on Thursday night, and while I was a student at Xavier, we'd have con-
certs on Thursday night. So I can picture coming from the concert. The concert ended at maybe eight o'clock, so I'd get there probably about eight thirty,
nine o'clock, and I'd be warming up, sitting on the stage. And there's a few
people, but it's kind of dark, so you know the people who you can recognize,
but you can't really make out everybody. I'm just warming up on the stage
and people walking into the club and you got one person over here. My sister Toya would come to the gig. And I'd be like, "Hey, Toya!" And she got her
friend with her, Nicole. And they got all the old heads like Eschew and Book
coming in, hollering at the band. We all hollering at Bittles. "Bittles, man, let
me get something to eat before the gig!" I used to get them ribs from Bittles,

Spug and Eric hamming it up at the Hi-Ho, August 4, 2011. Photo by Conrad Wyre.

man. And just hanging out with everybody before, everybody doing they little thing before the gig to get their mind right. Somebody smoking, somebody drinking, somebody hollering at females.

Just playing that first song on the stage, man. I'd say you can call it a Stooges tradition. We normally start a set off with like one of two or three songs. It's either "Freddie Hubbard," "Ghetto," or one other song to choose from. And it's just like, man, that first song, that's the icebreaker for the night so you want a killer first song, even if it ain't. Let's say the Hi-Ho could hold one hundred people. It ain't but fifteen people in there when you play your first note, but that's still your icebreaker for the night because you know anything you do after that, that's what you challenging yourself to. So like, "Oh, I can have a good time like this on the first song? Well let's see how much of a good time I can have on the second song." And it went like that throughout the rest of the night. After a while, it might have started off kind of slow with the whole band, but somebody knocked on somebody else and got them to dance. And you kind of nudge on somebody else and pretty soon the whole band is onstage and it's just camaraderie. That's what the Hi-Ho is; it just symbolizes that camaraderie. You just have a bad day and come to the gig and just knock a load off. But it's almost like you didn't need to hear the music for that part to happen! The music was just like icing on the cake.

KYLE: That's the way that a lot of people talk about second lines on Sunday. That's the time of the week when all the worries are out the window. You

Left to right: Glenn Preston, Eric Gordon, Walter Ramsey, and Garfield Bogan clad in Saints gear at the Hi-Ho, August 4, 2011 (three days after Walter's birthday). Photo by Conrad Wyre.

can forget about making rent or all the mundane bullshit you have to worry about in your daily life and you can just enjoy living for a little while. You can just kind of enjoy yourself out with music and friends and family and whatever else.

CHRIS: I will say this: Before actually working with the Stooges, I was afraid. I was one of those inside kids. Big groups of people scared me, so the first couple of second lines, I was walking around like, "Man, this is a lot of people. Man, there's a lot of people around here, bro." But that's another one of those things that I kind of appreciate for the opportunity, because playing with the Stooges allowed me to open up socially. That's probably the biggest thing that I could be grateful for, because I was real closed into myself. And you've met me as a stranger before, and it's like realizing that people just kind of want to talk to me just because they've seen me before or recognize me, you kind of got to open up a little bit more than you have. It's like you can see what years and years and years of not being open in that environment can kind of do to you.

✦ ✦ ✦

ERIC: Chris Cotton is the person who has *no* sense at all. Like, he will just do something. I'm the person that would start doing something crazy and then he would start doing it with me, but then say we'll be onstage playing a song, I might just jump into the crowd. I call myself "Kid Crowd Surf." I have crowd surfed several times. We'll be playing a song and Chris Cotton will just stop. As soon as we put our horns down, he'll run around the whole stage, doing push-ups or pull somebody's pants down. And you're like, "What the hell?" And the crowd is like, "Was he supposed to be doing that?" And the band's just like, "I don't care." We know something crazy's gonna happen. Every show something different is gonna happen. And Chris Cotton, me and him, that's how we were. Something's gonna happen—you just have to keep your eyes open. The whole time while you're watching this—pretty much the comedy show—you're still enjoying the music at the same time. It's cool.

KYLE: It's amazing that you can play as well as you do while people are being pantsed.

ERIC: It'll get crazy. Me and Chris, just randomly out the blue—I don't know if you've ever watched WrestleMania or something like that—we'll just be sitting up there and I'll get mad. I'll hit him in the stomach and I'll do a Diamond Cutter or Stone Cold stunner on him. And it'll be funny because I'll do that and he'll jump back and fall to the ground and then it'll be like, "What the hell?" He done fell to the ground and then I'll get on top of him and cover him and then somebody else will come and give a three count, like, "One, two, three!" And the crowd's like, "Yeah! This is a brass band show. What's going on?" It'll get crazy. And all the shows were like that. They all had something new that you never knew what was going on because everything was always instantaneous with the Stooges. I play with Da Truth and I played with TBC for some time, and the Stooges have something that no band I've ever seen brought to the stage or the streets.

✦ ✦ ✦

JOHN P.: We used to play at Hi-Ho. Of course you know that. But they had a lot of funny shit that happened in there, too. One in particular, I was telling you about the other day. We were playing and I can't remember what song it was. We were going so hard and the crowd was dancing and everybody was feeling it. I was feeling it. I don't know what happened, but I jumped off of the stage and I hit my eye on the ceiling fan and it just split wide open and I couldn't see for like three minutes and I was just trying to gather myself. They were like, "You stay down there. You get yourself together and then you come back up here." I think I really wanted to go down there to pass around the tip bucket and so I just jumped up and this shit happened. And it was like, "Damn!"

✦ ✦ ✦

SPUG: John Perkins jumped off the stage and Eric, he surfed. But John Perkins, I guess he was trying and hit the ceiling fan. "Eric's short and he can do that. You're almost two feet taller than him! You can't do that!" I won't forget that. The parties, the women! You know about Glenn that happened at the Hi-Ho?

KYLE: Tell me the story anyway.

SPUG: Well, we had a Pajama Party. It had a lot of women in there, but it just so happened Glenn Preston, being Glenn—I'ma say "Twice"—he came in women's lingerie.⁶ I understood what he was doing. I wouldn't have did it, but Glenn being Glenn, it just so happened at that same time, he had a warrant and the bounty hunters came for him and we're like, "What's going on?" Like, "We come to get Glenn." And we were like, "Ooh, uh, he's here, but please can you let him put some clothes on?" It wouldn't have been a good look for him. You don't want to go to jail in women lingerie with fluffy stuff around your wrists. Nobody wants to do that. You don't want to go to jail looking like that.

✦ ✦ ✦

WALTER: One day the owner came to me and he was like, "Hey man, you should buy the club. You're doing really good with your Thursday nights, and the club's starting to be successful because it's getting recognition around the world because people come down here to come to this Thursday night thing." I was like, "Nah, I'ma stick to music." I don't run clubs. I don't do that. I'm good at business, and prior to music, I owned real estate. But I'm like, "I don't want to deal with that." I don't drink. Then, a year later, he asked me again. He put the proposal up and the band members heard about it through the wind. They was like, "Hey, man. The guy trying to sell you the club. What's up? Man, we should buy this! We should do all this!" I was like, "No." But then they kept pressuring me. The Stooges is ran like a board of directors. You have maybe five to seven people at one time that's going to make decisions in the Stooges. The people in New Orleans just know of me being the bandleader and band owner of the Stooges.

KYLE: President of the board, maybe, I guess.

WALTER: Yeah. So the board going to be whoever it's going to be most of that time, but it range from five to seven people that makes all the major decisions, and not just me. They get together and they talk about it and they sit down with me and it's like, "We should do this." I'm like, "I don't want to

Walter playing at the VIP Ladies and Kids second line, March 5, 2017. Photo by Pableaux Johnson.

do this." But I voted, so I'm like, "Alright, cool. Let's do it, let's study it, let's get it." For two months, we did a lot of research and studying on the club and did this, and then after we got enough research and figured out a game plan, we went and bought it. It was a good venture, but what we didn't factor in: how much time it would take. It wasn't the money, it was how much individual time that we had to devote to that club. Running it, meeting the orders in the morning to get the beer, making sure the music there. And then the kicks part about this was one day the ASCAP and BMI people were there to pick up their check, you know, because you got to pay them for music. And we was a little opposite of that end because we usually getting that check from them. Owning a club, you got to pay them. And I remember the bill from BMI was $600 and ASCAP was like $400 or something. So you have to pay and it's monthly.

KYLE: That's more than my rent, both of those!

WALTER: Yeah. The club expenses came up to twenty grand a month. And so you have to make sure this club makes thirty grand or forty grand a month.

KYLE: I mean, that's a big overhead.

WALTER: Yeah, and that's just you selling alcohol. He had rented out a spot in the back for a food company at the time, which they had it before we bought it, and we honored their lease or whatever. It was cool, but it was a project. It was not the easiest thing to do, but it gave us a sense of learning more—especially for the band members, because those guys, they work in the band, but it's like they have to put their business chops on now.

CHAPTER 8

The Controversy

It's 2012, and I've scheduled my stay in town to last an extra day so I can go to my first second line. Approaching the starting point at the entrance to Armstrong Park, I don't really know what to expect as I see the crowd gathering. Vendors hock "cold, cold Heineken" and cold drinks. I buy a Budweiser from a guy with a cooler and hand him a couple American dollar bills that seem like Monopoly money to an unaccustomed Canadian. Cooling off with some sips of my beer, I see a black bus pull up. The crowd hurries to the vehicle's doors, leaving a small, uncrowded area where a brass band, decked out in black T-shirts featuring bright pink band logos and an image of the breast cancer ribbon on the back, begins to assemble. Two tubas players rip energetic blasts on their horns to begin the band's first song as members of the Original Four Social Aid and Pleasure Club emerge from the double doors of the bus in spectacular fashion, their bodies draped in matching blue shirts and pants, their heads crowned with name-emblazoned headbands. Most second lines involve more than one band, and today serves up two: the Stooges and TBC.

We soon arrive at our first stop, the Ashé Cultural Arts Center on O. C. Haley Boulevard. While members of the Original Four disappear inside to change outfits, the two bands take the opportunity to blow at each other. Each band trades musical barbs as onlookers align themselves with one of two sides. The TBC taunts the Stooges, singing, "Nah, nah, nah, we knockin' at the Stooges," occasionally swapping out "Stooges" for "Pooges," a name the band proudly inherited by stirring up trouble in the brass band scene. The Stooges answer

The Stooges A band cutting up in a battle with the Stooges B band at the Pigeon Town Steppers Social Aid and Pleasure Club second line, April 16, 2017. *Left to right:* John Perkins (background), Al Growe, Virgil Tiller, and Maurice "Sporty" Craig. Photo by Michael Mastrogiovanni.

with the Rebirth classic "Rockin' on Your Stinkin' Ass," loudly singing, "Stop talking that trash, y'all / We rockin' on your stinkin' ass!" As if to coyly relinquish responsibility for the musical skirmish, TBC returns the volley with their cover of Jay-Z's "Trouble," ("Trouble, lookin' for me / Trouble, here I am"). Lyrical fragments that appropriately capture the feeling of the audience send everyone into laughter or moments of recognition that one band has one-upped the other.

The battle quickly heats up, turning into a cacophonous duel as the bands simultaneously play different tunes at different tempos. I try to get my bearings in this sonic hall of mirrors, but the volume is disorienting. The whole scene is loud and chaotic as each band tries to outplay the other in a conflict of volume and pitch. The musicians push their instruments to their physical limits, the alloy of their horns vibrating to a near rattle. With their two tubas, the Stooges dominate the battle in the low end, while TBC, with their fiery trumpet section, delivers searing lines that soar above the Stooges' bottom-heavy groove. The victor of these battles is typically decided by onlookers, based on a subjective set of criteria and argued endlessly after the fact. In the era of social media, extensive debates about winners usually play out online in days and weeks after one band pulls up on another.

The battle with the TBC is just one of many the Stooges have been embroiled in over the years. This time, the TBC were on the come-up and actively trying to knock the Stooges off the streets. During their tenure at the Hi-Ho, the TBC would come blow at the Stooges from the sidewalk, a challenge that, because of its marketability, was welcomed by the Stooges. Even if that weren't the case, the Stooges can hardly complain. Three years prior to the above-described battle with the TBC, the Stooges had done the same to Rebirth, contesting their domination of the second line scene in a feud that became more heated than most.[1]

The battle with Rebirth began innocuously enough. After their fallout with the owner of the Rock Bottom Lounge and their subsequent move to Garfield's bar, they lost some of their audience. This caused frustration within the band because they had worked hard to build up their Thursday night momentum. Having lost the Stooges, the owner of the Rock Bottom sought another band to play on Thursdays, and as a favor to the bar owner, Rebirth's bandleader, Phil Frazier, began filling in the slot. The Stooges took this as an affront, since they had worked so hard to build up their Thursday nights and Rebirth was effectively siphoning off part of their audience. After discussing their options on a particularly quiet Thursday night early in their Hi-Ho tenure, the Stooges journeyed Uptown to blow at Rebirth. They walked into the bar during Rebirth's set, trumpets blazing. Their challenge wasn't taken kindly—especially because Phil had recently had a stroke and Rebirth's A band was out of town. The whole debacle was exacerbated by misunderstandings from both bands. Things got so heated that the Stooges' provocation came to actual blows at the Big Nine second line on December 20, 2009. At the time, Chad Honore, who cut his teeth with the Stooges, was playing for Rebirth. Fists swinging, he found himself caught in the middle of a feud he never wanted to happen. Brass band competition and controversy is common, but rivalries are usually playful and rarely ever escalate to the level of seriousness of that between Rebirth and the Stooges.

Musicologist Thomas Brothers makes the case that, going back to early twentieth-century New Orleans, public "cutting" or "bucking" contests were one means through which male musicians articulated masculinity.[2] While competition is an outcome of the free market and exists across genders, for the Stooges it expressed itself in a gendered sibling rivalry. Al framed the Stooges' beef with Rebirth as between "little brother" and "big brother," a fraternal feud spurred by the Stooges' rise in the scene and Rebirth's status as the city's preeminent brass band:

> It was big brother against little brother. And little brother—all the time big
> brother always used to help little brother, but at the same time, big brother let him
> know that he's big brother. And little brother got a little older and little brother

started smelling himself a bit and little brother did some things. Sometimes little brothers do things that they regret. Some things they don't. Some things was right, some things was wrong. We wind up squashing it and everything wind up turning out alright.

The typical rules of masculinity in the United States dictate that men be "strong, active, aggressive, reasoned, dominant, competitive, and in control."[3] The Stooges in many ways subscribe to this and certainly struck an aggressive note by going after Rebirth. Rebirth, after all, provided the germinal inspiration for the Stooges when Walter first saw them perform in grade school. The Lil Stooges also got their first big break in 1998 performing for Rebirth's fifteenth-anniversary parade. But the Stooges were strategic about going after Rebirth. They knew very well that there was no way they were going to supplant them as the most popular brass band in the city. The idea is to punch up or to the side, but never punch down. Sitting on the couch of his old apartment, Garfield explained to me that "the controversy made us get closer and better, made us want to do better, want more for the band." In starting beef with a band on your level, it's about consistent one-upmanship. Beefs with bands on a higher level are usually aspirational. What the Stooges knew is that controversy would get people talking, drumming up support for both bands, much in the way up-and-coming rappers release diss tracks aimed at artists of higher stature.[4] In the end, Rebirth's fan base would likely become more loyal and the Stooges would gain a larger following.

Though, as Al says, things eventually "turned out alright," there was bad blood for a little while. This chapter explores the use of controversy as a marketing tool, articulating the stakes of such high-level competition and showing how the band's decision to blow at Rebirth was controversial not only to the second line community but to the bandmembers of the Stooges as well.

✦ ✦ ✦

WALTER: We was playing Uptown at the Rock Bottom. And then we got into it with the guy there. We was like, "Look, bruh, we got to start making more money. We're bringing in a lot of people here. Start paying us more." He said no, so we was gonna take a few weeks off and let his business slow down. That's how we thinking, and then he'll realize that we part of a asset here. We stopped playing and the Rebirth went and played in there. Now, we got an alliance with each other. Rebirth play on Tuesday night, so none of us play on Tuesday night. Stooges play on Thursday; no band play on Thursday. Hot 8 play on Sunday. Like, this is our alliance. We breaking our alliance!

Y'all go play in our spot for us? Now the man ain't gonna suffer because the Rebirth come in and play. We built that up and we was just looking at them like, "Dude, for real?"

KYLE: Before the audience even realizes that you guys aren't there, they're there at another show.

WALTER: Right. They're there the next week! "Oh, cool. Stooges aren't here and Rebirth playing? Cool!" So then we was like, "Fuck it." People only want to hear them on Tuesdays so we gonna go Downtown and try to find a club and build our Thursdays up. We're a month or two months in this and it's not working, and Rebirth started playing on Thursdays at our spot Uptown that we built. So Ersel was like, "Man, we should go up there and just blow at them." I was like, "I don't know, bruh." At that time, Phil had just caught a stroke, so it was not good timing, and the real Rebirth was overseas. Phil had put the band together to keep playing. We was just like, "Fuck." Ersel was like, "Man, we should just go blow at them," so I was like, "I'm out. I don't really want to do that—me, personally." Me and Alfred was like, "Nah, that's stupid." But the band members was like, "Fuck it! I don't care. Let's go." So now I'm out, but cool—I got to go.

KYLE: You got to go with them. If they're going, you can't—

WALTER: Yeah, we got to go. So we just go in blowing at them. We got the people looking at them. They mad. Then we come outside and then one lady who live across the street from Flash say, "Flash said Walter said Rebirth can't be strong no more because Phil caught a stroke."

KYLE: You're the face of the Stooges and so anything negative—

WALTER: Or positive—it's gonna come. But no positive, it's gonna be all negative. I'm standing out there and they just said that. Phil's girlfriend Linda arguing with me and I'm saying, like, "I didn't say that! I just was in the hospital when he caught a stroke. I was with him in the hospital. Why would I try to capitalize off of him catching a stroke?"

KYLE: You're not gonna go visit him in the hospital and be like, "Oh, you got a stroke! Well that's good for us."

WALTER: Yeah! I don't wish that on anybody. So I was arguing myself, pleading my case. Now it's like, "Oh, now I'm back the enemy." And it's going hard now. So the other band want to come back. They were like, "Man, when we get back, we just gonna beat y'all up," and all this. That's how the controversy started.

✦ ✦ ✦

GARFIELD: I'm the black sheep of the group. I'm the Ninth Ward, I'm the guy that begets the controversy. I know how to start the fire.

Garfield proudly showing off his Stooges tattoo, a trend started by Arian, who got a "Big Stoogie" tattoo on his arm. Photo by Lisa Palumbo.

KYLE: Has that been your role oftentimes?

GARFIELD: Man, a lot of the stuff that we get into, we conquer. We started the two tubas. I was like, "Dude, look. We just fucked over a lot of people. We need to be ready at all counts. We have two people that can play tuba in the band, let's start bringing two tubas to the second line."

KYLE: But that started shit with other bands, too?

GARFIELD: They started bringing two tubas. Like, "We gonna have two tubas too, so when we roll up, it's going down!" The controversy with going to another band gig, we started that.

KYLE: Do you want to talk about the Rock Bottom and Rebirth? Did you have anything to do with that decision?

GARFIELD: Everything! Everything to do with that decision. One of the clubs that we played for had their coming-out party and they wanted us to play, but the Rebirth had started playing there on Thursday nights, and we was playing at the Hi-Ho on Thursdays, so we was like, "Your boy and them said they wanted us to come up there." "Naw, we ain't gonna do it." I said, "Bro, look. Let's go up there and blow at them bitches." They're like, "Huh?" "I'm serious. Let's go up there and blow." So the band looking around, they looking at each other like, "What we got to lose? The Rock Bottom was ours at first! We had the Rock Bottom popping on Thursday. We playing for that club that's coming out on Sunday. Let's go in there and do a grand entry."

KYLE: And this was after playing at the Hi-Ho?

GARFIELD: This was after playing at the Hi-Ho. We was like, "Hey, strap up. Let's go." We get to the Rock Bottom and the band standing outside and me and Walter, we look in the door, check out the scene, and they playing. Phil say, "Where your band? Go get your band!" He just didn't know we already had it cocked and locked. We was about to come in and do y'all something dirty, anyway. All we did was went outside and [*whistles*], "Let's do this!" Man, we came in that motherfucker and I tell you we tore the roof off. They could have shut the Rock Bottom down that night.

KYLE: But it was their B band though, right?

GARFIELD: No. We was—that's what it was.

KYLE: Because it was Phil leading it and everyone else was—

GARFIELD: Phil and a couple of other guys, yeah. Somebody else was out of town and so they felt like, "Y'all can't blow at Phil and he had the stroke and the whole band wasn't there." Yeah, I remember that. And so they felt some kind of way.

KYLE: Right. Which started a whole fucking big thing.

GARFIELD: That started something between us and the brass band world.

KYLE: Yeah, the entire Sixth Ward and everybody attached to it.

GARFIELD: Man, everybody that didn't fuck with us in the beginning, all that did was put a sour taste back in they mouth about who the Stooges is, what they was. "I told y'all them niggas ain't shit. Fuck them bitches we gonna cock suck fuck them." You know how they talk!

✦ ✦ ✦

CHAD: We was in London playing for the Olympics with Rebirth. So we at the O2 Arena over in London and we get a phone call and it was Phil. Phil is *angry*. It's like, "Man, calm down." He's so angry, he can't even talk. We don't even know what he's saying. Somebody had to call us back for us to know what he was talking about he was so angry. So then somebody finally explained it.

They was playing a gig at the Rock Bottom. It was this gig that Phil was trying to start up just to try and help the bar out, to help the bar get some money. It wasn't like a serious gig, but everybody know the Stooges play at the Rock Bottom on a Thursday night. But the Stooges messed that deal up, it wasn't the Rebirth. We didn't need that gig; we was helping that bar out. We got Tuesday night at the Maple Leaf that can pay all of they gigs for the whole weekend. We didn't need that gig. In fact, the only person that really wanted to do that gig was Phil. He was the only one that was there. He didn't

even go to London. He missed out on $4,000 cash to help these people out
and their bar, so it was disrespectful. The Stooges won't say it, but it was disrespectful for what they did.

KYLE: Oh, some of them will say that.

CHAD: It wasn't no beef or nothing. They was trying to come back and
they was trying to prove a point to us, which we don't give a fuck about.
What good is it gonna do to come and blow at us? If y'all really want to do
that shit, y'all should have brought y'all band to Tuesday at the Maple Leaf.
That's when you come and handle that shit because if we bring the 'Birth to
y'all gig, better believe we gonna leave with everybody in that bitch. Next
week, y'all gonna have nobody in the gig, you dig? We would never do that
to them, though. We knew what we capable of.

One thing I know—and it's been proven—Walter, he idolized Phil Frazier.
He wants his band in the Rebirth position. And what I told him, I'm like,
"You ain't gonna be able to force it." I don't think Walter wanted the fight to
happen, but it happened and he was one of the guys that got brought into
it. He wasn't trying to fight; he was trying to break shit up, too. He just got
brought into it because he's part of that band. He winded up fighting one
of the onlookers that was around. Like I said, when we started fighting, the
crowd started coming. So he wind up trying to protect his band and fighting onlookers. He wasn't really fighting nobody from Rebirth. And I know
because he didn't really want that to happen. It wasn't a good look for him.
That's what I always was trying to explain to them. I didn't even take part
in the fight. I was in charge of getting my band back together. After it took
place, I felt the animosity towards those guys. A lot of those guys didn't talk
to me for a while because of how they felt about the situation. But had the
original Rebirth band been at the Rock Bottom that night, would y'all still
come and blow at us? Would y'all had still came blow at us, or had we been
live Tuesday night, would y'all have brought y'all band to the Tuesday night
gig where y'all was supposed to bring it? Would y'all do it? And they said,
"No, we wouldn't do that to the Rebirth." "Well why would you do that to the
Rebirth on this day?"

KYLE: And it was also when Phil was having his health problems, too.

CHAD: Right, exactly. And so he was really mad about that. And it hurt
them in a lot of ways because, before that happened, Phil was a key catalyst
in giving them extra gigs. And you done cut a whole money stream away
from your band. Now TBC getting these gigs, New Breed, Kin Folks. We're
the biggest band in the city. Every weekend, we're giving away—I'm not
exaggerating—at least twenty gigs. That's a hell of a payday for these bands.
They stay relevant. That's how we keep it real. Y'all keep falling off now—and

they won't say it—but partly because of that situation. You can't bite the hand that's feeding you, that's feeding the whole culture, you dig?

KYLE: Sometimes it's better to shake it.

CHAD: Yeah! It's better to get ahold of yourself and think about it again and then come at this another way. But guys like Antione and Ersel, they do have hot heads. And they let their emotions take over them that day. Like I told them, we was done with it after that happened. We wasn't worried about it. It was y'all that kept it going even to where the next week, to the next second line. They at the second line like, "Fuck Rebirth." They saying this to everybody out in the crowd! You don't think these people coming back to tell us? This is our crowd y'all playing for. You got to remember these things. So yeah, it was disrespectful with them. We never talked nothing bad about the Stooges. You still don't hear the Rebirth say nothing about the Stooges.

✦ ✦ ✦

GARFIELD: I believe it was the Big Nine second line. We start at the Hi-Ho, coming on down. The craziest shit, it happened in front of Goody's. Like, Goody's is one of the stops that they gonna pass up.

KYLE: And you owned it at the time?

GARFIELD: I owned it at the time. And we're playing "Back Stabbers."[5] We like, "Yo, we gonna start off like we start off down and then when we come up loud, we gonna turn at them and give it to them!" So we playing and everybody know "Back Stabbers," so when we turned at them, we came out. Everybody's like, "Oh, shit! They fucking going at the Rebirth!" We played the whole song, man, and Glen Andrews that play trumpet, went up to the bass drummer at the time—I think it was Big Dwayne—and was talking shit: "Man, y'all better not fucking turn that way blowing at us no more!"[6] Because the crowd started coming our way. So Walter was like, "What's going on?" Now, we singing at the time, telling them, "Smile at your face / y'all backstabbing / such and such, whatever." He come by Walter and was like, "I said don't fucking blow at us! Y'all tripping! Stay forward!" I was like, "Man, you don't tell us what to do, man. Go back in the back. You tripping." I turn back, I'm singing and having me a good time playing and I look and I see them fussing. I'm like, "Man, what's going on?" So Walt trying to take the tuba off and he putting the tuba back on. And I'm like, "Man, look, y'all tripping." I turn back around and I get bumped by the tuba and them two tussling and I just hit Glen.

KYLE: Glen and Walt were tussling?

GARFIELD: Glen and Walter was tussling and fussing. He wanted to fight Walter while he had the tuba on, so I just hit him. The Stooges was the incident of incidents. Everybody wanted a piece of the Stooges, so I was just like, "Man, I'm tired of this shit." I just hit him. Boom! He looked back, falled back a little bit, and he looked at me like he was about to come at me. I hit him again and he fell. Kabuki ran up and he got into it with Chris. I think he just hit Chris and I pushed him. I went in Goody's and told my cousin at the time, I was like, "Look, man, we out here fighting with Rebirth. Come outside." So as I'm coming outside from telling my cousin that, Glen coming up the street. He got two horns in his hand. He got his horn and Kabuki horn.

KYLE: Which is actually Eric Gordon's horn.

GARFIELD: Which was Eric Gordon horn. He walking with it and as he walking up to me, he holding it and he biting his bottom lip. I'm looking and I keep walking. When he swung, I grabbed that horn and I hit him. Boom, boom, boom! Then he swung the other horn. I grabbed it, started hitting him with this one. Then, all of a sudden, a police on a horse grabbed me, pulled me and my daddy back. Because my daddy, at this time, he had done came and he was about to start getting some licks in. That's how that went. And we was like, "Y'all in trouble. Now we got y'all crowd, we done beat y'all up. We didn't want it to go like this, but y'all been asking for it. Now y'all got it and y'all better not come across the canal. Y'all better *not* come cross that water." We singing it: "Better not cross that water," coming up the street. They getting the message because, when I tell you the Rebirth did not come across the canal in that parade, they didn't come. They did not come cross the water. They got the message, but they wasn't the only ones that got the message that day.

We showed the brass band world, like, "Y'all not gonna push us around no more. We come to claim what's ours. We the kings of the street. We don't care if y'all put us in the back of the parade or put us in the front of the parade; we gonna have the crowd.

✦ ✦ ✦

KYLE: Were you in Rebirth when the actual fight happened?

CHAD: Yeah, yeah, yeah. I was in the Rebirth.

KYLE: Do you want to tell me a little bit about that and what that situation was like for you?

CHAD: That's two sides, you know what I'm saying? That's both sides.

KYLE: Yeah, that's why I'm interested in your perspective on that.

CHAD: The Stooges and Rebirth fight kind of happened over nothing. There wasn't really nothing that it was supposed to happen over. It wasn't like we were beefing with them or they were beefing with us, but at the time,

Eric Gordon and Chris Cotton at the Young Men Olympian Jr. second line, September 12, 2010. Photo by Lisa Palumbo.

the Stooges always fall off and then they come back. At that time, they was in the process of coming back and felt like they was head in charge on the street. Everybody know when the Rebirth on the streets, we king of the streets, hands down. Nobody coming and touch the Rebirth. At the time, we in the middle of a parade. First of all, we ain't even want to do the parade because we don't do parades like that no more. But we trying to get to the stop so that we can take a break and get some water and drink. Meanwhile, the Stooges stopped before the stop and they just playing. We didn't mind that, but now they just turned around and blowing at us. We trying to get to the stop and we telling them to move forward. They going crazy up there, blowing their horns. I'm like, "Man, I can't believe that shit. Look at these people, man." Glen went up there to tell them, "Man, look, we trying to get to the stop. Why don't y'all move up or do what y'all got to do so we can go?" It was one of the Stooges! Somebody was playing on the snare drum, I can't remember who, but I think it was Antione. He was like, "Fuck y'all! Fuck the Rebirth!" And Glen was like, "No, fuck you!" And he was like, "Man, what you gonna do?" And that's when it took place. He got out of the way with Glen first. I seen Antione swinging and then Glen swung and Kabuki ran up and then the fight took place between the band, or whatever. It got crazy for a little second. But we was able to settle it out and continue the parade or whatever. But it got real bad. It got *real* bad. I guess the Stooges feel like we feel some type of way personally against them.

Garfield repping the Ninth Ward while playing at the CTC Steppers second line, February 26, 2012. Photo by Pableaux Johnson.

KYLE: I mean, Kabuki was playing with one of Eric's trumpets, you know? I mean, you all know each other. A lot of you are friends.

CHAD: No, it's not like that.

KYLE: No?

CHAD: They don't know. I'm the mutual person. I'm the mutual person between both bands. None of those guys ever played with Rebirth or are friends with guys from Rebirth. They may have hung out and come see Rebirth at a bunch of shows, but not to be like a friend-friend, buddy-buddy. Certain members got certain relationships with certain people, but as far as Glen and Kabuki, they didn't know any of those guys. They know them as far as face, but not as far as friendship. So for us, it was like, "That's my bro." That's where Kabuki at with it. "That's my brother. Y'all gonna fight him, we gonna fight y'all." And it was gonna end up really bad. It could end up really bad because I know the Stooges people. They got people out there, too.

KYLE: And it's not so much the people in the band, it's—

CHAD: It's the people outside.

KYLE: Different friends and family and stuff.

CHAD: And that's where it was gonna get bad. The reason why shit didn't happen that day is because we understand that y'all have y'all people. Y'all have friends and family, but we got the whole city out here. So it was best that y'all just chill, split the band up. Go way to the front or it's gonna get real bad for y'all. We have to understand, but nobody gonna let y'all fuck with Rebirth. We didn't even have to fight y'all. After a while, the crowd started to fight them. You ain't gonna win, so you might as well just break this shit and y'all move forward.

KYLE: And you guys were in the Ninth Ward at the time, right?

CHAD: It was in the Ninth Ward. But no matter where it goes, most of our band members from the Ninth Ward. Just like how they had people out there, we had people out there, too. Everybody that's around us carries guns because they don't want nothing to happen to us. We got the illest killers that wanna hang with us. It's crazy, this brass band shit! And the Stooges have the same thing. All my cousins, I know these people. They're hit men. They hang around with Stooges. They're out there second lining and, damn, this one will pull out a gun and shoot you!

KYLE: It's like, "We're just playing music."

CHAD: Yeah, we're just playing music! But he will really pull a gun and shoot you! These dudes, that's how it is in New Orleans, man. Gangsters, they protect the music because we protect them. Sometimes it's the only thing anybody in New Orleans can do to even feel good: brass band, going to a second line, people *live* for that. For a second line on Sunday, just to come outside and smile and enjoy the weather and not have to worry about somebody or looking over your back and you having to get killed or something. You can come out there and enjoy your life for four hours. Some people look forward to that. That's the best thing some people have to do in New Orleans.

KYLE: It's kind of like a time-out from everything—

CHAD: Yeah, man. It's a time-out from everything. You ain't got to worry about making no drug sales, no nothing, because everybody got their own drugs at a second line. Everybody got their own alcohol at a second line, everybody doing their own thing at the second line. And you get to enjoy music and just live for a second. That's my job; my job is to make sure that before I put my horn back in the case, everybody around me is satisfied. And that's been my goal since I was with the Stooges.

✦ ✦ ✦

WALTER: Glen Andrews, which is the trumpet player for the Rebirth, he started going in Alfred and Virgil's ear, so I was trying to figure out what he was doing, because I could see everything. I'm in the back. I'm telling him, "Man, come over here and talk to me." I'm thinking he want us to move or do something or I'm not sure what the hell he was trying to say, but he came by me. He was like, "Man, I'm tired of y'all keep blowing at us and with all this bullshit. Y'all gonna stop this shit, y'all gonna learn, y'all gonna fucking respect us today." And he cocked back and tried to swing on me and I see the fist coming, so I just throw the tuba right there. He hit the tuba. Because he hit the tuba, all this forward motion pushed into Ersel, which is right in front of me. Ersel look like, "What the fuck is going on?" "He swung at me." So we just pushed him. I took the tuba off and my glasses off. We just pushed him into the neutral ground and we beating him up. So now his band members, they come running up. Kabuki punched Chris in the face or something. It was just like a brawl, but it was not really a brawl. So then it's me and Ersel fighting for our band. We get away. And then I see Glen's son and like four other dudes come at me and I'm looking at it like, "Aw, no. Y'all serious?" Like, this was real! Me, Ersel, all of us, we grew up fighting. And we ain't really had a fight in a long time, so I was kind of excited. I was like, "Oh my God! This is really real! Oh shit!"

KYLE: It's a little bit different when you get to be that age, though, because you can actually hurt someone really badly.

WALTER: Yeah, so four people running towards me. I'm ready because I ain't do this in a while. They swinging at me, they hitting me, I'm hitting them, and before you know it—I don't know how it happened (I got great strength)—but they all was on the ground. And they had a old lady coming telling me like, "Baby, how the hell you did that?" I was like, "I have no clue." It was just funny. I was like, "I don't want to fight no more. I just want to find my glasses now." Somebody had picked them up and brought me my glasses, and I was like, "I just want to play my horn." Kabuki hit the police horse with a trumpet and so the police got us all back to playing music. So now we still by each other. Now these *our* people, we from this area. So now people are getting wind of it. We just had a fight, so they want to go back there and they want to just bum-rush the Rebirth because they mad now. And I'm like, "Nah, it's all good. I don't know how this happened. It looks like we had a fight and it don't look like too many people messed up. We can still play our instruments. Let's just finish the parade." That was at the beginning of the parade. So then it was still too much humbugging because we was right by

Walter playing at the CTC Steppers second line, February 26,
2012. Photo by Pableaux Johnson.

each other, so then they wind up asking us to go to the front of the parade
and they stay at the back of the parade. But that was crazy.

After a while, we got it together and we were like, "Man, that's stupid." But
it was like big brother fighting little brother. I always explain that because
people want to know. All your life your big brother beating you at everything and then once you get to his height, his strength, and you able to beat
him, he mad now. So if he push you in the back of the head, you can push
him back now versus "Aww, he keep picking on me." That's how I look at it. It
didn't do nothing. But after a while, we started speaking back to each other
and everything was good. It took bigger people in the band. Derrick Tabb
would come up to you and be like, "Look, bruh, I'm not part of that. I don't

want to be part of that. We don't need fighting and stuff like that." And Stafford, who play trombone, he was—

KYLE: I mean, you guys are in Black Feather together, right?[7]

WALTER: Yeah! We like brothers. We Indians! So he didn't swing, he wasn't coming over there to fight. He was coming to break it up. But it was just constantly back and forth for years. And when Glen swung to try to hit me, that was like the icing on the cake. "Alright, now it's time to fight."

KYLE: It reached the boiling point.

WALTER: Yeah, you that mad now you ready to fight us. And then it's crazy because me and Glen's kids go to the same school. Our kids in the same class. So now they got to go to school and talk about—

KYLE: You have to tell your kids not to fight each other.

WALTER: Yeah, and his daughter and my sons are friends and now we got to see each other at the school. They go to school and they're like, "My dad had a fight with your dad." I'm like, "Oh, nuh-uh. This not good." They needed to see us hug and we're bigger than that. Because our kids are friends! That shit, that's crazy. Like, "I had a fight with her dad. I had to punch him." Nah. Like, "My dad beat your dad up!" "Well my dad said he beat yours." Nah, they wasn't like that. They was more mature than to go do shit like that.

KYLE: They're a lot more mature than you guys.

WALTER: Yeah, the kids was like, "Don't you think that was crazy?" I'm like, "Yeah, you're right. You're right. That was immature of us." But it's something that happened and it elevated us after that, too. We was already doing good, but now we on a national level. Bam! The Stooges had a fight with Rebirth and it made us big. And then it started the whole Red Bull–type thing coming about: Who got the best band for real? That's when Red Bull came down here and started that competition.

CHAPTER 9

Street Kings

Horns rang out in the cavernous space below the Claiborne Bridge as the Stooges paraded toward one of four stages. The bridge functions as an acoustic focal point of Sixth Ward parades, and the brass band battle that took place on October 23, 2010, took advantage of it for full effect.[1] As the Stooges paraded in, they declared their intentions to the other three brass bands with the words of "Wind It Up": "We 'bout to show you how to do it / We about to show you how to do it!" It was a cool and cloudy fall day, and they arrived at the stage after marching through a crowd of a few thousand. They were clad in crisp blue T-shirts, the words "Stooges Give You Wings" abutting an image of two bulls charging at each other. A riff on the logo and slogan of energy drink company Red Bull, the T-shirts were part of a ploy to win the battle. That day, the Stooges locked horns with the Free Agents, TBC, and Soul Rebels brass bands in a corporate-sponsored event that sought to crown the best brass band in the streets of New Orleans. In a hallmark display of provocation and tomfoolery, the Stooges brought wrestling belts and openly declared themselves victors before ever blowing a single note.

Why were the Stooges shirts adorned with the Red Bull logo, and how did this massive event come to be? In 2009, Red Bull was keyed into a number of regions, including New Orleans. Having only recently become widespread, Facebook had become the grounds for much of the competitive brass band banter that had formerly taken place face-to-face. Using social media as a platform for this competitive banter was like pouring gasoline on flames: *everyone*

The setup underneath the I-10 for the Red Bull Street Kings competition shows the Free Agents, TBC, Stooges, and Soul Rebels on their respective stages. Photo by 5040tos/Greg Rhoades.

had an opinion on who the best band was. Less than a year after their blowup with Rebirth, the Stooges by most accounts had the streets on lock, and the fight with Rebirth had been reduced to a simmer. But there's always another brass band vying for that spot, and the TBC were coming to the streets with fire. The heated arguments about the best band in the streets weren't cooled by the Stooges announcing themselves the "undefeated heavyweight champions of second line" online. Red Bull saw a marketing opportunity that could simultaneously bolster *and* capitalize on the city's brass band community. They went about organizing a massive brass band throw down, which came to be known as the Red Bull Street Kings competition.

While one might take a skeptical view of a corporate-sponsored event in which a multinational company seeks to piggyback off the work of the city's Black brass band musicians, this view should consider the on-the-ground response of the bands and most people in attendance. Red Bull's foray into the post-Katrina market may have been an example of "disaster capitalism" that sought to profit from Hurricane Katrina, but it was at least a form of disaster capitalism that was put to good use and finally gave brass band music the national audience many believe it deserves. The Street Kings competition was an event that, to quote Matt Sakakeeny, "hit all the right notes."[2] It was well researched, and those in charge were aware of desires within the second line community. Prior to the event, the Red Bull team, led by field marketing manager Scott Lopker, spent over a year researching the history of cutting contests at Tulane University's Hogan Jazz Archive, where curator Bruce Boyd Raeburn was impressed by "the extent to which Red Bull was willing to go to create an event that would have credibility within the New Orleans brass band community."[3] Red Bull Street Kings was a tour de force of word-of-mouth marketing that ran counter to standard forms of marketing in that it was "uttered by sources who are assumed by receivers to be independent of corporate influence."[4] In hosting the event, Red Bull injected themselves into the already-existing online discourse. In many ways, the company was doing exactly what the Stooges had done with their challenge to Rebirth: they were stirring the pot to gain recognition.

Though the Stooges' fight with Rebirth seemed to provide the impetus for the Street Kings competition, in a move suggesting their de facto dominance of the scene, the Rebirth never put together an application for the competition and instead left the bands underneath them to clamor for the title. With Rebirth out, it became clear that the Stooges were the band to beat. In a documentary Red Bull put together about the event, all the bands interviewed go after the Stooges. In interview clips with the Free Agents Brass Band, former Stooges trombonist Larry Brown exclaimed, "We call them the Pooges, man. You know what I'm saying? We gonna shut them *all* the way down. They can't even make it to the second round." Ellis, then the bandleader of the Free Agents, also went in on his former band. Holding his thumb pointing downward, he blew a defiant raspberry that faded to a smile. "We gonna eliminate them first."

The judges for the competition were Benny Jones Sr., Fred Johnson, Gregory "Blodie" Davis, and Mannie Fresh, and the competition was judged on five criteria:

Appearance (1st Impression & Presentation)
Material (Traditional Style v. Original)
Energy
Musicality
Innovation[5]

The Stooges sought to tick off every box. Their customized Red Bull shirts were meant to entice their corporate sponsor: appearance, check. They chose "Tiger Rag" (a "hot new traditional" in Eric's words) and the hip-hop-oriented "Why": material, check. Energy? Musicality? Innovation? That's kind of their brand. It helped that they were *the* band on the streets at the time, playing a majority of second lines throughout the season. During several rounds of competition, they swayed the audience and the judges and eventually walked away with the title, though not without controversy, of course.

When all was said and done, Walt, still with the same chip on his shoulder, proudly announced, "It take the people to make a Street King. The people of New Orleans is what announced us the Street Kings!"

✦ ✦ ✦

WALTER: Before Red Bull came in, I remember having a conversation with the Rebirth, because it was like, "Man, we tired. Y'all think y'all this and y'all think y'all that. We will never battle you until y'all put up some money." I remember this conversation. It was like, "How much money?" I'm thinking like a thousand. They come up with ten thousand. So Rebirth figure, "If we give y'all this high number, y'all gonna back down." But what they didn't know is I do real estate. I got money. And then we got smartphones these days. So they was like, "Man, y'all got to prove that. When y'all get ten thousand in y'all Stooges bank account, call us and we'll battle." And then they had little Chad playing with them who played with us. I was like, "Man, they serious? Alright, cool." So right then and there, I went to my Chase app and I pulled it up. "Show me y'all money. This good Stooges money." They looked. They had some other cats there and they could all look at my phone. It pissed them off. It was already heated because I think a long time ago Arian told them people something about they been in the game twenty years and ain't got shit to show for it, and they got upset at me and the rest of us for that. And we ain't said nothing! Arian was barely playing with us then. So we had heated battles.

AL: And then another thing with the Street Kings thing, I think it was right around the time the internet was popping up and we had Facebook and you start dealing with TBC.

VIRGIL: The storm really helped it, because at that time, everything that was New Orleans music, period. They wanted to see what was going to happen. So everything that started happening started going on YouTube. Everything started hitting the internet, everything started hitting the social media.

AL: And I think Red Bull—they used to have a lot of conversations on who was the best band that was in the street—and I think Red Bull picked up on that.

WALTER: And they met Ellis first.

VIRGIL: It was already a competition. It was already like that.

AL: It was already hot before. Before they even came to do that.

WALTER: Yeah, it was already. It was like we betting. We was putting up *money* money.

DREW: And Red Bull always had their ear to the ground for everything, especially anything that wasn't mainstream. They had their ear to the ground.

AL: Urban stuff, yeah. Skateboarding, everything like that. They know.

Al Growe, Virgil Tiller, and Walter Ramsey at the VIP Ladies and Kids second line, March 5, 2017. Photo by Pableaux Johnson.

DREW: Skateboarding, snowboarding, gliding, the whole nine.

AL: Yeah, I was telling Walt when they first came, I said, "Walt, man, them people saw what happened on Facebook." And it's just so ironic all that stuff happened on Facebook and all that stuff started happening with the challenges. They knew to come right at that time to pick up on it.

✦   ✦   ✦

WALTER: Red Bull come in and they talked to Ellis. Ellis was one of the front-runners. I guess they found some other producers. They got Nicole Robertson, which is a great producer out of New Orleans that do PR work. She works for big record labels and stuff like that. And they got this guy named Karl Washington, which promotes a lot of things. He got his own production company. At the time, they had a young lady working for the Stooges named Tyesha Jones. Tyesha was really like our secretary, just doing stuff, taking care of this, taking care of that. And because she have her own business and affiliated with a lot of stuff in New Orleans, she come about hearing about the Red Bull Street King competition. She called me up and was like, "Look, they gonna have this battle of the bands. It's gonna be something big. They talking about it gonna be under the bridge. I think you should do it." I was like, "Alright, I don't really care, but, alright, cool." She put together the press kit, the portfolio, all this shit, and she done a great job at it. Didn't even show it to me, but—

KYLE: Okay, so you needed like a press kit to get into the whole thing?

WALTER: Yeah.

KYLE: Okay, so it's only bands that really kind of have their shit together.

WALTER: Yeah, so each band had to have a press kit, and they pick four bands out of there. The only bands that didn't turn in stuff was the Rebirth, but all the other bands turned in.

KYLE: And why didn't they turn something in?

WALTER: I think they felt like quote, unquote, "too big for this." Which is respectable.

KYLE: That kind of makes sense. They've been in the game long enough.

WALTER: Yeah, they've been fucking thirty years by the time Red Bull come bringing a Street King competition. So, quote, unquote, "they ain't need to be in it." But Hot 8—everybody—turned in press kits, all the local bands. Then they picked four. I don't know how they picked them. They had this big old stupid process on how to pick it. They had all kind of different people—regular people—voting. And they picked the bands. So they picked the Stooges based off our press kit. They was like, "Yeah, your press kit was like the number one press kit they had."

KYLE: Of course you guys would have—except you didn't have anything to do with it!

WALTER: Right! So when they pulled it out, I was like, "Damn! This shit is nice." They started side-eyeing me. Like, "Yeah, man. This look good." Like, "Walt, you acting like this your first time seeing it." I said, "No, no, no, no. This not my first time." I had to call her up. I was like, "Damn, I'ma give you some extra money for that one." But her thing was, she worked for us, and she was young and doing her thing and having her own business, but she was great at it. And she put this together and she got us in there. I was like, "Damn, that's cool." And the good thing about her working for us at the time was we needed somebody to be secretary. And the thing about it, we didn't have to tell her what to do. She would figure out shit to do and just do it.

KYLE: That's exactly what you want.

WALTER: And she like one of the smartest persons that I ever had to work with doing stuff. Because you ain't need to tell her what to do. She thinking of shit to do and she just do it. And she'd take her own money or she'd take the money—whatever we gave her—and she'd just make shit happen. And it was good until she got married. Her husband took her away from us! But it's bittersweet because her and her husband have grown to do major things, and I'm grateful just for her to be in our presence in that short time. But that was good. She got us into the Street King competition. And then she told me, "Look, y'all in. I know you gonna win." Like, with *confidence*. Like, "I know you. I know how great you is. I know if you'd had to put this press kit together, you wasn't even getting in because you don't do that. But I know you gonna win." So then we started getting with the producers and a guy named Scott Lopker. He was like one of the main reps in the city for Red Bull. Scott used to come around talking, and then they started setting up the interviews because they made a documentary.

KYLE: Right, because they did the videos and stuff.

WALTER: It was funny, though, man. Now, you don't see the interviews from the other bands, you just see the interviews from our band. But how they chopped it up and put it together in the documentary was just so funny. They used to call us the Pooges. And they was like, "Man, they so poo. They play radio music." They'll say whatever. I'd be like, "Man, we the popular band so everybody gonna be charging after us." So when they got down to the four bands, it was just us, Soul Rebels, TBC, and the Free Agents. The Soul Rebels didn't rag on us because they're like, "Yeah, they're a young band. They came up underneath us learning some stuff." Which is true. You know, Lumar and them, the Soul Rebels are legends to me. They showed me a different side of this music: that you can play this music and you can still have something. They got this whole stage presence; they know how to entertain. I've learnt a lot from watching them and talking with them. Now, when we come in there with business, they come to us and be like, "How the hell you doing this?"

✦ ✦ ✦

VIRGIL: I think that even with the documentary, at first I was like, "Man, I don't know if we gonna win, because I like to win." When I get up there, first of all, I'm amped up on Red Bull, so I'm hyped. I get up there and we start to play. I'm looking at us and how we dressed and how we was having fun. And I'm looking at everybody—the other three bands—like, they were mad.

WALTER: Yeah, they was dressed mad. They got their eye black on, war paint.

VIRGIL: Yeah, war paint. And I'm like, "Why the fuck is y'all so mad? What's going on?"

DREW: What led to us winning that competition was something fair. When it came to that traditional category, we played "Tiger Rag." And everybody else was doing the regular repertoire.

WALTER: See, we was smart. We musicians and we the street musicians, so we could do both sets of things. I remember being onstage. Andrew was

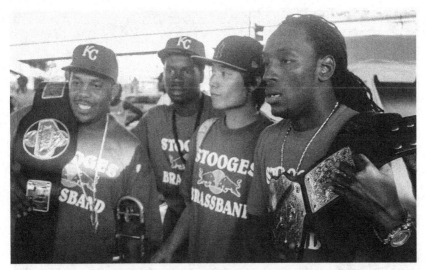

Garfield, Peanut, Makito Hashimoto, and Walter with a couple of wrestling belts at the Red Bull Street Kings competition. Photo by 504otos/Greg Rhoades.

traveling and doing other stuff too at that time, so he came to the competition and he was like, "Man, what traditional we gonna play?" "We gonna play 'Tiger Rag.'" That man was like, "Oh yeah?"

DREW: "Oh yeah? *That's* what we gonna do? Oh, okay." He was like, "No. Don't worry about it. I taught them. We learned it. I'm telling you don't worry about it. We learned it." I said, "Alright bro!"

VIRGIL: It came out good, too!

AL: And see another thing. I wasn't there. He says, "Bruh, they gonna do this competition." I said, "For sure, for sure! When it is?" "October 23rd." "I'm out. I can't do it. Man, that is my anniversary! The day after my birthday and my marriage anniversary. I can't explain to that woman."

WALTER: Because we've been around each other so long I'm like, "Man, tell her we got to do this! She'll understand." Like, this my cousin. He wouldn't know her if it wasn't for me! Like, "This is my cousin! I brought him to you! You owe me!"

AL: I told him, I said, "Bro, I'll do whatever I have to do to be able to take my spot, but I'm just not going through it. I'm not gonna go through that, because after that's over—win or lose—it's gonna be trouble in my house. But when I looked at the competition, I think really the people felt us the most. Between "Tiger Rag" and "Why," it was murder.

VIRGIL: Then we had this whole thing before then with the heavyweight champion belts! Because we were the masters of starting shit, we got the belt

The Stooges wearing their custom shirts at the Red Bull Street Kings competition. Photo by 5040tos/Greg Rhoades.

from one of them parties. Somebody had a belt, then I bought a belt, then we came in there with both of the belts already. We go up to the stage with the wrestling belts like the heavyweight champions.

WALTER: Man, we good at being great. That's what we do. The competition is what we build off. You ain't gonna be able to mess with us because we outthinking you. Ellis come from us, so it was like, "Man, alright. I know what I'ma do. I'm gonna go get the Mardi Gras Indians. I'ma go get this. I'ma go get that."

VIRGIL: The Baby Dolls.

WALTER: Yeah, "I'ma go get the Baby Dolls. I'ma win." He knew in his heart that we was gonna win. Man, I remember one time we looking at the Red Bull can before the competition. It was like, "There it is. We in. What they gonna want to see the most? Them, Red Bull. We gonna go get our shirts that say Red Bull. We ain't gonna ask them, because if we ask them, they gonna probably tell us no. We don't ask people nothing—we just do it." So we was dressed head to toe with the red bulls on the shirts. You cannot deny us of this! When we got there, the Red Bull marketing man was like, "Uh, where—who came up with the Red Bull?" I was like, "I looked at the can." I looked at Ersel, he looked at me, and he knew exactly what I was thinking. We good at marketing us. We know our strengths, we know our weaknesses and stuff like that, but we smart.

Hot off the recording session with Mannie Fresh in L.A. that they were awarded for their victory, the Stooges shared new material at Maison, April 28, 2012. Photo by 504otos/Greg Rhoades.

✦ ✦ ✦

CHRIS: Street Kings, honestly, I just kind of recall the actual day of it. A lot of the surrounding was a lot of smack-talking. That's where the name *Pooges* came from. And I used to hang out around other brass bands a lot. They'd play on different days of the week, so we'd go and hang out with each other and they'd be like, "Yeah man, that's them Pooges over there." It kind of got to me first, but I had to calm down because I was just like, "You know, we all hanging out." But the Street Kings thing, it was fun. I almost treated it like just another gig because of how we interact and perform with each other. Maybe that's one of the things that really helped us win in the end, but it was just kind of like another gig for us. Me and Eric went onstage dancing and having fun just like we do any other day. It was a lot of great music that day. There's a lot of talk about politics and all of this. "Walt paid the judges off." But no.

KYLE: It seems that Walt gets a lot of flack from people that aren't in the band. A lot of people think that Walt is somehow skimming money or that he pays the judges off or stuff like that. There's a lot of negative stuff directed towards the Stooges—more than a lot of other brass bands, quite frankly. Why do you think that is?

CHRIS: Well, I'm the type of person who feels like a lot of stuff is relatable, so I can relate what you just talking about with Walt being bad-mouthed and stuff like that. I can relate that to politics. When there's someone running for office, they'll say, "Hey, the other person is not as good as I am because they've done such and such and such even though they've spoken on such and such and such." It's mostly when you're getting in a band and people can tell that you're not happy in a situation. And just like everything else, they'll say, "Hey, it's not looking so good over there." "Well, it's better over here. The grass is always greener on the other side." Stuff like that may or may not be true to a certain degree, but hey, whatever it is. Because the grass may look greener on the other side, but is it real grass or is it spray-painted? Why is you so confident about this grass in the wintertime?

✦ ✦ ✦

ERIC: The high point, the career high, the highest thing that we ever did, was winning the Red Bull Street Kings. To be in front of everybody and win. The other bands were upset about that, but that was our glory. At that time, we already had claimed that we were the best band. And then to have a panel of judges say we were the best band was kind of like, "Okay, we proved it to you." At that time, some people thought we were arrogant, but we were the people's champs already. Had we not won it, still, we were playing the second lines every Sunday. We had the Hi-Ho going, which was a party every Thursday night. And nowhere we went, we could be beat. At that time, we would call out any band. If any band thought they were better than us, they'd say, "Meet us onstage." To be honest, in those years, I don't think any brass band in the city could have taken us—ANY brass band. Put that in quotations, big letters. "ANY." I'm not even going to say names. I don't think any band could have took us in those years because we were just hot.

KYLE: The years of like—

ERIC: From 2009 to 2010. Yeah. 2011.

KYLE: I mean, you guys were playing like every single gig on the streets, pretty much.

ERIC: Yeah, yeah. Yeah. We were self-proclaimed, and it was funny, because when we said it, we put it out there to every band. Every band could say, "Oh, well we don't like this. Y'all play radio tunes; y'all not real music." But if you put us with any band, the crowd would still be with us. You could put us at the YMO second line with six bands and we would have the most people.[6]

KYLE: I mean, you can't really argue with that.

ERIC: Yep. And then once you put us onstage—they actually put us with the best, the only bands that they didn't put up there were, I would say

The Stooges at Red Bull Street Kings. *Left to right:* John Dotson, Jerreau Fournett Spug, Virgil, Thaddeaus, Eric, Antione "Ace Free" Coleman, Chris, Maurice "Sporty" Craig, Walter, Drew, and Garfield. Photo by 5040tos/Greg Rhoades.

Rebirth and the Hot 8, which were legendary bands at this time. But we were the kings. And Walter had already had a championship belt made. He was wearing this championship belt saying we're the kings for maybe the past three months. "We're the best. We're the best. We're the best." And then they put us with the underdogs, which were the To Be Continued Brass Band. They had great music. They didn't have the stage presence, though, that we had. That's how we won against them. Then the Soul Rebels, which had us nervous because they're so talented. The Soul Rebels are very talented. But the thing that knocked the Soul Rebels out of the park, they were not in the genre that they needed to be in.

KYLE: Okay, like in what sense?

ERIC: They play a style of brass band music, but they don't play *street* music.

KYLE: You can't argue that the Stooges didn't play street music.

ERIC: And you can try and cover it up and twist it a little bit, but when you put the Soul Rebels in front of the street crowd, it's like a whole different type of problem when you're going against a street band. It's like a kickboxer versus a regular boxer. A kickboxer is used to using their feet. It's just two different things. You put someone in the ring and it's not their forte, it's different. Had it just been the Soul Rebels at a show, yeah, it would have been great. But your audience is the streets, the people that these other three

bands play for every week. And that took the Soul Rebels out of their ele-
ment, as great as they were. In that instance TBC thought they were better
than us, but they didn't have the stage presence. No one on the front row had
the stage presence. And the Free Agents, they had a little stage presence, but
their music wasn't strong enough at the time. But everyone didn't like the
Stooges because they thought they were better than us. And then to have a
panel of the city's best come along and say, "Well, we voted. Y'all played the
best traditional song because y'all had a hot new traditional." The stage presence was off the chain because when we did things with the crowd, we have
a tune where we start to march like a high school marching band and we do
a dance with it. And the whole crowd was doing the dance with it because
they know that this is our thing. No other band did that with the crowd—
things like that. Then once we won it with the judges, it was undeniable.

✦ ✦ ✦

WALTER: When it came down to Street King Competition, I study you, I
know what you gonna do already. I can defeat that.

KYLE: If you want to beat the competition, you got to know the
competition.

WALTER: Right, right. So then these other bands, which they just playing
music and think this is based off of music. No, no, no, no. It's based off the
right music, the right songs, the right way to get the crowd. Y'all ain't studied
nothing, so you ain't even developed this, and I'm not gonna tell you, I'm
just gonna beat you. In the documentary, you'll see them saying, "Oh, I hate
the Pooges." All this type of stuff and talking. And then you'll catch me in
the interview and I'd be like, "Well, we gonna win." And they be like, "What
makes you so confident you gonna win?" I said, "They call us the Pooges.
They don't like us. They think we arrogant or we don't know this, but we
gonna win. And I'm not giving them the secret of why we gonna win, but I
knew we gonna win based off of we know the science of this." So they gave
out the judges, everybody on the panel, who the judge is. I know all them,
the judges.

KYLE: And who were the judges?

WALTER: It was Mannie Fresh, it was Uncle Benny from Treme, it was
Blodie from the Dirty Dozen, it was Fred Johnson from a social aid and
pleasure club.[7]

KYLE: Yeah, he's Black Men of Labor, right?

WALTER: Right. And then it was Allison Reindhart who works with Roots
of Music. So Fred Johnson, he like traditional music. Blodie, he's straight

Chris Cotton with a joyful jump onstage at the Red Bull Street Kings competition. Photo by 5040tos/Greg Rhoades.

everything, and Uncle Benny's straight everything, but at the same time, I know I'ma pick a traditional song that's gonna be the hardest traditional that got like three parts. So we play "Tiger Rag." I know that's gonna win. Bam. I got them. Off the top, I'm gonna get them with that. Next thing is Mannie Fresh. He from the hip-hop elements of stuff. He gonna want to see how we could get the crowd into rapping and stuff. So "Why They Had to Kill Him" is going to get Mannie Fresh. It's relatable, it's a real story, it's rap, the whole crowd gonna sing it. This is hip-hop. Bam. And I just knew how to win. Like, none of y'all ain't got this. Y'all don't know. We *study* this. The icing on the cake was we had Red Bull shirts on. Don't this look good for TV? Now the next time they had the Street King competition, all the bands had Red Bull on their shirt.

PART IV
The Stage Band Generation

CHAPTER 10

I'm Just Doin' My Job

When I catch up with the Zulu Social Aid and Pleasure Club's anniversary second line, the Stooges are leading the crowd through the shaded area under the Claiborne Bridge playing a cover of Earth, Wind & Fire's "Brazilian Rhyme."[1] Years ago, the band added lyrics to the tune for their stage show, singing "Stooges 'bout to take a break / We 'bout to take a break" repeatedly. But here in the streets, the band doesn't sing the words and instead allows the instruments to carry the words' meaning. Soon after I enter the fray with my bicycle in tow, the band takes a much-deserved break at the Treme Bar and Grill. Groups of second liners huddle under crape myrtles and the shadows cast by buildings, seeking a respite from the cloudless afternoon sky.

I spot Virgil from across the neutral ground. His bald head is topped with a wet towel, and his lanky arms are exposed through a sleeveless white T-shirt. He snaps his head back when he sees me and shoots me a grin with his eyes nearly closed. We're both on break from the school year—Virgil as a high school science teacher working on his PhD in education and I as a PhD student also. Standing next to an overturned tuba on the sidewalk, we chat about his summerlong side gig, which I've been following on Facebook. Using a full arsenal of grills and smokers in his backyard (including one made from a recycled filing cabinet), he's been preparing dishes of pork shank, lobster, steak, and ribs for various customers in and around his home out in Chalmette. Although his cooking is in many ways a passion project, like many of his bandmates, Virgil entrepreneurially combines a number of different jobs to support his family.

"We have to have other things to do in order to support a family. And that's a shame because we should get paid more, but we don't," he tells me. In addition to music, the Stooges spend their hours making money in a variety of other occupational areas: Eric drives a taxi; Al works for Cox Cable; Garfield has at times run a car wash, a rental business, and a bar; Chad and Walter each invest in real estate; and the list goes on.

Our conversation about food and side gigs is cut short by a trumpet blast signaling that the break in the second line is over. We reemerge from our small patches of shade, and the band leads us back under the bridge through the remainder of the parade route. By this point, many of the Stooges have swapped their sweat-soaked shirts for fresh ones: marching for hours in the hot sun sometimes necessitates a shirt change. After four hours of parading, the second line disbands, and I begin walking back to my bicycle eleven blocks away. I see Virgil a couple blocks ahead of me, his tenor sax cradled in his arm, a bottle of water in his other hand. Virgil and Al would normally drink Hennessy during second lines, but the possibility of heat exhaustion in the ninety-degree weather makes their parading tradition unwise today. The rest of the band waits for Virgil in Al's truck, a black, two-door Dodge Ram named Justice, and Virgil hops in the back with his bandmates. Justice tears off around the corner as Al honks and waves. The band members and a tuba peek up over the side as they head back to the start of the route. From there, they get in their respective vehicles and prepare for a slew of other gigs, most of which will end in the wee hours of the next morning.

Making a living as a brass band musician can often be difficult, as late nights and early mornings bleed into one another—particularly on weekends when the demand for music is high. Combining performing with various other jobs, some brass band musicians are able to put together livable incomes through an arduous schedule that takes a toll on the body. Musical labor is physically demanding service work that necessitates occupational benefits that aren't provided when work is contractual and precarious.[2] Brass band musicianship is an occupation without healthcare and benefits, and its physical demands can be very costly, as there are no longer any public hospitals in the city.[3] For the core group of the Stooges who reached their forties while we were writing this book, their bodies can no longer bounce back quickly. After four hours parading in the sun with instruments, getting to work the next day can be a challenge.

Few people (professional musicians excluded) associate music with labor. This disassociation often obscures the fact that bands perform a service for audiences, a service that is subject to economic pressures like any other form of work. The Stooges make this point musically. Their cover of rapper T.I.'s "Doin' My Job" draws attention to the music's means of production repeatedly

Antione "Ace Free" Coleman (*left*) alongside Virgil Tiller at the Original N.O. Men and Lady Buckjumpers second line, November 29, 2009. Photo by Pableaux Johnson.

in the song's hook: I'm just doin' my job.[4] The refrain calls attention to overly romanticized discourses around music by revealing its role in the Stooges' strategic navigation of capitalism.[5] Simply put, music is work, too. As Virgil outlines in this chapter, the second line economy is intertwined with the city's broader neoliberal economy, in which the public good (what one would hope is the purpose of government) is sacrificed for the accumulation of profits as the government partners with private companies. Short-term rental companies—Airbnb in particular—have made housing increasingly unaffordable and affected the amount of money that social aid and pleasure clubs are able to spend on hiring bands. The rising housing costs associated with short-term rentals (and their deregulation), stagnant wages, and a minimum wage of $7.25/ hour all contribute to the depletion of the economic streams that musicians pull from. Paying a band isn't usually something you can afford when you're struggling to make rent and pay utilities.

Furthermore, the labor that goes into producing musical performances for audiences isn't limited to that which is visible onstage and in the streets. The band is made possible by a massive group effort that includes the band's family networks. While the Stooges often have kids around at rehearsals and performances, child-rearing work is also shared by various people in their families—partners, parents, aunties, and uncles. This labor is all too often rendered invisible to audience members, who are rarely aware of everything that goes into making a performance possible. This chapter seeks to peel back the veneer of performance, exposing *some* of the work that goes on behind the scenes and the physical and emotional demands of playing music.

✦ ✦ ✦

KYLE: I was thinking of opening a chapter with writing about when you guys were playing for the Zulu anniversary parade the other day because you guys played gig, after gig, after gig.

VIRGIL: Yeah, and then we played the Blue Nile the night before.

KYLE: Okay, so do you want to tell me about that day in particular, and the gigs that you guys had to go to?

VIRGIL: I had four black and white gigs that I had to do right after that because it was a Saturday. Saturdays are not really the days you have second lines because Saturdays are your gig days. I think that Friday night we had one, and Blue Nile was the night before. So that Friday night we had one gig, maybe two. And it ended at 12:30 in the morning. Generally, when you're younger, you can just pop up and go get it. The older you get, you really have to get prepared for that.

KYLE: And you made forty this year?

VIRGIL: Yeah, so you really have to get mentally prepared to do this. We woke up and we had to play Walter's aunt's funeral, so we actually second lined from Washington and Earhart all the way down to where the Calliope Housing Projects used to be. And we were still on Earhart and we went a mile or so, so we finished that and we played outside the house and we walked from there to the beginning of Zulu. Usually, a second line, when you're younger, we'll start drinking at that point. But when you get older, you understand that's not going to work.

KYLE: Al always has some Henny with him, though, right?

The Stooges playing at the CTC Steppers second line, February 26, 2012. *Left to right:* Cameron Johnson (sax), Chris Cotton, John Dotson (cowbell), Walter Ramsey, Maurice "Sporty" Craig, Flash Jackson (sunglasses). Photo by Pableaux Johnson.

VIRGIL: Yeah, but we didn't even drink that day. I was like, "Yeah, this is too hot for this right now," so I got a snowball. We were actually hydrating, so we didn't even pay attention to all kind of stuff. That really works out well. Once you know your body, physically there's certain things you can't do. You start hydrating, you eat a little something—not anything too heavy, but not anything too light. You've got to try and maintain yourself.

KYLE: So you started Zulu around two thirty or something like that?

VIRGIL: We started Zulu around one, one thirty, something like that.

KYLE: Oh, okay. Well that was the start of the parade, no?

VIRGIL: Yeah. Well, I don't know. It started before. The band came and met us then and we left from that bar on Washington and then we started, we went over the bridge. So we left. We been doing this for years. It's real hot and we know we have to go over the bridge.

KYLE: Okay, you go over the bridge where?

VIRGIL: Right off of Washington on Broad. So people have clubs and people have dancing. They tend to want to walk up the bridge, but it's slow. That *hurts.* So what we do is, we gonna stop, we gonna play, we gonna stop at the bottom. We gonna let the parade go in the front, we gonna let that go till it gets to the top. And then we see that, you just run up the hill.

KYLE: Like, hit a fast tune?

VIRGIL: Yeah, we play "Let's Go Get 'Em" and we go up there. Once we get up to the flat part of the bridge, we gonna slow down, gather yourself, and then we gonna start doing what we got to do, going down. Going up that bridge slow, it hurts you. People pass out like that and you got to think about it. All the fumes from the exhaust from the interstate and you breathing that in. And after you've gone up and done all that work, people pass out. Sporty got sick up there. I almost passed out twice because of that—going over the bridge. I really don't ever like doing that, but it's a second line; you got to roll with it. You have to know what you're doing. That's part of the work part of it.

KYLE: And do you really need to know how to do it when you're younger?

VIRGIL: You're younger, you don't understand because you're younger, you can do certain things. Whereas right now, we can't do that. I'm not playing with myself like that. I know. I'm not saying I *can't* do it, but why?

KYLE: And especially when you have a few more gigs at the end of the day.

VIRGIL: Yeah, so we finished that at Zulu, you get your money back, I got in my truck, went home.

KYLE: Wait, didn't you guys all get in Al's truck?

VIRGIL: Yeah, we got in Al's truck. He drove us to the beginning because the beginning was where Walter's aunt's funeral procession started. So we got in the car, bam. I went home, took a shower, put the black and white on and started my gigs for the night. I didn't finish until like one thirty in the morning.

KYLE: So they were just black and white gigs—like, funeral gigs?

VIRGIL: No, it was wedding gigs.

KYLE: So who were you playing with?

VIRGIL: Kin Folks. I play with them for the black and whites. I made money, but I ain't gonna lie to you, I was *out* for the next day. I didn't wake up till two o'clock. I had been going all day. For me, once I get past that hump of being tired, I can just go all night. After getting home at twelve thirty in the morning, my body's conditioned to wake up at six. No matter what time it is, I wake up at six.

KYLE: Your biological clock kind of gets you up.

VIRGIL: Yeah, and just having children and all that kind of stuff like that. It's gonna be like that.

KYLE: Gotcha. Wow. That's a long day, man. I don't know that I'd be able to handle that. I was just at Zulu for a few hours and the sun was killing me.

VIRGIL: Yeah, it'll beat you down.

KYLE: So what are some strategies to kind of keep cool?

VIRGIL: You want to eat, you don't want to do anything too sudden. If you're going to drink, drink in moderation. I'm telling you because Al and I, we drink. We drink Hennessy because that's what we do.

John Perkins at the Family Ties second line, October 3, 2010.
Photo by Lisa Palumbo.

KYLE: That's what you've been doing since you were younger.

VIRGIL: Yeah, we've been doing that since we started. We had one parade that we did. It actually came down Freret. It was in June. Man, it was so hot out here. If you think about Freret, there's no shade, and we came all the way from Washington to between Jena and Cadiz and ended up two blocks down. Ace—Antione—he had to go to the hospital. I think it was like heat exhaustion. He passed out on the street at the end. The next day, I was teaching summer school and I get to the board. I thought I was okay, so I was writing stuff on the board. My students say, "Mr. Tiller." I'm like, "What?" It's like, "You alright?" I was like, "Yeah. Why?" It's like, "What you writing on the board?" I turned around, I looked. That shit didn't make no sense *at all*. I said, "Alright, y'all, I'm about to go to the hospital." I had to go to the hospital for symptoms of heat exhaustion. I was still done from the day before, so I had to go. They put in an IV and all that stuff like that.

KYLE: I mean, it's menial labor, right? If you're doing landscaping or something in the sun, it's the same kind of shit. You're carrying your instrument and you're just *walking*.

VIRGIL: Just walking. When it's hot like this, it's hard. When it's cool, it's not that bad. The heat, it will do some things to you, man. It will make you see stuff that's not really in front of you. It will do some things. You got to know the signs. I've been there a couple times on the street. It will take you out if you're not careful.

KYLE: Yeah, so what do you do to keep cool?

VIRGIL: The first thing is, a lot of people, they have two shirts on, they'll take it off. I don't do that. I keep that sweat. It stays on that shirt. I have an undershirt on, the sweat will stay on the undershirt and I keep that on there. I keep that perspiration to keep the shirt wet. If you take off all too much stuff, the stuff is just evaporating off and you're just losing water faster. Cover your head.

KYLE: With like a wet towel or something?

VIRGIL: Wet towel, hat, something like that. Keep it off. And water. Don't try to drink anything like hard liquor. That's why we didn't even drink that Saturday. We didn't drink at all because it's rough out there. It'll dehydrate you faster. Make sure you eat. And the good thing about the Zulu is that at the stops, they had fruit, they had all kinds of stuff at the stops, so we *killing* that. They're like, "You want this?" "Yeah." That fruit helps you, too.

KYLE: Do most clubs do that?

VIRGIL: It really depends on the club. Recently, some of the clubs have been real stingy about how they feed the band or the crew itself. Even having the number of stops that they having. They start making it smaller and smaller. And that's kind of rough. You're going for four hours. If you've got two or three stops, that's not really a lot of stops. But they'll get mad when you stop playing. When it gets to the point where we look around and Walter will hold his fist in the air, we stop.

KYLE: So why do you think the clubs are having less stops now? Does it have to do with the increase in permits?

VIRGIL: I think a lot of it's a financial reason. It probably plays a part, raising the prices of the thing, but just financials, *period*, in society. Things are costing a lot in New Orleans. What people are being paid—their salaries—hasn't increased.

KYLE: It's completely stagnant, right?

VIRGIL: Yeah, but the cost of things has risen. So, I mean, that's the state that we're in. You can't fault them too much. I think some of the clubs have

Al, Maurice "Sporty" Craig, and Walter outside Sportsman's Corner at the Lady Jetsetters annual second line, January 8, 2017. Photo by Michael Mastrogiovanni.

rearranged their routes whereas you're going too far. To try to beat the time limit, you have to move a lot and so you don't have enough time.

✦ ✦ ✦

KYLE: Another thing that I want to talk about is working a job and then going out and playing gigs at night. That's a pretty serious grind. It must be really tough. How do you balance that and family life?

AL: Well, one of the things, you got to have a good wife. You got to have a wife that's understanding. And sometimes, she don't understand, but then a lot of times, you got to give and take. I *involve* my family. You see me at a gig, nine times out of ten, my wife's with me. I'm not just leaving her at home and she barely see me. Because I can't bring her to work with me, so when I get off work and I got five or six gigs with me that night, if I don't take her with me, then I'm not gonna see her for the whole day. It's a give and take. Now, some things I can't take her, but if I can't take her one night, if I ain't got gigs the other night, I take her out, take her somewhere. You got to balance everything. It's all about a balancing act.

KYLE: Okay, and your oldest is old enough that she can take care of the rest of them?

Al, his wife, Shawn Growe, and their daughter, Que'Lah Growe
(a.k.a. Piggy), at the Young Men Olympian Jr. second line,
September 12, 2010. Photo by Lisa Palumbo.

AL: Yeah, she can take care. But she's graduating right now. She's about to go to military. So, actually, Que'Dyn's the oldest now. I got good parents, and my wife parents watch them sometime when we need to go and do different things. We balance it out. Just keep everything balanced, try to make everybody happy. That's the main thing, just handling the business. And if I can't make the gig, I can't make the gig. If I say I'm on a gig, I'm on a gig.

✦ ✦ ✦

DREW: I had this discussion with my old lady actually and we were just talking about living versus lifestyle. That was the crux of the debate. The

Al Growe playing at the VIP Ladies and Kids second line,
March 5, 2017. Photo by Pableaux Johnson.

way I had been living was that if I spend the rest of my life making only
$30,000 a year, living in my $75,000 house, I'm fine. No matter what the
neighborhood is, I will be fine. Now, do I want more? Of course! But my
standard and my threshold between me living and my lifestyle—

KYLE: Like, your idealized lifestyle?

DREW: Yeah, my idealized lifestyle. My threshold is a little lower than
yours. So, yes, we won't see eye-to-eye on what house to buy all the time, or
what car to buy, or how much we should have in the bank, or how much the
engagement ring should cost. It's just like my standards and your standards
are totally different. My standards are like that for a reason. For me, I am
living the lifestyle that I have. One, because I don't put as much value in the
things that are expensive. But more importantly, I don't put that much value

on crossing that threshold as most people do. We're just living in a society that the dollar is glorified, romanticized. I think that was one of the main reasons how Walter and I were able to be friends for so long. We're road dogs, and the most important thing about that is we do for each other and we realize by doing for each other, our standard of living will always elevate. Not only are we doing it ourselves, but we have a network. As long as that wheel turns, it's like a boulder going down a hill. As the boulder goes down the hill, it gets bigger and bigger and bigger and you've got this massive glob that crashes into the wall.

✦ ✦ ✦

CHAD: We take this seriously. It's a lot of people's livelihoods, it's careers. I never had to work a nine-to-five before. This has always been my job, my horn. Practicing, playing, practice, playing, practice, playing. That's what it's been. This my life. For every brass band, I believe it's the same way. But some guys aren't in my position. Some guys have to play with smaller bands and do things because they have families and they want to stay grounded. I have two kids and everything, too, but it's all in the way of how you manage it. I always tell a musician—any musician—that brass band is good, but it's good to just get your hand into everything. *Everything*. You might as well because brass band—*just* brass band—is not gonna pay the bills.

You have to extend yourself to certain things, and that's what the Stooges did. We realized at a young age. Man, you doing these brass band gigs, we might do twelve gigs, at the end of the night, we might have $400 a man; versus doing two stage gigs, we'd have $400 a man. We learned that early. We know what route to go, it's just that it all takes time in building it. Some guys do feel—especially with the Stooges, man—it's like every three years the band change. With the Stooges, they'll get a good squad and then somebody's gonna lose it in the head, and mess that whole thing up. Then they fall off the streets for another year or two, then they get back on the streets with another good squad, somebody falls off again. Because I know where it was at. I know where it was at because I was one of those persons that fell off. But I always stayed afloat and moved up.

I just tell guys, "We making moves now." We got brass bands getting *Grammys* now. And I'm trying to tell everybody in the brass band community, it's more than just brass band now. Yeah, in New Orleans, brass bands rock crowds. But around the world, Rebirth rocking *crowds*. I'm talking about five thousand here, ten thousand there. Everybody's starting to get on to the brass band music, and this is the first time I ever heard Wynton

Marsalis give us credit. Like, brass band, *period*. He's from here and he love the culture, I believe, but I don't ever see him support it. The first time he supported it was the Rebirth. I believe we outsold his album by fifty thousand albums, so he had to support that shit. It was like, "We understand that y'all are heavyweights, but right now, we over that, you dig?" What make it sweet for me is that the guys that talk down to us and talk down to my brass band family, we ain't too far from getting the same payroll that they getting. It's just that brass band, we do it for the love, we do it for the people. We can't go to a family that's just burying their son and ask them, "We need to pay everybody $200 a man." So we got to do a few things to move some corners. That's why we have six gigs a day or five gigs a day. Because at the end of the day, we still got to feed our families, too. It's not that this guy's making more, we just work harder.

KYLE: It seems like there are only a few brass bands that make a living off of it, and I guess my question is, What does it take to do that, and then, how did your training in the Stooges prepare you to make a really good career out of it?[6]

CHAD: Well, I'll tell you. Walter always was like a big brother to me. I always look to Walter for advice and guidance and stuff. When I started with the Stooges, I didn't too much know anything about how brass bands even worked. I got to learn the business through the Stooges, and how it works. Pretty much every brass band works that same way. It was a taste of it with the Stooges and then when I moved with the Hot 8, it was the same thing, just a little bit better pay scale. I moved to Rebirth, it was the same thing, just a better pay scale. Like I said, it's certain levels, but in order for a band to make it to that level—the level of Rebirth—it takes time, dedication, traveling for no money, and time. I mean, just *time*. It take time to build that name, and that's why Rebirth name is exceeding itself now, because we do spend a lot of time on the road building that crowd. No other band doing that. And that's what's hurting a lot of other brass bands now. Y'all only still local because y'all scared to take that forty-five-minute drive to Gulfport to start off something that you can go back three months from now, you might get thirty people. And the next time you go back, you might get one hundred people. And the next time—that's how it works.

The interesting thing that I tell every brass band, when I go on the road and the Rebirth been around thirty-three years, I always ask the crowd, "How many people's first time seeing Rebirth Brass Band?" Damn near more than half the crowd always raise their hands. It's thirty-three years later, though. That's what I'm trying to tell them: "Y'all gonna be in the same position." Every time you go to a crowd ask who's the first time. Look at them. You got to feed those people so the next time they bring somebody else to your show. And the next time, they gonna bring somebody else, and then they might bring their kids and put their kids onto your stuff. You got to keep it rolling. I learned a lot from the Stooges, man. The Stooges, it was my first experience with hard work for little pay and my first experience with learning that every gig don't pay, learning that you still have to build to get where you're going. And it was just the first point in my brotherhood. Those guys still my brothers because I went through a lot of stuff with the Stooges—dealing with Katrina and everything. The Stooges was definitely the platform for me.

✦ ✦ ✦

VIRGIL: We could go out of town and make all kinds of money. But here? No. And it's because of the supply and demand. Some of the club owners don't care about the quality of music. They're pulling kids that's off the streets that don't really sound that well and put them in their club. And people will come in.

KYLE: Yeah. People aren't going to know the difference. It's like Vaso.

VIRGIL: Yeah, so they don't realize the quality because they got people in the club and they'll drink. They make money off the drinks and hopefully you as the band have to make money off the tips. And he might give you a little something. That's not just with Vaso's. A lot of places are like that. Blue Nile has been good to us. d.b.a. has been good to us in the past. But still, if you go out places, you'll get paid a lot more money to play.

KYLE: Can I ask numbers? How does it differ?

VIRGIL: I would give you a percentage. I would say I think we make double the money.

KYLE: You make double the money out of town? And I suppose they probably fly you, too?

VIRGIL: Yeah, and they might give you a per diem, they feed you food and everything else. Clubs here don't do that for us.

KYLE: Well, no.

VIRGIL: No. They don't feed you food.

KYLE: It's like, "You got a house, go there."

VIRGIL: Yeah, yeah. Some clubs, you pay for your own drinks. And you don't even get comps; they don't set you up with a greenroom. Some clubs, you just come up in there and they don't do anything for you. That's how we're slighted down here because there's a large supply of music. They're able to do it, where if you go somewhere like Jackson, Mississippi, they can't get that, so they gonna pay.

The Stooges pose for a group picture at a stop in the Single Men Social Aid and Pleasure Club second line, March 19, 2017. *Left to right:* Al Growe, Virgil Tiller, Thaddeaus "Peanut" Ramsey, Clifton "Spug" Smith, Mike Jones, and Peanut's friend Rickey Turner. Photo by Michael Mastrogiovanni.

KYLE: Okay, so what's a corrective for that? How do you fix that? That's kind of a crazy question, but . . .

VIRGIL: Well, one, I think part of it is not the clubs, part of it is it's the clubs *and* the bands.

KYLE: Because people undercut.

VIRGIL: Yes. I can ask $4,000 for a gig and they can go somewhere else and get it for $2,000. They will go with the $2,000. I might be better. It doesn't matter because on Frenchmen, you got walk-in clubs where they don't charge. They just gonna bar hop. Any club, that's how they do it.

Even second lines. If we charging $4,000, they say, "Well, we gonna charge $3,000 to do a second line." They gonna go with the $3,000. And that's what it is.

KYLE: Mind you, in the streets there's more of an appreciation for the different brass bands. They can discern better than tourists who a good brass band is, right?

VIRGIL: Yeah, but that money does control it. When we're in the streets, we were the ones that were upping the amount of money—not just for us, for everybody. Then you have bands coming behind us that were saying, "Hey, you don't have to pay them that, pay us this and get close to the same music. As a matter of fact, we will play the Stooges' songs." It's just unfortunate that it's like that. I'm not just going to blame it on all the clubs. It's the clubs and the bands. I think if we had a brass band union and we got together saying, "Hey, this is what we're charging. If you are with this, then we all go into these clubs with this price." There would be classes. Like, this is an A band, this is a B band, this is a C band, because I can't have a band that's just coming in making the same amount of money as an A band. There would be classes and we would have to figure that out, but right now, it's whatever. It hurts the musicians and it hurts the music, too. Some of the music that's being played onstage is—I'll be honest with you—really not good. We have cats that's coming from out of town—no disrespect for the people that come from out of town and learn how to play the music—and they think that brass band music or traditional music is just all some stuff where "I just got to learn a little head or whatever and then I can play it and they will like it." It's more difficult than that. Sometimes when I hear cats playing traditionals or sometimes I hear cats playing brass band music—or if I play with them, they call me for a gig and I turn around and I'm like, "What are y'all doing?" And they'll be like, "What? That's the song." "No, it's not!" This is not the correct way to play this. It kind of hurts you on the inside because, as a child, I had to learn how to play this music the correct way. And here, you can get a gig and get paid—and when I say "had to learn," I mean I had to go to gigs and *not* get paid.

CHAPTER 11

On the Road

The alarm wakes me with a jolt at 3:45 a.m. I shower and pack a couple of sandwiches and a change of clothes in my backpack before leaving the house. As I ride my bicycle toward the Stooges' studio in the dark, humid morning, my stomach feels uneasy and my muscles tighten after only a few hours of sleep. Five minutes after I arrive, production and road manager Royce "Flash" Jackson pulls up in a big white rental van, a menthol dangling from his lips. He enters the code to open the gate and, pulling up to the studio door, we load a keyboard into the already-packed back of the van, speaking few words. Flash gives Walter a call: "Where you at?" After a brief pause and the distant crackling of Walt's voice, Flash replies in annoyance, "I could have been in my motherfucking bed, man!" They told Flash 5:00 a.m. and he told me 5:00 a.m., but the rest of the stage band isn't set to arrive for another thirty minutes.

Coming from an all-nighter after a gig on Frenchmen Street, stage band drummer Roland "Rolo" Taylor soon shows up and offers me some hash browns from a grease-soaked McDonald's bag. He and Flash fuss at each other over a drum stool and Elliot Slater, the white guitarist, arrives in short order with his guitar, followed by Abdule "Duley" Muhammad, the percussionist, who wastes no time noting Flash's orneriness, telling us within Flash's earshot that he's afflicted with "old man syndrome." With the band's go-to Mercedes Sprinter in the shop, we pack into the rental, which smells like body odor and unwashed carpets, and head out to pick up Walter and Mike in New Orleans

East before driving to an afternoon sound check and subsequent 7:00 p.m. gig in Johns Creek, Georgia.

Spending time with the Stooges is nothing if not funny. Before we even get on the interstate, Duley unleashes a steady stream of words, carrying on like someone who's been awake for hours, much to everyone's simultaneous laughter and annoyance. Ever the clown, he delivers some good-natured ribbing to Flash and cycles through topics like local and celebrity gossip, old-school hip-hop, and mumble rap, punctuating much of it with jokes. As soon as we get on the interstate, the rest of the band instigates an arbitrary "no talking on the interstate" rule in an effort to shut him up long enough to fall asleep. With the van silent, everyone—Duley included—drifts off into much-needed sleep except for me and Walt, who is wide awake behind the wheel despite having stayed up the previous night at the hospital with his mother. Our conversation drifts from the humorous chat of our pre-interstate driving into more serious subject matter. With his eyes focused on the road, Walter tells me the story of the stage band's genesis during the storm—his business partner, the scamming contractors, the importance of music in returning him to some sense of normalcy. With only two hours of sleep, I'm amazed he has the energy to keep his eyes open, let alone drive for eight hours, but Walter is, as usual, determined and focused. "We ain't just gonna make money in the city, we gonna make *world* money," he tells me. Life on the road isn't often as glamorous as some make it out to be, and it comes with its own set of challenges. Making a livable wage in a brass band necessitates touring—especially during the summer months, when there are no festivals in town on account of the heat. Venues and social aid and pleasure clubs in New Orleans are not always willing or able to pay livable wages to brass bands, especially when bands often consist of eight or more musicians. The matter is only made worse by young pickup bands who are willing to undercut senior bands, a practice that can only be fixed by some form of unionization. Paring down the large brass band format and going on the road is just one means of making the brass band venture into a viable career.

A few hours later, Elliot, Flash, and Duley wake from their sleep, uncurling their bodies from whatever uncomfortable positions they'd been sleeping in. Elliot begins rolling a backwood and when we pull up to a gas station near Mobile, Alabama, he and Duley head out back to smoke it.[1] Flash stays around the front to smoke a menthol, Walter orders a breakfast sandwich from Arby's, and I unpack a PB&J from my backpack while Rolo and Mike stay sleeping in the back. Just as Flash, Walter, and I get back in the van, Walter spots a police cruiser, exclaiming, "Let's go!" with an urgency that catches me off guard. He honks the horn to alert Elliot and Duley, but they're nowhere to be found. We

This blurry cellphone picture captures the feeling of a 4:00 a.m. gas station stop somewhere outside of Atlanta, Georgia. Ah, the road life. Photo by Kyle DeCoste.

pull around the side of the gas station in the van and I see them speaking with the police. We wait for a few minutes to see how Duley and Elliot will fare with the officers, and they soon return to the van looking defeated. They express frustration at the confiscation of their blunt, noting that the officer they spoke with will likely smoke it later.

Such is the modus operandi of outdated drug laws and their enforcement. Cannabis use is one means of coping with the physical demands of touring, but it comes with a risk that, despite its humorous treatment in this chapter, can have serious consequences when police become involved. Marijuana arrests uphold white supremacy through policing, which the history of the drug and its connection to Latinx and Black people attests to.[2] Despite increased destigmatization of cannabis and changing drug laws, law enforcement practices haven't changed much since the days of *Reefer Madness*. As an ACLU study on racial disparities in marijuana-law enforcement in the United States attests, African Americans are 3.73 times more likely to be arrested for marijuana possession than white people despite comparable usage rates.[3] One might wonder how Elliot's whiteness may have affected his and Duley's treatment by the police officers that day—a question Flash alludes to in this chapter. When taken together with the need to tour to sustain a living, life on the road is fraught with hazards. Later that day, surrounded by sleeping band members in a greenroom in Georgia, Walter admitted to me, "That road ain't nothing nice, but we do it." Drifting in and out of sleep as we drove through the night to make it to Sunday church gigs the next morning, I had to agree.

✦ ✦ ✦

FLASH: Oh! I've got a story for you. I think we was leaving Ohio, and the battery had cut the transmission line. It was bumping into it and it burnt the battery out, so the van had broke down. This was about one o'clock in the morning. It's late. Walt was at home because he had to do a special gig, and we broke down on the interstate. We got a code: if we call you three times back-to-back, that means something very important. I don't care if it's one o'clock, two o'clock, three o'clock in the morning. That's something between Walt and I. If I call you three times back-to-back, something happened. "Walt, the truck broke down, man. It's not going into drive and stuff like that. And it's not doing nothing." He said, "Man, see if we can get a tow truck." I said, "Man, we tried to get a tow truck and everything." They asked him about money, I said, "Well, don't worry. I got the money part right." So Walt said, "I'm gonna see what I can do." At this time, everybody smoking, everybody chilling out. Guess what happened next? The fucking state trooper pulled up. I said, "Everybody chill. Everybody chill and let me talk." We had Elliot, the white dude, with us. So it was like, "Can I see everybody's identification cards and everything?" He said, "Do you have any drug paraphernalia or anything like that?" If you don't mind us searching the van, it's all cool and stuff. So I said, "Oh, shit!" I know we got weed in the van. I know because *I* got it. They went through the whole van and everything. So then another cop came and it was two white cops, but at the end of the day, they was cool as hell. They came, the guys towed the truck, and they found a town to go to and stuff. So the cops said, "Well, we can't leave you out here, so we gonna ride in the police car to the hotel," which is about five, six miles. The cops was racing on the interstate with the sirens on!

KYLE: Because you can speed with those things on.

FLASH: Yeah! And the cops, they were seeing who can get there first and stuff. So once we got there and everything, I said, "Thank you very much for your time" and everything. He said, "Flash, look, when you smoke that blunt, think of Officer Williams." That was so cute! He said, "Y'all be safe!"

✦ ✦ ✦

ARIAN: When I used to drive during the out-of-town gigs, driving and shit, it would be like six o'clock in the morning and it would be freezing fucking cold. Oh man, I used to wait till I get on the interstate and I used to be mad because they used to go to sleep on me. I'm driving. Now, Kyle, I've been driving all fucking night. I've been driving *all* night. I'm coffee'd up, blazing, wide-eyed and everything. I said, "Okay, you bitches want to go to sleep?" I press the gas, going down there doing 100, going straight down the interstate. I push the windows down, all the windows, they come down just like this. Boy, you talking about the cold air! Whoo! "Bitch, close that window! Close that window!" "No! Wake the fuck up!" "Close that window! Say, bro, Fat Boy tripping in here." "Man, I ain't tripping. Wake the fuck up!" I said, "I've been up all night!" And then Walter was like, "Man, y'all better wake up. That man been up all night driving. Now you motherfuckers think y'all about to let my cousin drive all night because he can drive a trailer. Fuck that." That's the only thing—he was on my side. I was on his side because he ain't trust none of them niggas driving his truck like that. I was the only one that could really drive it besides him. It was special because he had a truck with a trailer on the back and I'm the only one who can pull it, really, besides Walter.

So they be like, "Man, close that window!" Boy, it was freezing cold. I ain't gonna lie, Kyle, that shit woke *me* up. It was in the Twin Cities. Man, you know the Twin Cities is cold as a motherfucker. You can't even see the city because the smoke. So I was like, "Alright, you bitches want to go to sleep, alright, I'ma show you. And how beautiful it is, it was *blue* that's how cold it was. Everything was blue. Like, that freezing blue. Man, that time I rolled that window down, them boys said "Ooooooh!" They didn't have no jackets, none of that. They jumped up, they all jumped on the back, jumped in the front. Ersel looking at me, he's like, "Come on, dog. What's wrong?" I said, "Nothing. I'm just fucking with them." He goes, "Alright." So I just roll his window up thinking, "I ain't fucking with him, because that's my dog."

KYLE: Because he's gonna get you back later?

ARIAN: Yeah, right. He'll look at me like, "What the hell's wrong, dog?" I'm like, "Nothing. I'm just fucking with them." He said, "All right." So he cover up and go back to sleep. He know what I'm doing. That's my dog. I love him. He know my routine. The other two, man, I gave them the blues. They couldn't handle it. They were like, "Man, Fat Boy tripping today." I said, "No, I ain't tripping, It's just cold. You all want to go asleep on me? Now, suppose I fall asleep and all of us have a big accident?"

KYLE: That's no good. You need somebody at least checking up on you so you're not drifting off into sleep.

ARIAN: Yeah. We had one thing, Kyle, the goddamn fucking—somebody dropped a ladder.

KYLE: On the highway?

ARIAN: Yeah. We're talking about the one that you fold out. Man, picture the ladder. Wayne was driving and it just so happen I was up with Wayne, but I was sitting behind him. I don't know what we was coming from, but all of a sudden, I was like, "Wayne! Look at the ladder!" Wayne swerved, but I was like, Wayne, don't swerve too hard because you got that trailer on and you'll flip us. Walter had brand-new twenty-fours sitting on his truck, *brand-new* twenty-four-inch rims. He didn't even ride with us. He flew. And so we drove there. Man, the top of the ladder was almost inside the truck. That could have killed us. That ladder could be inside the truck and killed us.

KYLE: So did it hit the rims?

ARIAN: It hit the rim, but I'm saying if it had lifted up, the impact would have cut through the body of the truck and went inside the truck. And them boys was laying on the floor.

✦ ✦ ✦

MIKE: You know, they always have a stigma in the South that people that's from the country is slower as far as mentality-wise than people from the city. And we learned that that definitely wasn't true going to New York. We pull up to the gas station, man. And we pop out, we're having another smoke and shit. A guy pulls up next to us and he's like, "Man, I got these two Macbook Air Pros for sale."

KYLE: Typical thing to buy at a gas station . . .

MIKE: Yeah, but the thing is, the dude pulled up, he got a Best Buy shirt on like he works for Best Buy. So we're like, "Oh, shit. Maybe he fucking stole something from out of the job and he's just selling them." Walt like, "Man, fuck. I only got $100, man." He like, "No, I got two of them. I'll let both of them go for $375. I want $200 a piece for them." Walt was like, "Man, fuck it, man." He started waking people up because, "Man, this dude got these notebooks, we got to get it, man." I was like, "Man, I'm straight." I go to the bathroom, come outside and smoke a cigarette. I see Walt taking off in the van. I'm like, "What the fuck going on?" We call Walt. We give him like five, ten minutes. We're like, "Bro, where the fuck you at? What's going on?" "Man, dude got us out of our money!" I'm like, "What you mean he got you out your money?" Dude took a binder and put duct tape and cardboard and all kind of shit to make it heavy. And it legitimately looked like it really was lap-tops, like it was really fucking laptops.

Flash and Mike having a 2:00 a.m. smoke at a gas station outside of Montgomery, Alabama, July 23, 2017. Photo by Kyle DeCoste.

KYLE: So was he chasing him down the road?

MIKE: Yeah! He went to chase them to try and get our money back! And I was telling Walt, I was like, "Man, I'm glad I wasn't in the car." I'm glad I left my gun at home! Because I would have been out the window shooting this motherfucker! But my money wasn't involved so I can laugh about this shit! But it was real funny.

KYLE: Walt didn't catch up to him or anything?

MIKE: No. For some reason, we didn't take the Sprinter. We just took a van. I think the Sprinter got some problems going on with it. But we took a van and the van was too fucking slow. Dude was in an Infinity. And then it's his neighborhood. He's dipping through all the little streets and shit, so they lost him. Javan and Walt put up the money for it and Javan put up most of the money, so Javan was pretty heated about that shit. I was like, "Damn!" Everybody sitting up there quiet because everybody's pissed off. Walt don't worry about that shit. That's one thing I can say about Walt: he don't really stress about shit. But Javan was really pissed off about that shit. And it was funny because it seemed legit. Man, the dude had *an extension cord* that he had wrapped in some motherfucking bubble wrap to make it look like it was the charger. The thing that it was for a computer, the fucking hard drive,

I think for a computer. So it's quiet and I'm just trying to make light of the situation. I was like, "Oh, I guess I got to call Kyle." Like, "Call Kyle for what?" "We got some more to write in the fucking book." But it goes to show you because we was right outside Tuscaloosa or Birmingham or some shit. But shout-out to the guy who got that money, man! Shout-out to you, man! I hope we don't ever see you at that Lowe's gas station ever again, man. Oh, he lucked out, man.

✦ ✦ ✦

FLASH: Me and Javan in the last row of the airplane. Elliot's trying to say, "Look, ma'am, I'd prefer for you not to put my guitar down there, or put it somewhere where it's gonna be safe. This is my $6,000 guitar." Javan was like, "Oh, no, man, we can make enough room right here." She said, "Sir, no, it cannot go there." "Man, don't tell me! I'm telling you there's enough room!" She said, "Sir, please don't raise your voice." "You can't tell me how to talk!" So then the lady asked him to shut up one more time and the next thing you know, she's on that motherfucking radio. "I'm gonna ask you one more time, sir." I said, "Javan, shut up, bro, and let it ride." So he put his headphones on, right? "Sir, get up please." "Where you going? No, you're not taking him off the airplane!" Shiiiiiit. They took his ass off the fucking plane.

KYLE: Ooooh! They kicked him off the plane?

FLASH: They kicked him off the plane.

KYLE: So, wait, Javan was getting after them about storing Elliot's guitar?

FLASH: His guitar, yeah. Because he was saying that there's enough room behind the seat and you don't even need to lie back or nothing. But the steward was telling him, "We will find some room below the deck and secure it." But Javan was like, "I made enough room!" And he kept talking and then he was talking to the head chick. She said, "Sir, please moderate your voice, you ain't got to talk that loud." "I know my rights!" and all that shit. Well, they showed him his fucking rights, boy. That big tree trunk came out the front door, "Excuse me, sir, you need to leave. You need to get up." "I'm not going nowhere!" Shiiiiiit. Took him off the plane. But, you see, that could be a bad mark. That means you'd be red-flagged.

KYLE: Oh, for flying.

FLASH: Yes. And they serious on that shit, man. They serious on that shit. Man, we kept trying to tell him. Man, keep your mouth closed. Look, I'm right next to him saying, "Javan, shut up man." "But they can't tell me . . ." I said, "Man, Javan shut up." I said, "Man, I'ma talk to them."

Garfield, Walter, and Spug posing for an aspirational photo on the
Hollywood Walk of Fame in 2012. Photo courtesy of Garfield Bogan.

✦ ✦ ✦

WALTER: The longest drive was thirty-one hours. I remember we was on
the road—maybe 2015, something like that—and we was out for, shit, two
months straight. We was into at least the seven weeks out of two months.
We was in Michigan and then we had a gig in Little Rock, Arkansas, cancel
on us so we like four off-days now. Boy, I was like, we can party or we can
go home. Everybody was like, "Man, go home." We drove nineteen hours
straight from Minnesota all the way down to New Orleans, stayed for two
days, and then we had to go to New Mexico. It was crazy.

KYLE: The middle of the summer, too?

WALTER: Yeah, yeah. And that was like being on the road with everybody
for that long, I remember Javan and Duley had a fight.

KYLE: Like, a fist fight?

WALTER: Yeah, a real fist fight. It was in one little small little house and it went from every room. I even got punched in the jaw trying to break it up. And then after they finished fighting, they was outside chilling, laughing, and hugging like nothing happened.

KYLE: You get it out of your system, I guess.

✦ ✦ ✦

SPUG: Slater loves to party all the time. When we're on the road, he'll be like, "Hey man, I'll just catch y'all guys at the hotel." He never comes back with us, like, at all. He always out sleeping somewhere. Anything. He just loves to party. He was one of the last Stooges. Yeah, he's a white guy, but he loves to party. No race thing, but he party harder than all of us. I didn't believe it, but he party harder than all of us. That was on the road, pretty much, me, Garfield, Ace, Cotton, Walter. It was pretty cool. We may do one again. But my whole reason to stop traveling: I just had my son.

KYLE: Oh, okay. Congratulations!

SPUG: Yeah.

KYLE: Like, just really recently?

SPUG: No, he's three now.

KYLE: Okay, gotcha. I was thinking you meant just the other day. I mean, Al just had one last night—or this morning, or whatever.

SPUG: Yeah, he got about seven, eight, two dogs, a fish. He got a whole farm. But my youngest son is one.

KYLE: Oh, okay. It's hard to get away when you have little ones, I would imagine.

SPUG: Yeah, because when my first son was born, we flew in, a day and a half later she had the baby, the next day, we got to fly to Utah. It's hard.

KYLE: It's good that you were around for it, but then it's tough when you have go back out and you can't provide some support.

SPUG: Yeah. She held that for years against me. Like, "You left us?" I'm like, "I had to leave, I had to make the money. I have a family; I'm the head of the household." But I pretty much stopped traveling because of that, to be with my sons.

✦ ✦ ✦

VIRGIL: We started traveling real heavy at that point, and I experienced a lot of things through that period. The first time I saw a windmill was with the Stooges. I'm an educated person. I haven't traveled. I've been overseas because of the Stooges. I wore a kilt.

KYLE: You wore a kilt, saw a windmill . . .

VIRGIL: I've seen a moose. I just saw stuff people don't normally see. My students are like, "You saw this stuff? Can you explain it?" I tell my children about it. I've been to New York before, but I hadn't really experienced New York as a musician.

KYLE: And you were there for a while doing those studio things.

VIRGIL: Yeah, the studio things. Even when we were touring. We were there for like maybe four or five days.

KYLE: And the Brooklyn Bowl, too?

VIRGIL: The Brooklyn Bowl. That was this summer, 2015. They had every Monday and the rest of the summer for a month. I didn't do that, but there were times we were in New York for about seven days. I went everywhere I had to go in New York because I knew I may not get this chance again. The biggest joke when we go out of town is that at six o'clock, I'm up because I'm going to walk and try to find out what's going on. Mostly, I want to experience what's going on. I've never done those things. And to say that I'm educated, I have all these degrees, all these things. If it wasn't for the Stooges, if it wasn't for brass band music, I wouldn't have experienced half the things that I've experienced, and I think that that's unique to my life experience.

KYLE: Yeah. It takes you places.

VIRGIL: And I will tell you this. People respect you more—and I love New Orleans—people respect the music and brass band musicians more outside of New Orleans. We did those things. I'm in my 30s, bro, and so those are things that I *felt* like I should have had a chance to experience. I did all that with the Stooges. That's because of Red Bull, us being popular, going different places.

KYLE: And I'm sure you got lots of press coverage from a lot of people who were looking at that competition.

VIRGIL: We went to England, we played for a jazz festival and they had a whole magazine for the festival. We were on the front page. Like, the front cover in the kilts. And the kilts that they had us wearing for the shoot, they were designer kilts—$5,000, $6,000, $7,000 kilts. And they were showing us the pictures of the stars that came there to get those kilts—Kanye West, Vin Diesel, they had pictures on the wall. Like, "Damn. I'm in here with those people." That's kind of cool. So we are more respected after this.

KYLE: And going back to what we were talking about before with people looking down on brass bands—because it's not the case elsewhere.

VIRGIL: Yeah, it's not the case elsewhere. It's flipped everywhere else. Because you are a brass band, they won't pay you as much as a stage band. I

The Stooges' nontouring stage band posing for a portrait at French Quarter Fest, April 13, 2018. Photo copyright © Curtis Knapp.

think that's part of that marketing scheme for us: change it to a stage band so we can get to that upper echelon of money. I'm not saying we're doing the same thing, but it's the same concept.

KYLE: Is that the same out of town when you guys are touring?

VIRGIL: Yeah, it is. Unfortunately it is that, but we get paid more money than here. So they look at it as being, "Oh, you're just a brass band. I know you're from New Orleans." You get paid more than what you would get paid in New Orleans, but still we can't get that money. We can't get that Trombone Shorty money, and that's what we're trying to shoot for. There have been instances where the Stooges have gone out of town and we will go on before the act and we'll blow it out of the water and the act after us, the headliner, be like, "How the fuck we gonna compete against this?" "Well, you talk to the promoter about that." Sometimes they think, "Oh, it's just a brass band. They just gonna come in and whatever," but then we get up there and actually do our show—because our shows are high energy, high energy, high energy, high impact. Off of that, we end on a high note and so the other person has to deal with that. It's not our fault.

KYLE: Then it's almost like a question of what promoters are paying for. Are they paying for entertainment, are they paying for a show? Or is there some sort of weird aesthetic/value judgment when it comes to a brass band?

VIRGIL: I'll tell you this: Regular brass bands that go up there and play outside of the Soul Rebels and Rebirth, they go up there and they just play. Shows are dynamic, and that's not what the promoters are expecting. I think some people, maybe from New Orleans, are telling promoters, "Oh, this is what they do." Naw. We're more than that and we show them that. They come in with a different appreciation of us as being a brass band, rather than what they've heard.

KYLE: Trombone Shorty, he came up from the Stooges. It's the same type of show, it's the same energy, the same kind of antics onstage.

VIRGIL: Trombone Shorty, we used to open up for Trombone Shorty, and he liked it.

KYLE: He's probably one of the few people you could open up for, because it's high energy the *whole* time from the both of you.

VIRGIL: Yeah, because you can't get more high energy than Shorty. He enjoyed it. We would play right before Shorty and get the crowd hyped, and he would come right back on with that same energy and come all the way through.

✦ ✦ ✦

J'MAR: I think one of the funniest moments, we went to Tennessee University. I can't remember exactly what year it was. It was a Rebirth gig and we were gonna play at the college. When we got to the college, the people were so nice, man, and they were so excited. They gave us everything we would want between liquor and food. Me and Ejo was always the guys that was kind of different. We actually left the compound and the university and went by certain people's houses. We'd been there *all day* up until the time that we played. We supposed to be playing for four hours and we get there and we start playing and people enjoying the music. After we take a break, man, the guy came out with the Rebirth CD cover. He says, "Now, I know that y'all said y'all the Rebirth, but I don't see any one of y'all on the disc." So I say, "Well, look, man. This is the situation with the Rebirth." And it was a lie. I was like, "Rebirth, it's a huge band and it separates into different parts." I'm trying to think off my head. You got to grant that we been drinking all day, all night, out in Tennessee, for free. I'm trying to think of something to say. They getting kind of crazy, like, "I don't think y'all the Rebirth." In the process of that, we go back to playing. But as I look, I see the crowd kind of angry. I tell Big John, like, "Spread the word, man. Tell Walter somebody go start the van. One by one, we gonna have to get out this place, because these dudes about to go crazy." One by one, you just see a body disappearing because they go in the van, go in the van. Finally, I become the last person to go out there and they're not really paying attention because they're drunk. We take off because we don't know what to do.

Then after about three to four hours, man, we wake up. And I'm thinking we gone. And we probably about a mile away at some type of shopping center mall next to a dumpster. I mean, John driving and we didn't go nothing but a mile away for three hours of the night in the van. I'm like, "Man, we got to get out of here." That's one of the craziest moments I thought about.

KYLE: So that would have been I guess maybe early 2000s or something like that?

J'MAR: Yeah, that was early 2000s, man. The people was really upset because they *knew* we wasn't Rebirth after they got the CD cover. I guess they wanted us to play certain songs for them that was on the CD, which we could have played. But I guess when they grabbed the CD and was asking for the name, they didn't see none of us. And they were ferocious. Seriously.

KYLE: They probably wouldn't have known the difference otherwise—it's the only way they would have figured it out.

J'MAR: Yeah, because we there all day from eight in the morning till the nighttime. We was all over campus and all over the frat houses and they didn't say anything. They weren't glad to see me that night. I said, "Man, we might be in trouble."

KYLE: Did y'all have Rebirth shirts on and everything?

J'MAR: Nah, we didn't have Rebirth shirts on. We would usually at that time wear white T-shirts. That's probably what we had on, but we were representing as the Rebirth up until that night.

KYLE: I mean, it's good of the Rebirth to kind of spread the wealth.

J'MAR: Yes, sir.

CHAPTER 12

Stooges 101

Waiting outside the Fontainebleau storage facilities where the Stooges own and operate their two large studio spaces, I can hear a brass band working their way through "Just a Closer Walk with Thee." In the humid still of the night, the band's up-tempo rendition permeates the air with semirehearsed vigor. Al pulls up in his truck and he and his twelve-year-old son, Que'Dyn, jump out, toting a trombone and snare drum. "Hey, Al! How you doing?" I ask, "I was just about to call you." "I was at work, Kyle!" he replies, still clad in his blue-collared Cox Cable uniform, a pair of pliers sticking up from his back pocket. We dap and head inside the stage hall, where Virgil and Walter are already working with six young musicians: three trumpet players, a trombonist, a bass drummer, and a tuba player. The students are positioned on the drum riser while Walter and Virgil instruct from chairs on the hardwood floor. Walter hammers out bass lines for the tuba player while bouncing back and forth between a keyboard hooked up to the PA system and his valved marching trombone (or as Garfield calls it, a "trombumpet").

The chord changes to traditionals like "Just a Closer Walk with Thee" are much more technical than most of the contemporary brass band tunes that are played over repetitive funk-like riffs. In traditionals, the bass line follows intricate chord changes, and Walter is quick to point this out as the band picks up the tempo for "Closer Walk." Virgil later told me, "With tuba players, once you learn traditionals and stuff like that on tuba, any song you gonna play after that, it's easy. You're basically learning theory while you're playing it. Tuba players, they don't know that." Playing traditional hymns is essential to making money at funerals and weddings—gigs most musicians simply call "black and whites" in reference to the formal attire required to play them. It's also necessary for playing plenty of other genres. Navigating the chord changes requires either *very* intuitive ears or a solid foundation in music theory, which typically comes from school settings, or in some cases, through the patience of older brass band musicians like the Stooges.[1]

The band starts again from the top of "Just a Closer Walk with Thee," beginning it as a dirge with Que'Dyn and bass drummer Dorian "Tank" Jones providing the introductory press roll on snare and a few slow thuds on bass drum. In the corner, Al and Virgil show the trombonist the supporting melodic line to back the trumpet players. The band sounds good, but proceeds with much more hesitation than the Stooges ever do. After honing in on the tuba player, Al raises his fist to cut off the band and says to him, "You got it? Next week—go home and practice it." In the summer, the Stooges spend their Tuesday nights schooling young brass band musicians in the profession, running tunes with them and teaching them music theory on the fly.

But the traditionals aren't the only means of learning music theory, and the band begins playing "Can't Be Faded," one of the first songs Walter wrote while at NOCCA. A flex on the theory he learned in high school, the tune is loaded with fast runs that are challenging to play on horns and changes that aren't simple to solo over. The trumpets try to play the melody, sometimes ducking out of phrases rather than trying to bluff them. Halfway through the hardest of these, Virgil extends his open palm toward Que'Dyn and shakes his head. The band stops. Que'Dyn lowers his sticks and turns to Walter quizzically. "You got to listen to our music. Look, you don't play through our runs. You know how hard it is for us to play that? You *break* when we play that!" Walter instructs him, to everyone's laughter. Que'Dyn looks back to his dad with a little grin on his face, mouths something in half-hearted defense, and punctuates it with a few hits of the drum.

As the Stooges themselves like to say, they aren't just a band (or a *brand*, for that matter), they're an institution. Over the years, they've become a musical home base for many of New Orleans's brass band musicians and can regularly count probably thirty musicians who know the Stooges songbook and can sub at a moment's notice onstage or in the streets. Through their pedagogical efforts, they've also supplied musicians to nearly every brass band in the city and altered a musical landscape that, compared to when they came up in the school system, has fewer opportunities for young musicians to learn the fundamentals of brass band performance.

Since Katrina, the school system has been drastically restructured through what journalist Naomi Klein calls disaster capitalism, in which corporations take advantage of disasters and, in a time of need, privatize public goods and services.[2] New Orleans's education system was not immune. Public schools have now been entirely replaced by privately run ones that receive taxpayer money but have little public oversight. To determine the government's allocation of funding, they use standardized test scores. Charter schools are for-profit, and teaching to the test is profitable, regardless of whether tests are actual measures of a successful education. As John Cannon so bluntly put it, "All these corporations that are hiding this money in these charter schools, they don't give two shits about the kids that are there." Whereas pre-Katrina marching band education began in elementary school, it's now something that often doesn't take place until high school, if at all. As Matt Sakakeeny notes, due to the importance of securing funding through quantifiable test results, "the charter model supports a fully embedded arts curriculum only in specialized schools, with marching band as an option, often directed by teachers who are not full-time employees."[3]

Few out-of-town companies that run the city's charter schools are familiar with local music traditions, unlike the band teachers from the Stooges' generation. The children's teachers don't look like them, either. The school board fired most of the school board's Black middle-class teachers after the storm and replaced them mostly with young white transplants in the newly charterized system. In setting up an educational infrastructure for young brass band musicians, the Stooges attempt to provide some of the educational opportunities they were given in grade school, though the burden shouldn't be placed on their shoulders and needs to be prioritized at a governmental level. Musical literacy certainly isn't everything, though. In truth, it's only one aspect of a holistic education that needs to serve all of the city's children.

✦ ✦ ✦

WALTER: What we didn't know we had created was a school. We taught all these brass band musicians to the point where I saw Troy—he was introducing me to a saxophone player the other day—and he was like, "Man, this is such-and-such." I was like, "Alright, cool." And Troy was like, "He from wherever he from, out of town," and Troy told him, "Now that you know Walt, you got to join the Stooges 101." He was like, "What's that?" The dude looking at me. He was like, "You're not going to be able to get a gig in the city until you join the 101." It was just so funny. We was just laughing. And Troy was like, "I'm serious. He better go to camp so he'll know how to play." And this cat looking—I don't even know his name—but he looking at me weird, he looking at Troy weird, and he was like, "So, um, what's your number? What do I do?" If you got Trombone Shorty telling you what you got to do, it's like, "I must have to do this." He was like, "Man, I need your number so I can find out when practice is." I died laughing. But it's something that happens. It was never planned. We don't refuse musicians. A musician come out right now be like, "Man, I want to know how to play." We gonna start teaching them, we're going to show them, and probably get them in a brass band and help them get on a gig. Some of them need instruments. We even bought instruments for a bunch of kids. It's just teaching them and helping them. Eventually, they going to get out and probably play with somebody else or join somebody else's band. But you come learn. No one knows how to do this music. They might go out there and play or learn a song, but they don't understand the concept of what we're doing. We didn't invent the concept, we perfected it.

AL: We kind of broke it down to steps.

WALTER: We put the science to it.

AL: Or what the to-dos and not-to-dos. It's just stuff that you look at and, like, "Oh, they just know how to do that." No, they don't just know how to do that. One of the important things on the snare drum is we taught how to lead on progressions, how to lead to the next fill. A lot of people look at it like, oh, they naturally know how to—no, a lot of people don't. I played with a snare drummer the other night that didn't, and still don't.

WALTER: Yeah. They'll build up on the wrong part of a song.

AL: That's supposed to lead you somewhere, but it's not in the right spot. It's certain things like breaking a second line down for the four hours, how to make that work. Our main thing is if our fans is not grooving or they're not liking it, we're not doing our job.

WALTER: Yeah, we're not doing our job.

DREW: We learned our lesson *real* early.

AL: If the sidewalk is looking at us funny, we'll switch a song. Get out of this song, let's go to another song. If we got them jumping, hollering, doing chants and everything, we might stay on that song for a hour because we got them. It's just certain things we did as a band. We know how to take people from one spot to another.

WALTER: Like I said, we broke it down to a science. Not taking from any other band, but some bands that have been doing this longer than us still don't know how to do this. We didn't invent it, we gonna say it must have came from the Dirty Dozen or Rebirth, but we studied it and figured it out to where it can be teachable versus you just learning to play the song and you play it exactly how they play it. Versus, "alright, now you understand what you're doing and how to do it so you can add your own stuff to it and it still work."

Virgil Tiller and Cameron Johnson at the release of the Stooges'
sophomore studio album, *Thursday Night House Party*, on May 5, 2016.
Photo by Karen Lozinski.

VIRGIL: We made sense of the whole process. Before I even joined the
Stooges, I used to listen and follow so I'd know what to play, but the thing
that I appreciated the most, because I like structure, is that it was structured,
and everything that I had played before was unstructured, so I would never
know where I'm going. I know exactly where I'm going when I'm playing
with these cats. I know exactly what's about to happen. Even when I don't
know when it's about to happen—

DREW: You can feel it.

VIRGIL: I know. I can feel it if this is about to happen because I know this
is how we do this. I think it's a good time frame in which we came up with
the music. It was a situation where, when we were coming up, they weren't

so friendly to new musicians as they are—as *we* are—now. You had to really earn your stripes. You really had to figure out what it was.

✦ ✦ ✦

KYLE: What does it mean to you to have Que'Dyn picking up the torch and playing in brass bands?

AL: Oh, it means a lot. He come up from around this brass band thing and I can show you pictures and stuff with him as a little baby doing the music stuff. I never really thought he was going to pick up on it like that, but he start picking up on it and he actually love it, so I'm not going to stop him. I wish he'd have played a horn.

KYLE: Why do you wish he played a horn?

AL: He play the drums. Hey, he pick up on it, he like it. He actually gets more gigs than I do right now, so you got to keep doing it.

KYLE: You like to see him working?

AL: Yeah, some of his hours be kind of weird because he's just still twelve.

MIKE: I'm about to tell him, "Put *me* on a gig, man!"

AL: But I don't mind. I love looking at him and being able to say, "Damn, that's my son." And he *playing*. He not just pitter-patting, but he actually playing. So I love it. I love it. And I know one thing that kept me and Ersel and a lot of us from being in trouble is playing music. Music was our way of staying out the streets. We'd go play basketball or do something.

GARFIELD: Music kept me out of the streets more than I would have been. I was in the streets, but I was one of them cats that had a different upbringing, character. Al used to always tell us, "Say, bruh, you can either be a gangster or you can be a musician. You can't be both. You can be a gangster or a musician, you can't be doing stupid stuff on Thursday and Friday night. They know where you're playing at, they come, shoot up the whole club."

AL: Yeah, so you got to be a gangster or you got to be a musician. And I love the fact that I can bring Que'Dyn around young cats that love to play music.

KYLE: Yeah, a bunch of like-minded guys.

AL: Like-minded guys. They not really about no foolishness. And they getting paid! They getting paid *money*! My son bring home two to three hundred dollars a weekend—he's twelve!

KYLE: I mean, you can't complain about that too much.

AL: What I'ma say? He twelve! He ain't got no bills. Getting paid like that, two to three hundred dollars a weekend, he's coming with new chains, bikes, PlayStations.

Al and Que'Dyn at the final meeting for this book. Photo by Pableaux Johnson.

A portrait of some of the Stooges' kids at the French Quarter Fest. From left to right: Que'Dyn Growe, Que'Jyan Growe, Que'Elle Growe, Que'Lah Growe, and Marvin Henry. Photo copyright © Curtis Knapp.

MIKE: Say, remember the second line I saw you? I'm at the second line, I'm like, "Say, man, where you at, neph? Where ya accent? Where your trumpet?" He gonna say, "Where your piano?"

KYLE: Expecting you to be out there with your keytar or something!

AL: But that's pretty much our future, man. That's the way we try to raise our kids. I didn't have a father that actually played music, so I had to pick everything up by myself. It's good that I can set a legacy up. He got a little brother that's in there right now, and his little brother gonna look up to him. I would much rather have him looking up to a positive person than all the negativity that's out there now. I love the fact that he playing.

KYLE: So, like, how are some of the ways you teach him? Do you just sit down with him? Do you take him out to shows?

AL: No, honestly. It was hard for *us* to learn. We actually had to go to Donna's Bar and Grill. We had to actually go to the Maple Leaf. With him, I just set him up and let him know some different players, and he go up on YouTube. He go on YouTube, Pandora. With YouTube, he can actually see Derrick Tabb, or Glen "Budda" Andrews, or somebody like that playing. He can honestly look at what they're doing and pick up on it. Between that and me letting him go on Frenchmen Street and playing with the younger cats that's out there. I can't teach drums, I don't know how to play drums.

KYLE: You know how it's supposed to sound.

AL: Yeah, but I don't know the first thing about a drum. But I let him watch YouTubes and listen to Pandora. When we riding in the car and it's just me and him, we not listening to the radio, we listen to brass band. And it's not just me! *He* want to listen to it.

KYLE: Do you think—is that a much different way of learning it from when you guys were coming up?

AL: Yeah.

KYLE: Do you think it changes the music much?

AL: Not really. Well, it kind of do, because when we was coming up, we had to learn and listen to traditionals, too. They listen to what's going on. Now, what's good about him, one of the bands I was playing with was a traditional band, so he got to learn the traditional stuff in the midst of it.

KYLE: Is that Mahogany?

AL: No, no. I played with Mahogany—*you* was probably a kid when I played with Mahogany.

GARFIELD: You sounding old, Al!

AL: No, I played with Praline Brass Band. But he was coming up in that time, too, so he got to play a lot of traditional gigs and so he got to hear it. The kids now, they're playing traditionals, don't get me wrong. Sometimes

I go on Frenchmen Street, they're playing traditionals, but they just getting they chops on, they just learning how to keep tempo and keep different beats. He learning with them and he's usually the smallest one out there. And they let him go and play solos because they know he's cute. The crowd arrive, "Oh, look at the little bitty boy and he's really playing!" So they put more money in and they like that. Between that, and when we was getting it, we had to go to Donna's and sit in the back and hear it on our own tape recording, so we could go home and listen to it. With the new age YouTubes and the go-lives and all that, he can see Derrick Tabb anytime he want.

KYLE: Right. Is there anything lost in just seeing it on a computer?

AL: No.

GARFIELD: Not for him. Like, maybe some other kids, but not for him. Because of his daddy.

AL: Not for him because for him, the beat is not in his brain. For him, the beat is in his heart. He's *been* around it. You got to understand, he's been around second lines since he was two and three, and he never stopped.

GARFIELD: And he had competition since he was a baby.

AL: So it never really got out of him. Some people, music was taught to them. With him, it's just a part of him. He might play a song and I be like, "Man, you know that song?" It's in him! He's been playing it for so long, it's just in him.

✦ ✦ ✦

CHAD: All of the brass bands are learning experiences, but playing with the Stooges, it's more laid back, fun, educational. Walter will not hesitate to sit down and practice some shit that you won't know. That's the most musical band I've ever been in. Being around people like Andrew Baham or Walter or Jamelle Williams and a lot of these guys that's taken their talents to another level, it all started right there with the Stooges. It's a great inspiration, man. Them guys really know they horns. That's the difference between the Stooges and a lot of other brass bands. That's why the Stooges can fall off and then get a band back together and then come back and hit the streets together, because they serious about their horns.

KYLE: Yeah, and like they say, the Stooges 101. They're bringing people up and so now they have a really wide pool of people to pull from. When they do go through a rebuilding stage, they've already taught people, and they've taught them the technical aspects, too. Like, trombone should be on the fifth of the chord, trumpet should be on the melody.

CHAD: That's what I've said: that's the most musical, most educational band that I've been in. They'll really break it down to every note. Walter,

Andrew, even me—we'll sit down in front of the piano and figure that shit out. Ain't no other band I've been in did that shit. Because nobody else was even literate enough to sit in front of a piano and figure this shit out. If you don't know music, then you can't do it. That's the most musical band. That's what makes it all different, man. They play the chord changes and they playing the *right* chord changes!

KYLE: The way a lot of people think of brass bands, like there's either a really street, raw sounding band that maybe isn't so much into the technical sort of thing. They've got that feel, of course. And then on the flip side, there's the Soul Rebels or something where they're super, super technical, right? And it seems like the Stooges bridge that. There's both there.

CHAD: They bridge that. Yeah, I would say it's both. And that just come from knowing the music and having the background. The drummers we had were little cousins of Cayetano "Tanio" Hingle, Kerry "Fat Man" Hunter, and Terence Andrews—all the great drummers before them. They started playing at four or five years old so they came as a package: Wayne and Sam. When the Stooges was able to get they hand on them, they brought that brass band flavor to that technical jazz side that Walter and Andew knew. Once you put them two together and then they start composing their own music, they just started catching on.

✦ ✦ ✦

KYLE: So what have you kind of learned from being in the Stooges? A lot of guys talk about it being the Stooges 101. You come in here, and they're gonna show you how to operate as a serious professional musician, and they're gonna show you the ins and outs of the music.

CHRIS: You can quote me on this one. I had this in my brain real good a couple seconds ago. Here's where my testimony becomes valuable as a newbie. But Stooges 101, I learned a lot—business, musically. I guess we can talk about this on the record. I don't know if it's really a secret, but I know Walt likes things his particular way, and nobody else does it this way because he always has to explain it whenever there's a new transition or new person, but, "Build up on four and eight! Every four and eight, something got to happen musically!" This is what he tells the drummer: "Every sixteen—it's either a four, eight, or sixteen—something got to happen! Build it up!" That's one of the key things that the Stooges does. Of course, every band has their gimmick, but that transition or buildup is one of the things that holds the people's attention for a minute. I got that lesson and I'm not even the drummer. I've seen this as I analyze music. I'm a student at Xavier, so analyzing other music, it's actually relevant, it's a real thing. As a trumpet player, they may not be able to teach me nothing about the techniques, about playing, but as a entertainer and as a musician versus just being a trumpet player, I've learned many things from those guys. Al and Garfield and Walt (he's not always on the frontline, but when he is), they've just got this communication between each other and their MC game is really tight. I got that from them, and there's some theoretical stuff that I've learned from Walt as far as music goes. So it can be comparable to Stooges 101. I mean, business aspects, we haven't really talked business, but I've made my observations.

KYLE: Right. Walt is a very astute businessman. He knows what he's doing, and that's also not even brass band stuff. Where do the Stooges fit in musically in terms of their sound? It seems to me that they're very technical, but they can also bring a really raw street sound. And I'm kind of wondering where they fit in in terms of other brass bands. What differentiates the Stooges? What makes them the Stooges?

CHRIS: Well, one of the things that I mentioned about Walt was that I learned some music theory from him. I know it's not too much in these days, but in the beginning days of the Stooges. You can hear this on the CD in a lot of the tunes they wrote back then. Walt and a few of the original band members were in NOCCA, and I think they took a lot of the stuff they were learning in NOCCA and applied it to brass band music. When you get that *It's About Time* CD, you kind of get that almost nerdy brass band sound. I'm saying nerdy because of the technicality. And as they grew in age and band members mature, they kind of keep certain things and go away with certain things. So that's how you get that grungy street kind of vibe with the old technical stuff that they used to do. Honestly, I don't know what words to say specifically to describe the Stooges sound, but it's good music.

✦ ✦ ✦

JOHN P.: To this day, I couldn't see myself completely disassociating from the Stooges. I could move on and I could go and play and make more money with other people and do all these gigs and stuff, but if I'm free and they call me for a gig, that's nothing. Hands down, man, I'm gonna play. They know that. And they don't try to hold you back either because, of course, there's Drew Baham and Jamelle Williams who plays for Raphael Saadiq. And Drew, of course, is Drew, one of the baddest trumpet players ever. Chad Honore, he plays with the Rebirth now. All these dudes came through the Stooges. They had their tenure with the Stooges, and if Walt called them and he needed them, they would be like, "Yeah, come on, man. This the Stooges, man. Let's go. Let's hit this gig."

KYLE: So how did you end up in the Stooges? Like, how did that come about?

JOHN P.: One day, I went to the Hi-Ho and they had already heard about me. They heard me from the Free Agents, and Al pulled me to the side of the Hi-Ho—me and Cameron, as a matter of fact—and was like, "Look, I know y'all two dudes, y'all promising, y'all some good musicians, and we would like to have you in the Stooges." I told him straight up, "I was thinking about making this move, anyway, if y'all would have had me." The Free Agents was going through that little rough patch. Man, there was a time that—and all the dudes in the Free Agents can attest to this—that we didn't get paid from a big gig for an entire year. I had to bring it back up and be like, "Oh, we need this money." It was supposed to be, like, $800. It was during Mardi Gras, so we kind of just let it breeze by and we forgot about it. But then a year later, I'm like, "Man, remember that gig at Eiffel? What the fuck, bro? We need to get that money." Of course, I called the guy up and I was like, "I need my money." And he was like, "Alright, boy, I got you." These musicians and their problems.

KYLE: Yeah, and so it was kind of Al that brought you guys in? And you did an audition?

JOHN P.: I think I was out of the audition era because I know that Bogie, he did a audition. I kind of did my audition. I know that I played one gig with the Stooges back when I was in high school, and I did a practice before the gig, and that may have been my audition. I learned a song and we played it. It was just like, "Oh, you know how to play," but I really wasn't that good. I was just getting into it. So then after I went through my incubation period in other bands.

KYLE: You hatched from your egg.

JOHN P.: I went into my cocoon and came out a beautiful butterfly! I came back to the Stooges and they were like, "Man, you really progressed over the years." "Yeah, motherfucker. I've been practicing!" I'm one of those musicians that can say I did a lot of practicing and I didn't fall victim to a vice that hinders me from getting better or from having my mind focused at all times. I do drink, which is normal, but I don't overdo it. I'm not a alcoholic. When I was a kid, my mom had to work two jobs because my dad wasn't around. So I spent a lot of time inside and the trumpet was that thing that helped pass the time, so I practiced a lot. When I first started playing, I practiced every day. I don't practice every day now. I'm ashamed to say it, but I don't. But it was at least four hours a day. Sometimes I was doing eight-hour days practicing. And I was dedicated to learning how to do what I say I want to do. If I say I want to be a fucking trumpet player, I'm not gonna half-step it, I'm gonna be a good trumpet player.

Walter, Al, and Garfield at the first annual New Orleans Original Brass Fest in Congo Square, March 16, 2019. The festival is organized by the Save Our Brass Culture Foundation, which is run by Garfield. Photo by Michael Mastrogiovanni.

✦   ✦   ✦

SPUG: Younger brass bands, they're not following the structure of, I guess, what was gave to the Stooges.

KYLE: Okay, how so? Like, how do they differ? Is there something that they're just not getting?

SPUG: They just don't understand. They need to be taught. It's hard to explain. It's not—they just don't get it.

KYLE: That's something that brass band musicians have been saying forever. It's always like, "Those young guys don't know what the fuck they're doing."

SPUG: Yeah, right! "Look at y'all, y'all gonna figure it out. We want to teach y'all." Some of them just hardheaded. You try to give them everything to keep our tradition going, but some of them do good, some of them fuck up. The ones that fuck up, they pretty much freelance. They're not really a part of a solid group.

KYLE: Fucking up in terms of like life decisions and stuff, or in terms of just learning the music?

SPUG: Learning the music. I'ma say it's some life decisions as far as every-thing it's easy to get down here—drugs, money, firearms. Me, Cotton, and Eric, coming under the wing of Al, Garfield, Walter, they help you to not go down that path they probably had some of they friends go down. You know what not to do. If you wasn't taught, they're gonna make sure: "Don't do that." In certain respects, you never want to see a person down, but once you click to somebody that you enjoy and you look up to them, most likely, you gonna follow in their footsteps.

✦ ✦ ✦

VIRGIL: My grandfather taught me. He played with Olympia and the majority of them were from Treme, but then also he taught me the music and he was from the Treme. I had that. Other band members had other people that they could go to, and so when it was time for us to go play with those bands, they were like, "Man, you ain't from the Sixth Ward. You can't be in this band. I don't want you around here." That's how a lot of those bands formed outside of the Sixth Ward. Our whole band was generally Ninth Ward people.

KYLE: But kind of defined as being *not* from the Sixth Ward.

VIRGIL: Not being from the Sixth Ward. So that's how we just got our bands together. Walt said, "Look, we ain't worried about that. We gonna do it. We gonna get a band and we gonna make sure that we better than them and we gonna take their money." That was our goal and you can't stop us from doing this. I think a lot of it is the mentorship as far as you have to pay your dues and you have to really use your music. That's true with the Pres-ervation Hall Jazz Band. Now, you can't just get up there and play with Pres-ervation Hall. You have to know that music or you not gonna play. Some of those other bands that play there, they will tell you it's a rule. If I go to try to sit in, I don't sit in on the first set. I ask. I'ma listen, I'ma sit down, I'ma bring my axe with me, I'ma look, you gonna see me with the axe. After the first set, I'm gonna ask can I get up, and then the second set, I get on. I do that to this day. It's not like that now. Cats just want to get up there and just start playing. I think it's part of that pageantry of how you do that. The protocol, it's been lost.

KYLE: It's like manners.

VIRGIL: Yeah, yeah. Somebody come up there and they're trying to get it. And the thing about grandstanding and stuff like that, you don't do that on somebody else's gig. Even today, if I go to a Soul Rebels gig, before I even leave my house, if I'm gonna bring my axe, I'll call Erion Williams and be like, "Erion, look, I want to come down and sit in." He's like, "Bro, why do you call me every week to ask me if you can sit in? Bro, you *know* you can sit in." It's just me, who I am. "Man, bring your horn and you can play." Sometimes I sit there on the first set like, "Man, come up on the first set." I'm like, "Aaaah-hhh . . ." Like, "Man, come on, bro. We know who you are. Come on, come play." So I'll play all the sets. I generally don't do that. It's just the way I was raised in that music. I think it's part of that. And if you couldn't play traditionals, you had to get out the Square.[4] If you couldn't play, you had to go. And they would run you out of there—*physically* run you out of there. Like, "You can't come here." If you can't play, no, you got to go. You got to go home and learn how to play, and maybe they let you come back next time and then you can play, but *anybody*, that's just the problem.

They got a couple of cats that can play up there, they got the music and stuff like that. But it's just not the same as it was before. It's just not the same. I think that's more of the problem as far as understanding protocol, respecting the music, respecting it enough to follow what was laid before. That's what we had for the music. We had respect for the music. Right now, it's like cats just playing. They don't really care. They got some bands that don't even know how to play "When the Saints Go Marching In" correctly. When I play "When the Saints Go Marching In," there's a correct way, what's supposed to happen in what series.

✦ ✦ ✦

DREW: I remember I had what ended up being an argument with this cat, Kerry "Fat Man" Hunter from the New Birth. He was going off on this diatribe about the young cats, "Man, these motherfuckers, they just going on Canal and Bourbon and just playing, and they playing nothing but the marching band stuff and they're playing no traditionals." I said, "Well, hold on, bro. You're right. They aren't doing any of that. The question you need to ask yourself is why." I said, "Here is the difference," and I told him my vision. My vision has always been that there is always a hierarchy when it comes to the development and the passing on of the tradition. There's you. You're this young, strapping guy or band who just wants a chance at stardom. You're doing all the necessary things. You're working on your craft, you're trying to get your business together, but you're hitting brick walls at every turn. Why? Because you're patterning yourself after big brother. Big brother is usually the ones who's doing what you want to do. But they don't have the time nor the patience to show you what that is, which would put you in a sort of frustration.

KYLE: Right. You're trying to mimic or emulate that sort of thing, but there's no instruction coming directly from them.

DREW: Right. And to fill that void, in comes the elder. The elder will tell you, "Come here, young brother. What you doing is pretty good, but let me show you how to make money doing it." The elder is the one who teaches you how to become big brother, and then you become yourself the elder.

KYLE: I don't want to stereotype that there's this "wisdom," but maybe with age comes a deeper understanding of how it works and realizing that you don't have to be in competition necessarily.

DREW: Right, because it's kind of like the elder has done what you're trying to do three times over. They've been around the world ten times before you even pick up the horn. As the elder, his job is just to impart the wisdom onto you just as the elder above him gave it to big brother. And it's a constant. As you gain wisdom, as you gain experience, as you gain all these things, you move up in the process. And then it cycles over. So I was like, "Fat Man, who can you say was your elder?" He said, "Tuba Fats." I said, "Good. Who can you say is the elder for this young generation?" He couldn't answer me. I said, "There's your problem." They have no elders.

✦ ✦ ✦

JOHN C.: Roots of Music and some of these other middle school bands are trying to fulfill the void, but not having music in elementary school, middle school, *and* high school, a lot of these musicians aren't being prepared the way they should. The other side of it is the band directors today—and this is only my opinion—don't really have the same compassion for the music as the band directors of old. The band directors of old would put half of their leg in your ass. "I need it done. I don't care." It's just the way it is. Band directors now, "Oh, if you don't want to do it, you don't have to do it." No! That don't go like that. That's what we all come from. Kennedy used to practice at six in the morning doing field shows. They had to do that because 50 percent of their band population was in NOCCA. So they *had* to do it. Mr. Hamp would start band practice in the summer. He didn't give a shit whether or not you thought it was too hot outside. You going outside to march. And now they have it to where kids say, "Oh, I'm not going to go to band camp, I'ma just go to school and get in the band after school start." It's like you're doing the band a disservice. When you see them for Carnival and other events, that's why they look the way they look, because nobody don't really give a shit no more.

KYLE: And do you think part of that has to do with the way the school system was changed immediately after Katrina?

JOHN C.: Well that's all of it! That's all of it. The charter schools are only focused on one thing: financial dollars. Write-offs. You know, all these corporations that are hiding this money in these charter schools, they don't give two shits about the kids that are there, the programs that are there. One of the problems is this: Say you go to ABCDE charter school. You're the head principal, but I have six principals under me, I have five administrators under those principals. Then I get to the staff. My curriculum says we're gonna study this, but in the middle of the school year, we have to take a test and study this. So this is standardized state testing that we have to take and federal testing. The curriculum doesn't meet this; however, at some point in time in the school year, we have to stop this curriculum and teach this. Why isn't this the curriculum? And then you have time for band and all of these other things. When you start talking about all these fifty- and sixty-thousand-dollar Teach for America salaries for these people from all over the world. This is New Orleans.

KYLE: Who don't even know the culture.

ELLIS: Don't know the culture and they're not even teachers.

JOHN C.: One, they don't know the culture and they're not even for the culture. They're not here for the culture. They're here for happy hour and to say, "I live in New Orleans." And to have that $200,000 house in the neighborhood where the people can't afford one, but you have that $60,000 salary, so you don't really give two shits. Years ago, the teachers cared. "I don't want to hear that shit about you don't want to do this, that, there, or the other. Get your horn and play. You're in my music class, this is a grade. You have to get your grade." I mean, now, a D student is curved to a B student.

KYLE: And that's to get funding through standardized testing?

JOHN C.: So what happens is if we drop the standards, then we'll get a better turnout on passing kids. Everything in the charter school is about numbers, so you have to have a percentage of kids passing. If I say my curve is now a forty-point curve and not a ten-point curve, well you can be a D student, but on paper, you have a B. Because the students that are F students and the ones that really have problems, they'll be a D student under this program. They'll be failing.

KYLE: I hate to boil this down to music and how that affects the musical landscape here, because it's a lot bigger than that, but what do you see students doing now if they want to play in a brass band or do that sort of thing?

JOHN C.: You have different programs that are set up. Jazz and Heritage has a program. Satchmo has a program—

KYLE: Like, Class Got Brass?

JOHN C.: Well, Class Got Brass was something that was implemented into the schools through the Jazz and Heritage Foundation. But there is the Don

"Moose" Jamison Jazz and Heritage School of Music, and it's at the Jazz and Heritage Center. It's every Saturday, every Thursday. They teach you if you wanna learn brass band or if you wanna just learn the standards of jazz. They're teaching theory, they're teaching everything that a kid needs to get to the next level. That was taught to me in elementary school.

ELLIS: Right. But for those kids that don't have access to that, you might see them in the French Quarter, you might see them on Frenchmen Street.

JOHN C.: Or they might be in Roots of Music.

KYLE: Jackson Square.

JOHN C.: But here's the thing, some of the older guys that are in Jackson Square, they're not there anymore.

KYLE: And some of them you don't want to be mixing kids up with.

JOHN C.: Oh, well that's the other side of it! You think about if, as an adult in this industry, we have an issue with drugs, we have an issue with alcohol, what do you think that mean for the kids? That's all they have to look up to. They see that as, "Oh, I can do this and I'll be fine! Because if I do that, at least I'll get to go to Paris or Switzerland and my band will be able to travel." Some of these guys, if you write them a check, they won't know the name on the check. That's a *big* issue.

KYLE: Yeah, that's a huge issue.

JOHN C.: Yeah, that's a big issue. That's a big issue.

ELLIS: Not knowing how to sign your name . . .

JOHN C.: I mean, not knowing how to count. That's a big thing. If I tell you you're on a six-hour gig and I'm going to give you fifty dollars an hour, and then I turn around and write you a hundred-and-fifty-dollar check and you're excited about it, that's an issue because I'm not keeping my promise to you. A lot of people know that and a lot of people now are monopolizing on just that very thing.

EPILOGUE

Can't Be Faded...

The afternoon rainstorm was just beginning to dry as a gentle breeze carried the scents of the French Quarter through the air. Aided by the fresh rain, the smell of magnolias cut through the familiar funk of fried food and tobacco. I furiously typed as Arian dictated his biography to me. His first words were perhaps the most direct and honest: "My music speaks for itself. My heart is pure." His music certainly could speak for itself—in literal terms, even: he had an unmatched ability when it came to making his tuba laugh. In conversation, he always wore his heart on his sleeve, and today was no different.

He stood on the sidewalk outside his mid-nineties Chevy Suburban drinking a tall can of sweet tea, his large frame draped in a purple XXXL polo shirt and shorts. I sat on the passenger-side seat with the door wide open, my laptop perched on my lap and my recorder in the door. It was no small feat that Arian was standing of his own free will. When we met one summer earlier in Jackson Square, he was showing young musicians the ropes in a pickup band and was aided by a walker. He needed help carrying his tuba, and I gladly obliged when we sought shelter from the rain. At thirty-eight, his body had already been through the rigors of touring, a myriad of health issues, and significant personal loss, but he always remained outwardly optimistic and proud of his ability to stand through all of it. He stood for the entirety of our one-hour meeting.

Arian was usually reflective, but I found him even more so on this day as he had just come from visiting his grandmother, Betty Ann, who was in the hospital. An accomplished gospel organist and vocalist, she was responsible for pushing Arian off the porch and into a world of music. He told me about the last time he recorded with her and the Hot 8 Brass Band. In that recording, his grandmother sang prescient words of love and loss in a regal tone over Arian's joyfully bouncing tuba playing: "We will stand on the banks of the river, where we'll meet to part no more." Though his grandmother's poor health hung above our meeting, it was nonetheless a joyful occasion and time for reflection. Speaking to me, he made his grandmother's profound influence on his life known in no uncertain terms. With her in mind, he told me he didn't want to come across foolish.

Arian also insisted on honesty. As our conversation meandered, he spoke of touring with his former bandmates in the Stooges. Cursing like a sailor, he told me stories of life on the road in his earnest, stuttering baritone. He was a great storyteller. He called me by name frequently, and his cadence soared with each accentuation. He referred to his bandmates jokingly as "motherfuckers" and wholeheartedly as "brothers," often in the same breath. With little effort on his part, he had us both laughing big, warm laughs. His was an honest kind of love that I found hard not to appreciate. When we wrote the end of his biography, he insisted on thanking his cousin Walter, with whom he had plenty of differences over the years: "I'd like to thank my cousin, Walter, for being the arrogant, competent guy he is. I'd like to thank him for being who he is, because without him, we wouldn't be the brothers we are."

When I committed Arian's biography to my computer and we had done some editing, I read it back to him to confirm that I was getting everything right. "That sounds like me," he said, as he wiped tears from his eyes with his shirt. Wrapping up our meeting, I promised to send him the finished biography so he could read it to his grandmother at her bedside. Heading back to my bicycle, Arian yelled to me, "Tell Walter I want to have an old-time cookout with you and everybody! He'll know what I mean!" As with our last meeting, I left laughing.

Two months later to the day, when I was back in New York, I found myself choking back my own tears as I read on Facebook the news of Arian's death. Among his bandmates in the Stooges, I saw a rollercoaster of feelings run their course. First, disbelief that he was gone. Then, sadness as the loss set in. Finally, and most importantly, a resolve to celebrate the importance of his life. I circulated his biography on Facebook as a tribute and, at Al's request, sent recordings from our last interview to his family. In a showing of love, musicians quickly coordinated a second line that night in his memory. It ran from St. James Church to Tuba Fats Square in the Sixth Ward and was followed with many more parades over the week leading to his funeral. The voice of Arian's grandmother on that final recording took on an even more powerful mean-

Al carries a white rose and walks alongside Fat Boy's casket. Chad and John Cannon can be seen in the background. Photo by Karen Lozinski.

ing: "We will walk through the streets of that city, where our loved ones have gone on before." Arian was valued and loved. His friends and family refused to let his existence go unrecognized. That night, I watched on Facebook as tuba players and other brass band musicians paraded through the streets, sending up an exuberant eulogy to "Fat Boy."

Ten days later, a mass of tubas sparkled in the sunlight as his bandmates laid him to rest after his funeral. Arian Jr. bravely played among the sea of tubas. Musicians, friends, and family sent Arian Jr.'s father off in a tribute befitting the effect he had on everyone's lives. I couldn't help but continuously replay our last interaction in my head. "Tell Walter I want to have an old-time cookout with you and everybody." I hadn't mentioned Arian's idea to Walter, and that regret moved through Arian's absence into a general sadness at the foreclosure of possibility. The past has a horrible way of shortchanging the future. But seeing and hearing those tubas fill the air with music—even while I was in New York—somehow made Arian feel even more present than he had been before. Garfield raised a large cardboard cutout of Arian into the air, and his loved ones adorned their bodies with memorial T-shirts and ties. The shirts read "Jammin with the Fat Boy." We're still jamming with him to this day.

With Arian's passing came a renewed urgency and a reminder of the importance of documenting the stories that *Can't Be Faded* holds. One night while on the back of his pickup after a gig, Al told me that he spoke to Arian ahead of our first meeting. "He knew he had to talk to you because he didn't have time," he said, acknowledging Arian's foresight. Though *Can't Be Faded* is a history of the Stooges Brass Band, it's also the story of so many brass band musicians in the city over the past couple of decades. Arian's memory is just one piece of the *collective* memory evoked in these pages. As a written document, it can hold onto the past for a future that extends beyond the last reverberations of Arian's tuba. Arian isn't physically with us anymore, but his self-representation and memories are imprinted in these pages. *Can't Be Faded* is a story of lives lived and experiences had. Whereas musical recordings provide one means of fighting against the erasure of death and the fading of memory, this book provides another type of trace through the written word. It bounces through hardships with laughter and a sustaining joy. Despite all the controversy and the trials of living in a beautiful yet structurally flawed city, as the Stooges' first original song proudly declares, they can't be faded, and their story can't be faded either. More than two decades after their founding, they're still standing—as vibrant as ever.

ROLL CALL

Walter "Whoadie" Ramsey
(b. August 1, 1980)
Bandleader, tuba player, and trombonist from 1996 to present

It all started in 1980 when I was born to my father, Walter Taylor, and my mother, Demetrie Ramsey. My maternal grandfather helped start a band called the Dirty Dozen. He was actually the triangle player in the band with a bunch of young kids. They used to rehearse a lot and my mom used to be around it, so I guess I was born into New Orleans culture, which is second line music, Mardi Gras Indians, and social aid and pleasure clubs. My father at the time was also a president of one of the leading social aid and pleasure clubs Uptown, called the Scene Boosters. They was very known for the fancy clothes they wore, and they kind of stamped the way people dress today at social aid and pleasure clubs.

I remember back as far as when I was three years old, I started parading with my father and his club. And I remember one particular birthday party I had. I was five years old and my parents paid to block off the city streets at my parents' house. I had a brass band play for me called the All-Star Brass Band, which, at the time was a bunch of young kids featuring James Andrews, Terence "T-Bell" Andrews, Kerwin James, all these guys that I didn't know at the time, but further along in my career, they became some of my idols.

I remember getting a gift from Eddie Bo Parish, which is a trombone player. He bought me two snare drums that day. And I can remember seeing pictures when I was five, beating on the drums. And from there, I continued second lining and being around second lines with my father. I was in elementary school one day and we had an assembly and the Rebirth Brass Band played at the assembly. I was really fascinated with a brass band being onstage. I'm used to seeing them parade up and down the street, but me seeing them play onstage that week did it for me. It was like, "Wow, this is what I want to do." The very next year, I asked the band teacher can I join the band. He asked me what instrument I know how to play and I told him I have a drum. He had a lot of drummers, so I couldn't play drums. I had a cousin that played trombone. He was marching for Weston at the time, but he wasn't playing the trombone no more, so I brought him one of my snare drums and asked can I borrow his trombone for a little while so I can learn how to play it. We switched instruments and I immediately started learning how to play trombone in elementary school with a band director named Mr. Knight.

When I got to junior high school, I joined the band, and one Saturday I asked the band director if it was possible, could I clean out the back practice room where all the band equipment goes. And I asked if I do a good job, could you give me one of the old, broken tubas. She said, "Yeah, I don't know what you gonna do with it." I told her I wanted to start a brass band and I needed a tuba. I cleaned the band room and she gave me one of the broken tubas. I had no money to get it fixed; I just kept it at the time. And I started doing my best to acquire all the instruments that was in a brass band. After that, I got to high school. Around tenth grade, I started finding the musicians who could help play those instruments I had.

By sixteen years old, me and my friends, we founded the Stooges. It was based off of two rival schools—our school we went to was John F. Kennedy High School, and the other guys went to St. Augustine High School. One of the founding band members was named Andrew Baham. He was like, "Hey, man. We got to audition for NOCCA." So we all auditioned for NOCCA and we got accepted.

We worked hard trying to develop and come up with all kinds of ideas to get our band name known around the city, and so we kept playing, we kept practicing, we kept trying to get better. We had a lot of adversity and stuff that we had to go through with other bands out here, but we didn't let that stop us. We kept pushing. And one day, the Rebirth Brass Band, which is the band I saw at my elementary school, asked us to play for their fifteenth anniversary parade. We was so excited because we was just teenagers no more than eighteen or nineteen years old. So we played for their parade and it gave us a lot of notoriety.

Looking back at this, I'd like to thank all of my band members. I used to be hard and a tough leader to be in front of, so it's just a beautiful thing.

Andrew "Drew" "Da Phessah" Baham
(b. July 22, 1980)
Trumpet player and producer from 1996 to present

I was born in 1980 to my mother, Patricia Baham, and my dad, Andrew Baham Jr. I was raised in the historic Pontchartrain Park, one of the first neighborhood developments for working middle-class Black folk. It had a golf course, designed by one of the most well-known Black designers, Joe Bartholomew, and I spent my young years playing football and baseball there.

My mother has a bachelor's degree in music education from Dillard University, and my dad played snare drum and timpani in Ms. Yvonne Busch's bands at George Washington Carver High School.[1] My first memories include having an upright piano in the living room. That was my only justification to be able to go in there (back then, in Black homes, you didn't go into the living room, lol). The first song I learned was the melody line from Sheila E's "Glamorous Life" (hint: it was all the black keys). I played it so much, my parents would always have to replace the black keys every couple months.

My dad had a record collection in the den that covered a whole wall. Whatever genre you could think of (except metal) was there. When he would come home from drill (Army), he would sit me down (and my friends who would spend the night) and he'd put on Donny Hathaway's *Extension of a Man*. He would be a little tipsy, so he was emotional: "Son, I just wanna let you know," as he started ducking in and out of consciousness, "Daddy loves you." The albums that interested me the most were two albums: Louis Armstrong's *Hot Five and Hot Seven* (Reissue) and Freddie Hubbard's *The Love Connection*. I kinda knew then that I would play trumpet.

I picked up the horn in fifth grade, at W. C. C. Claiborne Elementary. It actually was a cornet from the pawn shop, but it was cool because nobody else had one. I learned my basics through the tutelage of Donald Batiste. Since my mom was a music major, she always sat me down at the piano and gave me ear-training tests (I didn't realize it at the time though). I used to beat the shit out that piano, I swear. But I was in my world—when I wasn't playing video games with the buddies, of course. Needless to say, her work would pay off.

By the time I got to Gregory Junior High, I was starting to get the hang of this music stuff. So much so that in seventh grade, I started to write arrangements for marching band. They sucked, but the bug was in me. A couple friends and I learned some traditional tunes and would go in the French Quarter to try and make a little money. We had a lot to learn. By ninth grade, I started attending the New Orleans Center for Creative Arts, commonly known as NOCCA.

I honed my skills in writing, arranging, and playing jazz from the tutelage of the late Clyde Kerr Jr. I also was able to take lessons with trumpeters Nicholas Payton, Wendell Brunious, Terence Blanchard, and even Wynton Marsalis.

But I really cut my teeth on the streets with the Stooges Brass Band. I learned one of the most important lessons about music: Always try to find a way to connect with your audience. Out there in the streets, doing second line parades, parties, weddings, funerals, etc., you learn what makes the people feel joy, what calls them to action, mourn a loved one, all that. It made me understand that all the formal training in the world is nothing without connection to the people. Not only did it make me a better player/performer, it made me a better person. A more communicable person. My experience with the Stooges has helped me develop my approach to music. The band has served as the backbone of my existence as a musician. I am forever grateful for our music and our culture in New Orleans.

Ellis "Ejo" Joseph
(b. November 30, 1979)
Bass drummer from 1996 to 2001

I was born in 1979 to Joakima Marie White and Patrick Joseph. I spent most of my younger years with my great-great-uncle James and aunt Sister. My mom's parents died before I was born, so I never had the chance to meet them. My mom's mom died when she was four, and her dad died a year before I was born. My mom's dad's sister and her husband basically raised me up until the age of eleven. They passed by the time I got to college. My stepfather was—and still is—a hardworking dude, and he really stepped in and handled his business. I have always admired his work ethic and his extreme need to pay attention to details! I knew my dad throughout my life, but the majority of my early life experiences came from 2410 Gentilly Boulevard. This address was across the street from Dillard University, where I learned about college life, fraternities, sororities, and a bunch of things that I shouldn't have seen at such an early age. During my stay at my grandparents' house I met people like Smokey Robinson (as an infant), who wanted to hold me, so I puked on his mink coat (my cousin sang backup for him for many years); James Brown; and Rosa Parks, to name a few. My great uncle (who I knew as Gramps), was a United Methodist preacher, while his wife, Sister, was a devout Southern Baptist, so we had an organ in our front room. There would be days when I would come home from school and my cousins would be having straight-up church going on while my grandma (Sister) would be watching Oprah and cooking one of my favorite meals. They instilled greatness in me. My grandpa whipped me if I did wrong and also acknowledged me when I was right. My grandma bought me whatever I wanted, but made sure that I handled my business at school and in whatever other endeavors I was pursuing. So I was basically a Theo Huxtable. Meanwhile, on my dad's side of the family, I was exposed to life on life's terms: the hood, the art of hustling, and making a way out of no way. But I received all the love a person could ever get. Being the first grandchild to my grandma and the first nephew to my aunts and uncles was the recipe for some of the best experiences ever! This is where I learned to work on floors with my dad and grandfather. I learned to love public speaking and entertaining from my uncles, who later gave me my first job in radio.

Moreover, I began playing music in elementary school at Gentilly Terrace, starting off with the recorder, then the clarinet until I got to St. Paul the Apostle. Once I went to St. Aug, I began beating on the desks along with my best friend Buzz and started playing the bass drum professionally with the Lil Stooges Brass Band at fifteen years old. Although I marched in the color guard in the Marching 100, I still maintained my spot in the brass band playing in the streets of New Orleans. I then got recognition for being a bass drummer and started playing with the St. Aug brass band called the Ace of Spades, making gigs all around the city and state. I graduated from high school and began traveling the world before I started my first day of college at Nicholls State University. I always had a hustle; my dad and his dad did flooring work. I kept money in my pocket since a youth. I would wonder why my Grandpa Pat (All Profit) would take me from the labor work and bring me to do the paperwork with him. Now owning my own band and having to do contracts and paperwork, I see why. But the original Stooges were all leaders, so to say. We all have been booking gigs since I can remember, traveling and handling business since we were kids.

We all strived to be the best people we could possibly be. We always knew that we had others looking up to us. So we made it a point to set good examples for those who came up under us. To add to that, I began working with kids. From family and friends, in the neighborhoods (hands-on) to professional settings doing workshops educating children about our rich culture in parts of the world that I will never see again. My goal has always been to inspire the youth and increase the amount of young entrepreneurs throughout the world. My great grandma told me New Orleans has always been very violent and very religious. We have seen so many of our friends die, be killed, die from drugs—just so much violence and negativity. It's sometimes hard to keep going, but the music is what keeps us thriving and going as hard as we do. I think we are a very compassionate city, we love hard, and we react as a result of our feelings. Everyone has a story, and this is ours. I'm tired of hurting; I'm tired of seeing so many others hurt. My ultimate goal is to help as many as I can!

J'mar "Buzz" Westley
Snare drummer from 1996 to 2003

My name is J'mar, a.k.a. Buzz Westley. My love for what we call second line
music started at the age of six. My auntie is one of the founding members of
the famous Lady Buckjumpers, Lottie Irving. During that time, I used to watch
videotapes of their parades, learning how to second line. Simultaneously, I
was playing the drums in elementary school. From an early age I got good at
my craft, playing the drums. Up to high school I became one of the greats at
playing the snare drum. There wasn't a place you couldn't find me with a pair
of sticks. I was one of the guys who was a part of the Stooges who went to St.
Aug. While attending St. Aug, I was one of the members who was a part of a
band by the name of the Ace of Spades, which were guys who were attending
St. Aug. But one day my best friend Ejo mentioned something about a band
called the Lil Stooges. Not to brag, but I was so good at playing marching
band and second line music on the snare drum, he asked me to come out and
practice with them at his house. Upon me going to practice, after a few songs,
the Stooges wasn't going to let me go. I actually liked the guys and the vision
Walter saw, therefore I joined the band. At that time we were a young group
trying to find our sound, but actually we were following our big brothers the
Rebirth. I loved and was great at my craft, but I can finally say I really look up
to Derrick Tabb, the snare drummer from the Rebirth. I mean, this guy plays
the snare drum in a way that even today I believe he is the greatest second
line snare drummer of all time. I know when he reads this book he is going to
be shocked, because every time I ran across him I always wanted to challenge
him, but if anybody ever watched me play, I sounded just like him.

Sometimes when Ejo and myself used to play with the Rebirth, the front
row used to always turn around because we sounded like Derrick and Shorty,
the bass drum player. Shout-out to them—we learned a lot from y'all secretly
(lol). I was one of the outspoken ones in the band. When Walter said in the
song "Why," "I remember when Ejo and Buzz used to fuss about their cash,"
boy, he couldn't have said it better. I mean, back then we used to play gigs for
hours—several throughout the day—and we used to walk away with about
thirty bucks (lmao). I couldn't understand then, but we had to put in a lot of
work for the brand the Stooges have now. To the new Stooges: wear that name
proud because we had to work hard to get the Stooges out there. Back then a
lot of bands hated us because we might not sound all that good, but we always
stayed what they called swag out. We probably was the only band with our
own personal limousine driver. Shout-out to my brother, Walter. Even though
we didn't always see eye-to-eye, you always try your best to help me, luv u bro.

Right now I am incarcerated for a robbery charge; at this point I have been locked up almost fourteen years. Hopefully I don't have too much longer. Much luv to everybody who continues to support me constantly during this tuff time in my life. I promise when I return I won't let y'all down. You know B-U-double-Z got some hits. Get ready, 1.[2]

Ersel "Garfield" Bogan III
(b. March 14, 1981)
Trombonist, drummer, and vocalist from 1997 to present

My name is Ersel Bogan III, known as Garfield, better known as King Garfield. I'm originally born in New Orleans, Louisiana. I grew up in the Ninth Ward on Mazant Street. Back then, I was a church boy/trying to get my stripes in the street/mama's boy/the prodigal son. My daddy's watching out for every move I make, my mom is protecting every move I make, making sure I don't go down this route or that route. It was a tug-of-war which made me the person that I am today. I had a strong foundation with families. I'm this family kid, so I have a love for people. That gives me my personality being a people person, because I was always around people. I have two sisters that was raised with me, but I have other sisters outside of the marriage.

I was brought up in church and went to church every Sunday, where I started playing music at the age of five. I played two songs every Sunday for the Young Singers for Christ, which was the kid's choir at Rosedale Missionary Baptist Church. My cousin Romond was the church drummer. As he got older, he moved up to the piano and organ, so I became the church drummer and started playing around different places.

The Stooges came in high school. I went to F. W. Gregory Junior High School, and then I went to John F. Kennedy, which was like Gregory's high school. I started playing tuba at Gregory for three years under Mr. Edwin Harrison and Joseph Torregano. He was a very good teacher, very stern. John Cannon took me under his wing and showed me everything as far as tuba. When I got to Kennedy, Walter Harris, better known as Doc, was my band director. John was actually the tuba player for the Stooges when I first got in the band. When I got there, I was going to NOCCA with Brian, Walter, Sam, and Andrew. I was a drummer going to NOCCA for jazz, but I was playing tuba in the marching band. John was busy and they said I could play tuba with them. One day we were at this gig I'll never forget. It was about nine of us at the Palace Hotel on Canal and Claiborne, which is now empty. It was time to play and Big Sam had to use the bathroom. He told me to hold his horn. I started playing. To my knowledge, I sounded pretty good on it. I was playing the notes in the song and I liked the way the slide moved. My sound was pretty fat. I was like, "I like this. I can do this." Two trombone players turned into three trombone players, and two tubas turned into one.

Then Alfred came in the band, and I learned some tailgating with Alfred because he came from a band that played traditionals. Stooges as a band was never a traditional brass band. We had a lot of people say we didn't play in the tradition. We came up the lane the Rebirth created. So when Alfred got in the band, at first it was a little controversy because Walt was upset with me at the time. It wasn't a pretty sight, because he was coming to take my spot. He couldn't do what I could do and I couldn't do what he can do. We started calling ourself PNC. We connected.

I'm in my second marriage. Before I got married, I had three kids. My oldest's name is Ersel Bogan IV, then I had Alexis Maya Bogan. My third child came from a chick that was president of 9 Times Social Aid and Pleasure Club, Chiquita Surtain. So I was pretty much doing "king stuff." I ended up with the president of the club, and we have a beautiful baby by the name of Paisley Rae Williams. My first marriage was to my best friend. I thought it would work. I felt like if it don't work in two years, it ain't gonna work in twenty. Walter will say I'm the two-year champ. But I tell him it's one year for them and one year for me. My wife right now, her name is Jevon Bogan. She is my queen. She is the match from heaven. We have a son now named Jamison Prince Bogan. And that name comes from my mom's maiden name and my last name. Now we have a Brady Bunch. My wife is forty-four this year so I have with her eight kids total. I have four grandkids. I'm doing stuff different and I have to make an inheritance for my kids and their kids. I'm a landscaper, a travel agent. Everyone gets a business.

I started the Save Our Brass Culture Foundation in 2018 to help musicians continue to be musicians and not have to work. We're trying to get jobs, teaching in schools, setting stuff up with NORD and the churches. We also put on Brass Fest. And that's pretty much my life. I'm a happy pappy, a loving husband, and I'm still a musician.

John Cannon IV

(b. January 11, 1980)

Tuba player from 1997 to 2001

I started my career on tuba (sousaphone) at the tender age of eight in third grade at McDonogh 15 under the direction of Preservation Hall bassist Walter Payton. I always tell people my horn chose me, I didn't choose it. I started out a drummer like every other young musician, however the lack of tuba players paired with having one of the greatest teachers—how could I pass?

In 1991, when I made it to Francis W. Gregory, is when my brass band career started. Andrew Baham and I were in a group call the Blue Jays, a band we put together to do school events. Also while at Gregory in the following school year (1992), Ersel "Garfield" Bogan was in my section. The band would play for pep rallies and on- and off-campus events.

In 1995, after being promoted from Gregory to the St. Augustine High School, I began playing with Ace of Spades Brass Band, where I met Virgil Tiller, who was also a drum major for the St. Augustine Marching 100. After being together for one school year, I then joined the Stooges Brass Band. They were known then as the Lil Stooges, but as for the sound, there was nothing little about it. Being classmates with J'mar "Buzz" Westley and Ellis "Ejo" Joseph made our sound untouchable.

After twenty-plus years, multiple festivals, numerous parades, funerals, etc., I can honestly say my life is and was designed just for me. In fact, eighteen years ago while playing a local theme park with the Stooges, I met my wife, Tonya Boyd, who later became a top-twelve contestant on season 8 of NBC's *The Voice*. That was at the summer of 2000 at Jazzland Theme Park, which later became a Six Flags Park and was destroyed by Katrina in 2005. I would say it was the ideal job for a guy right out of high school. From this unit, we have two amazing teenagers: Jonte', my singing and dancing daughter, age 17, and John V, the percussionist.

Being able to travel to other countries such as Russia, Germany, Brazil, Switzerland, Pakistan, and Tajikistan has been a highlight. We had numerous road trips and some were brutal. I believe my musical journey is not just for me, it's for everyone I'm connected to. Whenever I'm out traveling, I bring a little of me to the rest of the world. It's the same thing I bring home when I return.

Alfred "Uncle Al" Growe III
(b. October 22, 1977)
Trombonist from 1998 to present

I started off my musical career at Livingston Middle School. The band director was named Daryl Dickerson. He was the first person who put a horn in my hand. It was actually a trumpet. It had to be 1991. I started off playing in the marching band. I used to listen to Tannon Williams. He was the trumpet player for the High Steppers Brass Band at the time. He was one of our big brothers that we looked up to at Livingston. Then I went on ahead to McDonogh 35, and

I was in the marching band under Mr. Lloyd Harris. Mr. Herman Jones took over and I went from trumpet to marching baritone.

I still was into just marching band for a while and then I started hearing Tannon, Tyrus Chapman, all those guys playing with the High Steppers. Me and my friends Malcolm and Marcus decided to make up our own little brass band. We made up the band called the Be'Be' Kids. That was the first brass band we actually did. We played little gigs for our parents. We was able to go into the French Quarters. That's when I started meeting a lot of people that played in brass bands. I met a guy named Bruce Gates. He was the guy that brung me around the Sixth Ward to meet a lot of the guys that played with the Lil Rascals Brass Band. I met Itchy, Bo Monkey, Coon, Eldridge, and Alto.[3]

Then when I was sixteen, we started going to Donna's Bar and Grill. All the brass bands used to play Donna's other than the Rebirth (they may have played now and again). You had the Lil Rascals, Soul Rebels, Treme. That used to be our hub, with Miss Donna and Mr. Charlie. We was young so we really couldn't go in all the other clubs and see the Rebirth and all of those. Mr. Charlie used to have a little back area where his kitchen was. All the young guys that wanted to see the brass bands play, we used to come in before the band started and go in the kitchen just in case the police came. There used to be a whole group of us just hanging out in the kitchen. Every now and again, we would come out the kitchen and walk around the band in the front. Miss Donna's still here, but Mr. Charlie passed.[4] But that's how it started. We started playing in parades.

I went on to college at Southern University. The band director was Isaac Greggs in 1995. I marched in the marching band for four years, and I was going back and forth. I was doing gigs with Arian. We was called the Hot Boys Brass Band. That was right after my freshman/sophomore year. I met a guy named Brice Miller of the Mahogany Brass Band and I started playing gigs with them. Brice actually took me on my first overseas trip to Nice, France. When I came back from Nice, I went to a parade and I run into John Cannon and he said, "We looking at doing some things with the Stooges." I said I'd come and try it out, see what's going on. That's when I met Walter and Ersel and them. Me coming in the band, I was actually taking Ersel's spot. But after a while we got to be best friends. That's when I started my career with the Stooges in 1998. Being cool with Walter, he brought me around one of his cousins whose daughter was having a birthday party. That cousin wind up being my wife. I was playing for my oldest daughter's birthday party. She was three. Then after that we decided we could come together and get married. She got pregnant and Katrina happened. We was living in Michoud. She just had my son Que'Dyn and we moved to Baton Rouge first, then we went to Atlanta. When we got married, a couple of months before Que'Dyn was born, I got a job with Cox Cable.

When we came back to New Orleans, the Stooges didn't split up, but we were in different places. When we came back, a couple of the guys that originally started the Stooges, we created the Free Agents Brass Band. We made a CD, *Made It through That Water*. And then Walt decided he was coming back for good and so we decided to start the Stooges again.

Other than that, it's plain and simple. My daddy worked hard, my momma worked hard. I grew up in New Orleans East. Thanks to my mom, Emma Growe, and my dad, Alfred Growe Jr., for raising a good kid. Shout-out to all my band directors for teaching me everything about music. Shout-out to my wife for having all my lovely children. To my son, keep playing music, keep the music going. I'm the first generation of Growe men to play music, so I'm the start of a heritage of music in our family. Keep the music going, keep playing. And to all the young brass bands out there, keep making new music. Keep the streets rocking.

Arian "Fat Boy" Macklin
(b. July 23, 1979, d. September 13, 2017)
Tuba player from 1996 to 2006

My music speaks for itself. My heart is pure. Love for music is a family trait that came from my great grandfather on down. My great grandfather, Frank Lastie, was the first man to put drum set in the church in New Orleans.[5] It came down from my great grandfather all the way down to me and my brother. Now, I have my son and he's into it. It's a beautiful thing.

I've been through a lot over the past couple years. I've had two major knee surgeries. And it was so funny because when I came out of the nursing home, all I had was my tuba. And when I was in the nursing home, the people would love it. I used to go to the French Quarters in my wheelchair. Some of the cats used to tell me how I was strong for coming out there in my wheelchair. And someone who gave me inspiration was Terrell Batiste.[6] He had a bad accident where he lost his legs. Terrell gave me motivation to stand up right now. He gave me motivation to move again, because I didn't know what I was going to do. He said, "Don't get used to that wheelchair. Get out of it." I'm a living testimony.

My main focus is to teach guys who want to play tuba under me. Instead of just teaching them the horn, I'd rather mentor them. I want to show them everything. When I teach the guys that play tuba these days, I don't just show them how to play the horn, I see where their head is at. You can go far in music—as far as you want to go—but please have a backup. The crime in the city is very high because children don't have anyone to follow. If we can play music and travel overseas and show children that we can do things and go places, that would be a beautiful thing. Instead of watching rap music, listen to jazz, listen to us coming from church and with God-given talents, putting it into our instruments. If we can do that, it would be a beautiful thing.

Let the children understand that it comes from the church. If you don't have faith in God, you won't strive for excellence. And us playing music, we learned it in the church. My grandmother was an organist. I always had to be in the choir stand or on the drum kit with my grandmother. I can understand it more clearly now. The last recording that my grandmother did was the Hot 8 twentieth anniversary CD, and I was on the album with her. The song was "We Shall Walk through the Streets of the City." I think that made the rest of my century, because it was a blessing looking at my grandmother. Besides me playing the drum set, I play my horn. She taught me how to be the man that I am. She used to fuss on me to iron my clothes. She kept me and my brother Joe's heads together. When she found out that we wanted to play music, she let us off the porch; she pushed us off the porch.

And I would love to thank my uncle Herlin Riley, my cousin Joe Lastie, and the New Orleans Sound for giving me opportunities to play music with them and enjoy things with them. That's one thing I always wanted to do was play music with my uncles, and I finally got to play with my cousin Joe. And to my brothers in the Stooges, I love y'all to death. Anything I can do for them, no problem. And I'd like to thank my cousin, Walter, for being the arrogant, competent guy he is. I'd like to thank him for being who he is, because without him, we wouldn't be the brothers we are.

Chadrick "Chad" Honore

(b. July 10, 1987)

Trumpet player from 2001 to 2006

I'm Chadrick Honore, trumpet player for the Rebirth Brass Band at the moment. I started playing music at McDonogh 15 Creative Arts Elementary School. My band director was Jerry McGowan. I was a part of a young, talented group of kids at McDonogh 15. We consisted of a lot of young guys doing well in music right now like Kris Royal, Troy Andrews, and Joe Dyson. Throughout McDonogh 15, we learned the basics of standard music theory and basic standard jazz theory. Ultimately, that led up to me getting accepted into NOCCA the summer of my seventh-grade year at Thurgood Marshall. NOCCA just had a summer camp. You couldn't go to the school until ninth grade, but for kids who are gifted, they started a camp.

My first brass band was the Real Untouchables Brass Band. Then, I started a band with a couple of my high school friends called All for One Brass Band. I started with the Stooges in high school in my ninth-grade year—January 2001. Walter's stepdad, Michael Buck, was best friends with my uncle, Paul Honore. They paraded with the Black Men of Labor Social Club together, and they'd been friends for a while, too. I met Walt through my uncle, and at the time the Stooges needed a trumpet player. And that was my first time being in a professional brass band. Walter gave me an opportunity to be in the Stooges and I took it. What drew me close to the Stooges was that the style of music was different from what everyone else was doing. These guys were playing in any key and the music that they were playing was inspiring. So that inspired me to join their band, and it worked out good for me because I still haven't played with a band that plays as much technical music as the Stooges.

It started for me with the Stooges on a Thursday night. They had a Thursday night gig we used to do at the Family Ties Bar. It used to be home of the Stooges. Thursday night was my learning grounds with the Stooges Brass Band to learn the songs and get them under my fingertips. After I got a feel for the music, I grew to the lead trumpet role after Andrew started gigging with others. My first time getting on an airplane was with the Stooges; we went to Japan. I was fourteen. It was going to be a fun trip for us, but we had just lost Arian's brother, Shotgun Joe, the day before we left. At the end of the day, we all love each other like brothers. That was my first time on an airplane. We wind up writing "Why They Had to Kill Him" in Japan. From the moment we played the song till the funeral, it was an emotional song. Everybody smiled, cried, laughed.

They were already doing second lines, but when I jumped in, I guess I gave them a fresh outlook on the band side as far as young cats. Like today, the bands got together to blow at each other, trying to be big and create our own name. And we took that and learned from each other. We made sure that we stayed like brothers. It was a brotherhood. I experienced Katrina with the Stooges, and most of us moved to Atlanta together and stayed in one big house off Austell Road. We developed a new sound to what the Stooges band uses today, which is called the Stooges Music Group. We took the stage approach and got the pianos and drum set and formatted the brass band tunes into hip-hop and funk-based tracks. We had a hidden project that no one knew about, but we did a performance at the Source Hip Hop Awards. Well, it wasn't the actual awards, but it was a hip-hop ceremony. The group was called JumpShive. I think the music was way before its time. People liked it but didn't understand the struggle. They haven't had any catastrophic events. They felt the music, but they didn't understand the pain. We got opportunities to produce for ESPN. We produced the *College GameDay* and the *SportsCenter* theme songs.

They had great musicians in the band—Big Sam, Drew Baham, Jamelle Williams, Ersel Bogan, Alfred Growe. They're like my big brothers and they taught me a lot about the music game. With Walt, he taught me how to work for myself. When I say that that's my brother from another mother, that's as real as it gets. He taught independence. He was always the first person to do something. I stayed under Walt just to learn how he do shit. It was more than music for me. I enjoyed the music, but I always wanted to be on the business end. That's how you learn to make money for you. Walt was one of my main influences with that. And Andrew Baham, he don't know, but he's probably my favorite trumpet player. It was a blessing to get to meet Andrew. That's the most humblest, charismatic dude. His mind is unmatched. Still to this day, they're all my big brothers.

Virgil Tiller
(b. January 27, 1977)
Tenor saxophonist from 2003 to present

My love of music started in New Orleans at the age of seven at the Sallier School of Music. I began my classical piano training under the careful watch of the city's most well-known piano instructor, Patricia Seals. During my weekly visits to the music school, my grandfather, Edmond Foucher, a well-known jazz trumpeter for Olympia Brass Band and Preservation Hall Jazz Band, introduced me to traditional jazz music. He took me to some of his band rehearsals and sometimes just allowed me to listen to jazz on the radio. My interest was piqued, and I began taking clarinet lessons at the age of nine. At the age of thirteen, I was accepted into the world-famed Purple Knight Marching 100 under the direction of Edwin H. Hampton and became a two-term drum major at the age of sixteen. While at St. Augustine, I became the principle clarinet player in the symphonic band and the principle piano player in the jazz ensemble under the direction of Carl Blouin Sr.

My professional career started at age fourteen when I started my own New Orleans traditional brass band, Ace of Spades, with my school peers. Some of the musicians then included Terrence Taplin, Ellis Joseph, John Cannon, Keith Green, and Tommy Curtain Jr. After high school, I attended Xavier University of Louisiana, where I earned a BS in biology. I continued to pursue my musical interests fervently with the help of famed clarinetist Dr. Michael White and well-known percussionist Herman LeBeaux. I often listened to Dr. White's practice sessions in Xavier's music complex as I tried to emulate his style. Dr. White also introduced me to the music of Sidney Bechet. This was a defining moment in my life; I switched from clarinet to soprano saxophone and tenor saxophone. During that same period, Mr. LeBeaux gave me jazz piano voicing instruction and a chance to perform with Xavier University's Jazz Ensemble as a second tenor saxophone player.

I also became fascinated with the technological side of music during my twenties. I joined a local music production group, Sound Lounge/Black Souls Entertainment, led by Raymond Duplessis and Michael Spears, in 1999 while pursuing a master's of biology at the Southeastern Louisiana University. Duplessis taught me everything about music production, engineering, management, and performance; we worked together for a number of years. My involvement with the company earned me production credits on jazz trumpeter Jeff Sutton's album *Sunday Drive*. In 2002, I manufactured my own home studio in my Lower Ninth Ward home in New Orleans and used this as a means to produce new local artists in the genres of jazz, R&B, and hip-hop.

January 2002 was my transitional time period to become a music educator in New Orleans. My first job as a music educator was at Alfred Lawless Public High School in the Lower Ninth Ward. With only a handful of members, I built a music program at the school that boasted seventy members in less than six months. The program then added a concert band that received excellent ratings in the Orleans Parish Schools Music Festival. While teaching music in 2003, I became the tenor saxophone player for the Stooges Brass Band. I performed regularly and regained my passion for brass band music, all while developing my soulful sound with the Stooges. In August of 2005, Hurricane Katrina ended my dream of transforming Lawless into a powerhouse secondary music program as well as my individual performance career. The storm left my house inundated with water and destroyed all my musical equipment except for the one tenor saxophone I took with me to Baton Rouge. While in Baton Rouge, I gigged with local bands. I also traveled to New Orleans often to perform with the newly formed Free Agents Brass Band. Eventually I became employed by the Baton Rouge public school system as a certified science/music teacher at Scotlandville Magnet High School. I then became their interim band director when the other band director abandoned the kids of the music program. I taught the kids tirelessly, and within six months they effortlessly placed first in the Marching Sport Battle of the Bands in Houston (2006). My next musical endeavor would be returning to my alma mater in New Orleans and taking on the monumental challenge of restoring the famed St. Augustine Purple Knight Marching 100 music program from 2006 to 2010. With support from the Tipitina's Foundation, Coca-Cola, alumni, and other benefactors, I was able to restart the musical legacy of St. Augustine High School's music program. The legendary Purple Knight Marching 100 Band has been known throughout New Orleans and across the entire country. It serviced over 115 young men and participated in a plethora of functions across the city and has even been invited to perform at many events in Washington, DC. Currently, I am a science teacher at Booker T. Washington High School and the principal tenor saxophone player and management team member for the Stooges. In addition to my personal music career, I still find time to mentor and promote the much-needed music education of today's youth.

Eric "Bogie" Gordon Jr.
(b. February 4, 1987)
Trumpet player from 2007 to 2011

I was born February 4, 1987, in New Orleans, Louisiana. My dad was a drummer, and I picked the drums up from him at the age of six or seven. In sixth grade, I started playing the trumpet. From elementary school, I was at Mary D. Coghill and then Thurgood Marshall. From there, I went to Warren Easton.

Tenth-grade year, I met a guy named Keanon Battiste, and we started off All for One Brass Band in 2003. Christopher Cotton, I met him at Warren Easton. My grandfather used to always tell me to play my horn. Cotton used to stay across the street from my grandfather's. We would sit there and blow all night at each other. Me and him, we kept each other going all through high school. And we used to go to the Stooges Brass Band practice.

After Katrina, I got with Da Truth Brass Band and formed my own brass band named the Next Generation Brass Band, which consisted of musicians like Ashton Hines (a good friend, and I'm still mad he was nominated to the *OffBeat* Best Trumpeter before me), Jeremy "Mojo" Phipps, Joshua Phipps, Edgar Little, Errol Robertson-Marchand, Jay Galle, and John Perkins. I look at people like John Perkins, who is one of the greats, and I actually taught him about brass bands; like Louis Armstrong said, "You'll know much more than I'll ever know."

In 2007, I wound up getting with the New Birth. That's the chapter that everything took off. By that time, I was in the big leagues and I had been practicing a lot. Around the summertime, that's when I hooked up with the Stooges. We hit it off. At that time, they had just come back from Atlanta and they needed trumpets. They trained me to be the lead trumpet player, and they had picked up Glenn Preston from the TBC Brass Band. That's when we had the clubs like the Rock Bottom. It was a hole in the wall. We also played Goody's, which was Ersel's spot, before getting into the cream of the crop, the Hi-Ho.

Around 2009, I quit the band. Me and Walt had some funny words and I fell out. At that time, Chris Cotton had been sitting in. And four months down the line, I was with the Stooges again. In 2009 and 2010, we was headed to the top of *our* game. We were playing the second line every Sunday, booked up on weekends, and with our weekly residency booming. That's when the controversy started. Around 2009 and 2010, the Hi-Ho days, the Red Bull Street

Kings competition came along. That kind of set in stone our dominance of the streets at that time.

Me personally, my whole concept between the music and just brass band culture, I do what I can do to keep the brass band culture alive and moving forward. Even playing every instrument: snare drum, bass drum, trumpet, trombone, and tuba—whichever is needed to keep the music alive at that moment. No matter which band you see me with, I'm going to give my best effort and just keep pushing the music forward and do my best to keep the crowd entertained and into it—and also by letting other musicians sit in, whereas traditionally, before, they couldn't. And I try to keep the holy trinity of brass band in sync: the social club, the band, and the sidewalk.

Shout-out all the instructors I had: Michael Pierce, Charles Brooks, Michael Torregano. My number-one inspiration was my grandfather. He passed around 2003 right before I got into brass band, but every time I got to my grandfather's house, he would say, "Go play that horn." That inspiration always kept me going. Thanks to walking home in New Orleans East. Just about every day, I used to take a twenty-minute walk home and I used to take my horn and it gave me time to practice after rehearsal. Thanks to everyone who supported me. Thanks to Walter Ramsey with the Stooges Brass Band for all the opportunities and giving me the chance to start my own endeavors with my own band, Eric Gordon and the Lazy Boys.

Chris "Rocc Out" Cotton
(b. December 24, 1987)
Trumpet player from 2009 to 2013

Let me tell you how I picked up the trumpet. Actually, I wanted to play drums. I don't know what drum, but I wanted to play the drums. First day of school at Green, which was my middle school, they put me in the art class. I wanted to be in music class, but the art teacher said, "If you want to go to band, raise your hand. They got drummers all covered." I was like, "Damn! I'm gonna play trumpet." One of my close uncles played trumpet, and he let me borrow it for a while. And I got into marching band. For the next six years, that's where I got all of my trumpet lessons from—band directors and friends. While I was at Green doing marching band, I really enjoyed it. In the band, if you get an end, you're a big deal because everybody gets to hear the person on the end. We had two full rows of trumpets already, so they had me in the middle on the tuba row. When you're in the middle, you don't care what people think. I was having fun dancing and playing—all the old heads in the band were even entertained. That's where it all started. From there, I rose in the ranks of the trumpet and became "Rocc Out."

In high school, it's kind of the same way. When I got to Warren Easton, I was the last person walking in the band. I learned the fundamentals of jazz and stuff like that. That was the first glimpse of learning jazz, and it changed my life forever. All I really wanted to do was play the trumpet and rise up the trumpet ranks. I became section leader my senior year. The whole experience growing up in high school, everybody's looking for something they're going to do for the rest of their life. I know money needs to be made and food needs to be consumed. Following the trumpet hasn't gotten me wealth, fame, and fortune, but it fed me, kept me clothed and housed. Plus, I don't complain as much about my job as my friends with six-figure jobs.

After high school, Hurricane Katrina happened. I followed behind my trumpet friend (Eric Gordon) and ended up at Texas Southern, where I studied music till 2009. And the same thing happened. The school semester started in August and here I am walking into the band room for the first time in October. Our band was funny, because the hierarchy is supposed to go first trumpets, second trumpets, and third trumpets, but I got placed in the second trumpet section. Eric was first trumpet. If you were someone, you got placed on first or third trumpet. Second trumpets were right in front of the mellos. I also got private trumpet lessons for the first time, and that's where my trumpet playing really took off. I started a brass band in Houston, Texas, with some band members. There were some band members from New Orleans and some from Houston. It was called the Voodoo Brass Band. We had a nice run for three years from 2006 to 2009.

After that, I came back to New Orleans and studied music at Xavier for a few years. It was around that time when I hooked up with the Stooges Brass Band—about April or May 2009. The brass band industry or scene—I like to call it a community—is like the barbershop. We network with ourselves, but we haven't industrialized as far as the rest of the world and with the music business. The music business is so intricate, but we work together. Everybody works with the next band, and you become more aware of that when you travel. The last couple of years, I've been traveling with the Hot 8 Brass Band, and people remember me from their visits to New Orleans with other bands. I've traveled with the Stooges a lot. You become more aware of the community and the network you have with musicians in the brass band scene.

The Stooges and Hot 8 have been the two big-name bands I've played with, but I've had gigs with the Free Agents, Da Truth, All for One, Voodoo (we never made it to New Orleans, but it's something real), Baby Boyz, New Breed, TBC, Most Wanted, New Wave, 21st Century, Street Legends, RoCC Out, and Free Spirit.

People always say—I guess this is when you're talking to adults—people always say it's hard or tough. I never thought that about anything I did in my life, but especially the trumpet. That's something that never deterred me. I probably would have been the same way if I played the drums. But it's always been fun—even when it's time to work and take care of business. I've lived my life based around music. Anything I did, it was to better my music career or get better personally on my instrument. I tend to follow my trumpet around. I'm playing it, so it's me, but I'm following it. Like Toucan Sam—follow your nose. If I just play my trumpet, I can't go wrong.

Clifton "Spug" Smith Jr.
(b. January 2, 1986)
Tuba player from 2009 to present

I was born in 1986 in the beautiful city of New Orleans. I was introduced to an instrument called the sousaphone in 1995 at Martin Luther King Elementary School. My first band director was Alonzo Bowens, with whom I studied for five years. I'm an alumnus of George Washington Carver School under the direction of Wilbert Rawlins Jr. I also attended Texas Southern University in 2005 under the direction of Richard Lee and assistant band director Clarence Gibson, who is now the head band director at Texas Southern. In 1998 in middle school, we started a brass band called South Park Soldiers. We were a group of kids trying to be like the Rebirth Brass Band at that time. At that time, they had a band called Stooges; they were new on the scene. We had a school function in which I knew Walter's mother, who asked him to come and hear us out at the school talent show. Meeting Walter in 1998, he asked us to practice with them and come under their guidance. Upon entering high school, South Park Soldiers broke up due to Hurricane Katrina and us attending Texas Southern. At Texas Southern, we started a band called Voodoo Brass Band. The musicians in that band were Eric Gordon, Lamar Heard, Christopher Cotton, Joelle Washington, and Josh Rogers.

During the summer of 2008, the Stooges were playing at the Rock Bottom, and I came to support Eric Gordon, Christopher Cotton, Superman Frank on bass drum, Little Charles on snare drum, and Al and Garfield, who were all members of the band. Later that night, Walter asked if I was available to attend practice. At that time, I was traveling back and forth from Texas to New Orleans. Walter asked me if I was moving back home. I said, "Yeah, next year." At the end of summer 2008, I moved back home. I let everyone know I'm back for good and called Walter. He said, "Great." Second line season was approaching, and he asked if I could play the first line, which was the Young Men Olympian (YMO). After that parade, I was asked to join the band. Later, there was a competition with four bands in New Orleans. After winning the competition, the Stooges recorded at the Red Bull Studios, which put them in a position to start traveling. One of my memorable times with the Stooges was when we was in New Jersey. They treated us to a game of Jägermeister shots, and the only person who couldn't handle they shots was Chris. Me and Eric had to carry him to the car, in which his last words were "I made it through the show."

I'm currently thirty-two and a father of two sons, Jeremiah Smith (six years old) and Christian Smith (three years old). I'm also a future husband to Rashana Thomas. It's a wonderful experience being a father. I encourage them to follow their dreams and to know that I always love them. I am now a current member of the Big 6 Brass Band with former Stooges members Lamar Heard, Chris Cotton, and Eric Gordon, as well as Thaddeaus Ramsey, Chris Terro, and Pierre Carter.

Mike "Dizzle" Jones
(b. July 3, 1991)
Keyboardist from 2012 to present

I started playing the piano when I was five years old. They used to have this radio station in New Orleans called 102.9, which is the old-school station. They had this song called "I'll Take You There" by the Staple Singers. So that's the first tune I started fumbling around on the piano. I started playing it not knowing what I was playing. What happened after that was my grandmother was sitting on the couch watching TV and my grandfather came out of his room asking, "Why is this radio station playing this song over and over again?" My grandma was like, "That's not the radio; that's your grandson playing." So my grandfather calls me from up the street and he put me in piano lessons. He said, "You're going to piano lessons, you're going to make me rich." They say you get rich or you die trying. He died trying! So, the next day, he put me in piano lessons with this guy names James McField. And James McField played with Michael Jackson. So I did piano lessons till I was about eleven years old.

After I stopped taking lessons from James McField, they had this other guy named Steven Foster who I started taking lessons from. Steven Foster is a great guy. And that was my first time playing at Jazz Fest, at the Kids Tent, with him. And I started going to lessons. By me starting to be around him, it kind of took me from out of the streets and it took me to a place where I was like, "Okay, I can do better with myself." And I remember I called him one day, and he called me and the first question he asked me: "How many sharps are there in the key of F?" I said, "Mr. Foster, there is no sharps in the key F. There's only one, and it's a flat, B-flat." "That's one of my students. If you would have said the wrong answer, I would have known you wasn't one of my students." So he did that, he put me on a gig with him at Jazz Fest. So every year, I started playing Jazz Fest. And then a stronghold came upon me where I stopped doing it and went back to the streets.

Katrina just brought up a lot of different emotions, and I was at a crossroads figuring out what I was gonna do—if I was gonna play music or just put both feet in the streets. Because at this point, I was selling drugs. And I talked to my spiritual mother, Charmaine Jackson. And I would always go by her house because it was fun and everyone there would try to keep me going in the right direction. You don't want to talk about music when your mom is talking about the lights getting cut off, the water getting cut off. And when I told my mother that, she punched me right in the chest. She was mad—"All this money people invested in you, you're talking about quitting?" I always made sure I kept a church gig. So I just started playing at different churches. That's when I met Walt, and my dad was looking for a bass player. Ersel was playing drums. And Ersel brought Walt on to play with the band, and that's how Walt and I got cool. I was fifteen or sixteen years old at the time. When I came of age, that's when I started touring the world.

John Perkins Jr.

(b. September 28, 1990)

Trumpet player from 2011 to present

I was born on September 28, 1990, in New Orleans, Louisiana. I got my start into music around the fifth grade. My first instrument was the snare drum. I learned to read rhythms while playing the drum, but I never became proficient at playing it. When I arrived at Thurgood Marshall Middle School, I switched to the trumpet. I quickly learned to play, which astounded my peers. The first day, I learned to play my scale. I was sent home with a fingering chart and the next day I knew all of my notes. In about three weeks, I learned all of the second and first trumpet parts to every song. The co-section leader at the time noticed my hasty progress and urged that the band director put me on first trumpet. So within a month's time, I was already at a decent playing level, more so than a few of my peers that had been playing longer.

When I arrived at McDonogh 35 College Preparatory Senior High School, I quickly showed my dedication to the craft. Even though Hurricane Katrina struck the city in 2005 (my sophomore year), I was able to salvage my trumpet and practice while in Texas. When I returned, I was better than ever and ready to prove my worth. By my senior year, I was able to earn the role of section leader. After graduation, I received a scholarship to attend Texas Southern University. I quickly moved up the ranks. By my second semester, I was already co-section leader in the marching band, first chair in the wind ensemble, and lead trumpeter in the big band. I was set to be the section leader had I returned the next year, but life had different plans for me.

In the year 2009, I returned home from Texas to further pursue a career in music. I then enrolled at the University of New Orleans. During my tenure as a music student, I played with various brass bands around the city. One of the bands that was especially influential in my growth as a musician was the Stooges Brass Band. They taught me a lot about the music and business. By playing a lot of second line parades, I was deeply immersed into the New Orleans second line culture, and it became a way of life. I immensely grew my musicality as well as my overall knowledge of this specific genre.

The Stooges took me on adventures that I never imagined. I traveled to different countries like Pakistan, Kyrgyzstan, Tajikistan, and Colombia, where I served as a cultural ambassador on behalf of the United States. I was asked to do seminars, where I basically regurgitated the information that I just learned in school. This helped me remember the information that I thought wouldn't be useful. All the seminars that I've done help me to teach the next generation.

In the year 2015 I taught at the Jazz Exploration Camp located in the Treme area in New Orleans. I then realized that I wanted to gift the future musicians all of the knowledge that I had acquired. So, I started what will be a music school in the future. The name of it is Art Is Music. In short, we'll just call it AIM. The mission statement is "Developing the minds of tomorrow's leaders through the avenue of music." I want to make AIM a household name in New Orleans for various reasons. I want it to portray musicians in a positive light and build a strong foundation for musicians to stand on—musically and in the music business.

I always worked hard at my craft, and though I can be quite silly at times, no one can ever deny that. I never believed in limitations, which is why my progression as a musician was swift and direct. This has always been who I was, and it is who I will continue to be!

Royce "Flash" Jackson
(b. January 21, 1961)
Production manager from 2010 to present

My name is Royce "Flash" Jackson. I had a vision of owning my own production company. Back in the 1980s, we didn't have the internet and multimedia. What is available now was not available back then. I met Walter Ramsey June 16, 2006. I had worked on one of his properties because he had a bad problem with his bathroom. He said, "Look, I'll pay you half right now and I'll bring the other $200 in two or three hours." He brought it to me and then he said, "What do you really want to do, Flash?" I told him I wanted to be an audio engineer, because a lot of people don't realize that, before it reaches BET, VH1, MTV, or YouTube, it starts in the studio. I wanted to see it from start to finish with every song. The process of making the track is very interesting.

Walt left and went to Atlanta for six or seven months and he moved back. He had a band he created called JumpShive during Katrina to make money. The band moved back to New Orleans and started to have practices at 1933 Bartholomew Street at Drew's house, and they would practice at ten. Walt had said, "I have to figure out how I'm gonna get you in." So I would get there by eight thirty or nine, move all the furniture around, and have everything set up, but I would stay in my lane. Somebody said, "Yo, Walt, you need to go turn me up." So Walt said, "Damn, Flash, you want to be a sound engineer? Get your ass over there and start turning the dials." And so I got my foot in the door and the rest was history. If necessary, Walt and Drew would have financed my training at Grambling State, but Delgado had just started offering the audio engineering class, and the VA paid for my first two years. Walt and Drew needed somebody in the studio who could stay at home and record and still have money coming in, because they had started touring.

And so I started traveling with the band and doing gigs. I remember one distinguished gig we played on the corner of Orleans and Claiborne. We had just started and Alfred said to Walt, "What's that old man doing over there?" And Walt said, "I want a person on my team like that that's a perfectionist. His cords have to be rolled up a certain way. I don't have to tell him nothing. That's his passion and I want a person like that on my team." And big shout-out to Al. That's why I'm here. Cut the check.

But the ball really started rolling in 2010. We ran the Hi-Ho for about a year and we were there every Thursday. I was the production manager. Everybody was aware that I had glaucoma.

Then we started putting together the Stooges Music Group, which is called the stage band. That was the early band members like Garfield, Virgil, Cotton, Ace, Spug, and Walt. Those were two sets of totally different Stooges. It was a transition. When I got to the band, I was green; I didn't know none of the slang or what things meant. And they was cracking jokes on me and stuff, doing pranks on me while I was sleeping, videotaping me snoring and putting me on Facebook. We started touring with that group and then, down the line, everyone had changes in their life, and that's when the other set of Stooges were put together. Elliot, Roland, Mike, Javan, and Duley. That was a package I was not ready for. But as times goes on, we learned to adjust to each other. We traveled to 276 cities in 2015. We've had the opportunity to play at major venues across the United States: Brooklyn Bowl, Vegas, and many more.

Then I fell in with the passion of live production of how a show goes on, how to work the lights, how to work CO2s. Then it came to a point where I started creating different light effects on different songs like "Fire" and "Sir Duke." I focused more on the sound engineering aspect of it. I continued going to Delgado for a degree in music production. I found out what financial aid meant. From that point on, I acquired $35,000 worth of my own sound equipment, and at this point, I am at the end of my dream. I have a very nice, spacious rehearsal space called the Stage Hall, which is at 90 percent completion, 30' × 30'. And my lounge is 90 percent completed. I have had the opportunity to work with artists like Master P, Silkk the Shocker, Denisia, Curren$y, and many more. But I mostly want to give a big shout-out to Mr. Ramsey, who believed in me when I was right or wrong and gave me the opportunity to step out. Shout-out to Big Al Da Godfather, Garfield, and Mr. Virgil Tiller, Mr. Cotton, Ace Free, Duley, Rolo Polo, Poppa String, Pretty Boy Javan, Spug, Mike Jones, Whoadie, and Flash. Thank y'all for the journey—especially myself, Flash, because, yes, I put a shout-out to myself in my own biography.

BAND MEMBER ROSTER

Abdule "Duley" Muhammad (percussion)
Al "Big Al" Huntley (trumpet)
Alfred "Uncle Al" Growe III (trombone)
Andrew "Drew" "Da Phessah" Baham (trumpet, production)
Andrew McGowan (keyboards)
Antione "Ace Free" Coleman (snare drum)
Arian "Fat Boy" Macklin (tuba)
Arnold Little (saxophone)
Brian Gerdes (trumpet)
Bryant Gair (trumpet)
Cameron Johnson (saxophone)
Chad Honore (trumpet)
Chris Cotton (trumpet)
Clifton "Spug" Smith Jr. (tuba)
Darryl Jackson (snare drum)
Devin Phillips (saxophone)
Dorian "Tank" Jones (bass drum)
Dwayne "Big D" Williams (bass drum)
Dwayne Finnie (trombone)
Eddie Christmas (drums)
Edward Lee (tuba)
Elliot Slater (guitar)
Ellis "Ejo" Joseph (bass drum)
Eric "Bogie" Gordon Jr. (trumpet)
Errol Marchand (snare drum)

Ersel "Garfield" Bogan III (tuba, trombone)
Floyd Gray (percussion)
Glenn "Twice" Preston (trumpet)
George McCray (snare drum)
Gregory "Chachi" Warner (trumpet)
Herbert Davis (tuba)
J'mar "Buzz" Westley (snare drum)
Jamelle Williams (trumpet)
Javan Carter (tuba, trumpet)
Jerreau Fournett (saxophone)
John Cannon IV (tuba)
John Dotson (percussion)
John Perkins Jr. (trumpet)
Joseph "Shotgun Joe" Williams (trombone)
Juvon Pollard Sr. (trumpet)
Lamar Heard (trombone)
Larry Brown (trombone)
Maurice "Sporty" Craig (trombone)
Mike "Dizzle" Jones (keyboards)
Noel "Dooby" Freeman (trumpet)
Nori Hirata (guitar)
Raymond Holmes (trumpet)
Roland "Rolo" Taylor (drums)
Royce "Flash" Jackson (production manager)
Sam "Big Sam" Williams (trombone)
Sammy "Lil Sam" Cyrus (snare drum)
Shamarr Allen (trumpet)
Thaddeaus "Peanut" Ramsey (bass drum)
Tommy Curtain Jr. (trumpet)
Travis Carter (tuba)
Troy "Trombone Shorty" Andrews (trumpet)
Virgil Tiller (saxophone)
Walter "Whoadie" Ramsey (tuba, trombone, bandleader)
Wayne Lewis (saxophone)
Wendell "Cliff" "Cumberbund" Stewart (saxophone)
Yorel "Yogi" Gardener (trumpet)

NOTES

Preface: Making "The Stooges Book"

1. *Black* is capitalized throughout to acknowledge its status as a term that, per the *The Chicago Manual of Style*, describes a national or ethnic group—specifically people of the African diaspora. In this sense, it is not unlike Chicano, Arab, Hispanic, or Acadian, which are all capitalized without question in publications. While I acknowledge that race is a social construct and that blackness is by no means monolithic, I hope that capitalization brings Black in line with these other usages, acknowledges the realness of race in lived experience, and emphasizes the positive associations many have with blackness.

2. DeCoste 2015, 2017b.

3. This is just one of *many* definitions of ethnomusicology, and I'm not particularly wed to it. The term references ethnography (systematic writing about people) and musicology (the study of music), but some ethnomusicology doesn't include people and some isn't about music, as the field of sound studies shows. I have absolutely no interest in defining or delimiting ethnomusicology, but simply offer this definition for those unfamiliar with the term. For a canonical list of definitions for ethnomusicology, see Merriam 1977.

4. To be clear, the "degree of access" I have to this group of Black musicians as a white ethnographer isn't something to be celebrated. "Native" ethnographers of color have long been institutionally discredited as "subjective" for their proximity to the communities where they claim some belonging (see DeCoste 2017a). To be celebrated for my degree of access perpetuates a cycle of white privilege.

5. This point about the distinction between writing and inscription is cogently made in Bejarano et al. 2019. They argue for a decolonized ethnography, a part of which is the attribution of authorship.

6. Collaborative anthropologist Luke Eric Lassiter (2008) notes that, in collaborative ethnographies, "both ethnographer(s) and consultant(s) must be willing to make concessions so they can work together in the first place; but they must also be willing to open themselves up to a dynamic knowledge exchange, to stick it out, and to discover in their work together emergent counderstandings, cointerpretations, and coinscriptions (which will always include points of disagreement)" (76).

7. Lorde 1984, 45.

8. My whiteness is both a reflection and recapitulation of the predominately white institutions where I've studied (Bishop's University, Tulane University, and Columbia University). Though my positionality is a problematic colonial norm (white researcher and Black subjects), it's a reality that is hopefully pushed against by this collaboration.

9. I say "we think" because who knows what the book's life will be like!

10. For other collaborative music books with varied audiences, see Cape and Guilbault 2014 and Muller and Benjamin 2011. In our collaborative approach, we take particular inspiration from New Orleans's own Neighborhood Story Project, which has published multivocal and community-oriented books (see Barnes and Breunlin 2014; Breunlin, Lewis, Regis 2009; Regis, Breunlin, and Lewis 2011; and Nine Times Social and Pleasure Club 2009).

11. This phrasing comes from an interview I conducted with one of my mentors at Columbia, Aaron Fox (DeCoste 2016).

12. If I codeswitch into jargon at times, it's more a byproduct of my training than my intentionally reaching out to an academic audience.

Introduction: Wind It Up!

1. Michael Buck was Walter's stepfather.

2. Like "The Funky Broadway," "The Wobble," "The Bus Stop," "The Twist," and many other instructional dance songs, the words explicitly guide the audience through the dance steps. For an in-depth look at the history of African American dance-instruction songs, in which "Wind It Up" can be placed, see Szwed and Banes 2005. I would expand this to include dance challenges on social media platforms like TikTok; the #BeforeILetGoChallenge or #TheGitUpChallenge are prime examples.

3. Normative masculinity, as it functions in homosocial male groups, hierarchizes relationships through competition (Bird 1996). This is made apparent in the New Orleans brass band scene not only musically through demonstrations of virtuosity, but also—in an exceptional case—physically through the Stooges' staged push-up competition. The Stooges bring this into their stage show.

4. There are exceptions to this in at least two social aid and pleasure clubs. Prince of Wales and the Ice Divas both have white club members.

5. Regis 2001, 755.

6. Knowles 1996; Sakakeeny 2013a.

7. Knowles 1996, 21.

8. Today, bands say that other bands play "radio tunes" (covers) as a dig. The goal is to make original music that receives play on the radio, but covering radio tunes is always popular with audiences.

9. Bruce Boyd Raeburn (2009) says it best when he states that "because Barker did not set limits on how his students could negotiate their stylistic identities, preferring instead to inculcate basic values such as discipline and self-respect, his plan to resuscitate what appeared to be a waning tradition succeeded. But rather than view the phenomenon as the *loss* of a tradition (as some conservative brass band musicians have), one must recognize that Barker was conforming to a tradition of experimentation, which is precisely what has kept jazz-oriented brass bands alive and culturally relevant in New Orleans for more than a century" (10). For more on tradition and innovation in the brass band tradition, see Sakakeeny 2013a.

Chapter 1: School Days

1. Sakakeeny 2013a, 54–60.

2. The parallel knee bend was brought to New Orleans by way of Edwin Hampton, who picked it up at Indiana University. This was written about by St. Augustine High School's first principal, Matthew O'Rourke (2003). The unofficial slogan of St. Aug is "with bended knee." Kudos to Will Buckingham for pointing this out.

3. The term *sidewalk* has a populist connotation and refers to all non-club/nonmusician participants.

4. Brian Gerdes, one of the original trumpet players, is now the owner of Gerdes Architectural Roofing. Trombonist "Big Sam" Williams is the bandleader of Big Sam's Funky Nation, of which Drew Baham is also a member.

5. Kennedy was never reopened after Hurricane Katrina and was demolished in 2017 by the Recovery School District (Hasselle 2015; Bruno 2017).

6. There are plenty of neighborhood borders in New Orleans, but the ultimate one is between Uptown and Downtown, traditionally divided by Canal Street. For information about NOCCA, see Shiels 2013.

7. For a more in-depth look at the life and legacy of Clyde Kerr Jr., see Kennedy 2002, 115–28.

8. Wayne Lewis, who is not featured in this book, played saxophone in the band. He is currently an associate professor in the Department of Educational Leadership Studies and an affiliated faculty member with the African American and Africana Studies Program at the University of Kentucky.

9. There are a number of bands called the "Marching 100." St. Aug's band is not to be confused with the marching band of the same name at Florida Agricultural and Mechanical University (FAMU). For an in-depth look at the founding of St. Aug's band program, see Chenier 2000.

10. For more on the role of band directors, see Sakakeeny 2015.

Chapter 2: Where Ya From?

1. The library, which was founded in 1915 to serve people of color, closed in 1965 and is currently owned by the Dryades Street YMCA. For more, see Cherrie 2014.

2. Directions in New Orleans don't follow the typical north/south/east/west model. New Orleans is surrounded by Lake Pontchartrain to the north and the Mississippi River to the south. Cardinal directions in New Orleans are lakeside, riverside, uptown, and downtown.

3. Ricky B is from the Seventh Ward. Ned Sublette (2009) dramatically describes "Nolia Clap," which features a roll call of projects no longer physically existing at the time of its release, as sounding "like a dancing skeleton, with graveyard air whistling through the bones" (300). Hip-hop archivist Holly Hobbs (2015) notes that the "ward roll call," a "traditional hallmark of bounce," has been adopted by brass bands. The boundaries between bounce and brass band music are porous (Sakakeeny 2013a; 2013b). The Stooges and the Soul Rebels are perhaps the two bands that currently do the most to muddy the distinction between hip-hop and brass band music.

4. These shout-outs are all to Uptown (UPT) neighborhoods. The Mag, Melph, and Callio are short for the Magnolia, Melpomene, and Calliope projects, respectively. Gert Town, Pigeon Town, and Hollygrove are all Uptown neighborhoods.

5. This section is adapted from Partners-N-Crime's "Pump tha Party," in which they chant, "Five plus four, and what do you get? / You get a Ninth Ward n**** running in yo' shit!"

6. Virgil Tiller's grandfather, Edmond Foucher, was a trumpet player with the Olympia Brass Band. Virgil credits him with teaching him about traditionals and showing him what was financially possible with a career in music.

Chapter 3: The Process

1. *48 Laws of Power* (1998) by Robert Greene is a popular treatise on power and a widely read text in some hip-hop communities, read by hip-hop moguls including Kanye West, Jay-Z, and Drake.

2. With regard to ending welfare, PRWORA did away with Aid to Families with Dependent Children (AFDC), a New Deal program that provided financial assistance for children in low-income households.

3. For more on PRWORA and the stereotypes that led to it, see Jordan-Zachary 2009.

4. Harris-Perry 2011, 114.

5. Harris-DeBerry, Shervington, and Govan 2014.

6. Angela Davis (2012) notes that "in 1991, the Sentencing Project released a report indicating that one in four of all young black men between the ages of 18 and 24 were incarcerated. Twenty-five percent is an astonishing figure. That was in 1991. A few years later, the Sentencing Project released a follow-up report revealing that within three or four years, the percentage had soared to over 32 percent" (38).

7. Dowd 2000, 73.

8. Robin D. G. Kelley (1996) points out that this type of strategy within capitalism is neither emancipatory nor revolutionary. It is "a range of strategies within capitalism . . . intended to enable working-class urban youth to avoid dead-end, low-wage labor while devoting their energies to creative and pleasurable pursuits" (45).

9. For the *XXL* article, see Linden 2007. On BET, the Stooges have done music for *Sunday Best*, *The Celebration of Gospel*, and *BET Jazz*, among other shows.

10. Music videos they've appeared in include Les Nubians' "Makeda," Jessica Simpson's "Angels," Jadakiss's "Times Up" (feat. Nate Dogg), T.I.'s "Ball" (feat. Lil Wayne), and Lloyd's "Set Me Free" (feat. Mystikal), among others.

11. Sakakeeny (2013a) writes about brass band musicians and social mobility in much more detail.

12. Although the Stooges didn't learn music business at NOCCA, historian Al Kennedy (2002) notes that "there . . . is a practical side to Clyde Kerr Jr.'s jazz instruction at NOCCA. He stresses the importance of learning the business side of music. He has seen too many musicians living in poverty because they never learned to manage their money. They spent what they earned without saving, planning, or investing. Kerr also cautions his students with tales of other musicians who never paid attention to the business and consequently are 'still getting ripped off.' NOCCA plays an important role in preparing artists for the business world" (118).

13. "Black and white gigs" include weddings and funerals and are labeled as such because they require formal attire.

Chapter 4: It's About Time

1. Nice 2013.

2. Matt Sakakeeny (2013a) notes that the Rebirth had a similar process with the recording

of "Do Whatcha Wanna," where their "initial performance was augmented with tambou-rines, cowbells, clapping, and vocal whoops and hollers that decontextualize the recording out of the studio and into the streets and intimate spaces of live performance" (43).

3. Osvaldo Oyola (2013) explores these manufactured markers of authenticity in recorded popular music, calling them "call outs to 'liveness.'" Louise Meintjes (2003), in her canonical ethnography of South African studios, defines liveness as "an illusion of sounding live that is constructed through technological intervention in the studio and mediated sym-bolically through discourses about the natural and the artistic" (112).

4. Wyckoff 2004.

Chapter 5: Why They Had to Kill Him?

1. Also written as "Why Dey Had to Kill Him."
2. For a more in-depth look at Joe's life, see Sakakeeny 2012.
3. Sakakeeny 2012.
4. Quoted in Young 2004.
5. Frankie Beverly and Maze tunes can be found throughout brass band repertoire, including the cookout classic "Before I Let Go."
6. Shavers was a snare drummer for the Hot 8 who was shot and killed in 2006. Saka-keeny (2013a) has written about his life and death. His sister, Nakita Shavers, now runs the Dinerral Shavers Education Fund in his memory.
7. Alexander 2012.
8. As Angela Davis (2016) puts it, "The purpose of the police is supposed to be to protect and serve. At least, that's their slogan. Soldiers are trained to shoot and kill" (14).
9. Here, I was channeling the insight of Bennie Pete, bandleader of the Hot 8, who said, "You have more drugs going on at Tulane University and Loyola University than any ghetto neighborhood. . . . And guess what? They cannot do them college students nothing" (quoted in Sakakeeny 2013a, 157).

Chapter 6: Made It through That Water

1. Johnson 2011, xvii.
2. As Walter Benjamin famously claimed, "The tradition of the oppressed teaches us that the 'state of emergency' in which we live is not the exception but the rule. We must attain to a conception of history that is in keeping with this insight. Then we shall clearly realize that it is our task to bring about a real state of emergency, and this will improve our position in the struggle against Fascism" (Benjamin 1988).
3. This can be described as "eventalization." To eventalize, in Foucault's (1991) words, is to "[make] visible a *singularity* at places where there is a temptation to invoke a historical con-stant, an immediate anthropological trait, or an obviousness which imposes itself uniformly on all" (76).
4. Studies have shown that the storm disproportionately affected those in the city's Black neighborhoods. Sociologist Patrick Sharkey (2007), for example, notes that, when account-ing for age, "the group of neighborhoods with the highest death counts and highest num-bers of residents who are still missing were, on average, about 80% African American. The neighborhoods hit hardest were not necessarily the poorest in New Orleans, but they were

the most segregated. This conclusion confirms that Katrina's impact on African Americans is not attributable to the fact that the storm happened to strike a city with a large Black population; rather, I find that within the city of New Orleans, Black neighborhoods and Black residents were disproportionately affected by the storm" (498).

5. For information about infrastructure failure, see Heerden 2007. For information about the governmental response, see Schneider 2005.

6. See Adams and Sakakeeny 2019.

7. jackbrass 2005.

8. jackbrass 2005.

9. Al explains the origin of the New Orleans term *shive* thusly: "Back in the day, with old folks, you could be shipe—it comes from sharp. So you got sharp and the old folks used to say, 'Oh, he's shipe,' meaning, 'Oh, he's tight.' And the generation after them came with something that said, 'Well, he not shipe, he's shive. He's shive.' Jive—shive. To 'jump shive' means you wake in the morning and put on your stuff. 'I'm jumping shive.' So they just named the group after jump shive."

10. The term *resiliency* oversaturated conversations at most government and corporate events to commemorate Katrina. These conversations, while important, occasionally drown out others about governmental failure and structural change.

Chapter 7: Stooges Party

1. I borrow the term *Black public sphere* from Mark Anthony Neal (2003), who gives as its examples "black church and civic organizations as well as barbershops, beauty parlors, and dance halls" (1). For ethnography of one neighborhood club in New Orleans's Black public sphere, see DeCoste 2017b.

2. For more on the gig economy, see Heller 2017.

3. Their weekly residencies leading up to the Hi-Ho are, in order: Kemps (at Washington and Lasalle), Baby's (at 7th and Dryades), Lee's Tree (at Washington and Magnolia), Family Ties (at Conti and N. Dupre), Club N'Finity (at Basin and N. Robertson), the Rock Bottom (at Tchoupitoulas and Peniston), Jo-Ro's Café and Lounge (at Orleans and N. Claiborne), and Goody's (at St. Claude and Louisa).

4. Perry 2015, 103.

5. Van Syckle 2012. The venue was eventually sold to Jeff Bromberger and Russ and Brian Greiner (the owners of popular Frenchmen Street venue the Maison) in 2013 (Woodward 2013).

6. "Twice" is the nickname of Glenn Preston, one of the Stooges' trumpet players who joined post-Katrina.

Chapter 8: The Controversy

1. Sakakeeny 2013a, 64–7; Cotton 2009.

2. Brothers 2006, 202–11.

3. Mutua 2006.

4. A historical analogue can also be found in the advertising wagons that bands performed on throughout the city in the early twentieth century (Brothers 2006).

5. The song Garfield references here is "Back Stabbers," the title track from the O'Jays' 1972 album.

6. This Glen Andrews is not to be confused with his cousin, Glen David Andrews, who plays trombone.

7. Black Feather is a Mardi Gras Indian tribe that Walter occasionally masks for. His little cousin, Thaddeaus Ramsey, regularly masks for them as a fly boy.

Chapter 9: Street Kings

1. Sakakeeny (2010) traces the history of the bridge and shows how second liners, through their sound and physical presence, reclaim the space underneath it.

2. Sakakeeny actually describes the *second* Red Bull Street Kings event, held in 2013, as "hitting all the right notes" (Sakakeeny 2013b). But the first event, where the Stooges won, seems to have had a similar response. At the second coming of the event, the Original Pinettes Brass Band, the city's only all-female brass band, won, changing the name of the competition from "Street Kings" to "Street Queens." For more on the second competition and the Original Pinettes Brass Band who won, see DeCoste 2015, 2017b.

3. Raeburn 2013.

4. Buttle 1998, 243.

5. Red Bull 2010.

6. YMO stands for "Young Men Olympian." Founded in 1884, it is one of the oldest social aid and pleasure clubs in the city. Their club has many divisions and features the most bands of any annual second line, so having the largest crowd at YMO is a significant feat. For a brief history of the club, see Walter, Sibert, and Rocco 2012.

7. Blodie is Gregory Davis.

Chapter 10: I'm Just Doin' My Job

1. For more on the significance of the bridge, see Sakakeeny 2010, 2013a, 21–35.

2. Sakakeeny 2015, Adams and Stiffler 2014.

3. The New Orleans Musicians' Clinic stepped in to try to ameliorate the inaccessibility of health services to musicians and other cultural workers in 1998.

4. Sakakeeny 2015.

5. Writing around the time of the Stooges' founding, Robin D. G. Kelley (1997) explores the divide between work and leisure that exists in much scholarship on the Black working class. He suggests that "the pursuit of leisure, pleasure, and creative expression is *labor*, and . . . some African American urban youth have tried to turn that labor into cold hard cash" (45).

6. Though brass band offers some local fame to most musicians, only a small percentage is able to professionalize. Sakakeeny (2013a) writes that "the brass band circulates as a symbol of local distinction, but only a few of the musicians have been as successful as Rebirth in exploiting this potential" (67).

Chapter 11: On the Road

1. A backwood is a blunt (a mixture of tobacco and cannabis) rolled in a tobacco leaf from a Backwood-brand cigar.

2. Dating back at least to the 1930s, cannabis use, at least in the imaginations of many white lawmakers, was tied to Black jazz musicians. For example, Harry Anslinger, the DEA for over 30 years, was virulently racist and adamant about the damages of both jazz and cannabis, tying them together quite explicitly (Hari 2015). For a primary source example of Anslinger's racism and delusional view of cannabis, see Anslinger 1964. Pembleton (2015) productively reframes the beginning of the War on Drugs long before the Reagan era and shows how the Federal Bureau of Narcotics operated propagandistically.

3. See Edwards, Bunting, and Garcia 2013.

Chapter 12: Stooges 101

1. In addition to "Just a Closer Walk with Thee," popular brass band hymns include "I'll Fly Away," "What a Friend We Have in Jesus," "Down by the Riverside," "By and By," and "Lily of the Valley."

2. Klein 2008.

3. Sakakeeny 2015b, 298.

4. "The Square" is shorthand for Jackson Square.

Roll Call

1. Yvonne Busch was an incredibly prolific music educator who was an accomplished musician in her own right, having played with the Swinging Rays of Rhythm. For an in-depth look at Busch's career and life, see Kennedy 2005, 49–81. For more on the band on the Swinging Rays of Rhythm, see Tucker 2001.

2. This is shorthand for "one love."

3. Al is referring to Dewon "Itchy" Scott, Corey "Bo Monkey" Henry, Gregory "Coon" Veals, Eldridge Andrews, and Charles "Alto" Taylor.

4. For an interview with Donna Poniatowski-Sims and further recollections of Donna's Bar and Grill, see Burns 2006.

5. For more on the musical legacy of the Lastie family, see Berry, Foose, and Jones 2009.

6. Also known as "Burger," Batiste is best known as a trumpet player for the Hot 8 Brass Band.

BIBLIOGRAPHY

Interviews

Baham, Andrew. Interviewed by Kyle DeCoste. Personal interview. Rook Café, November 10, 2015.

Baham, Andrew, Walter Ramsey, Ersel Bogan, Mike Jones, John Cannon, Al Growe, Que'Dyn Growe, Virgil Tiller, John Perkins, Javan Carter, and Ellis Joseph. Personal interview. Livin Swell Studio, June 30, 2019.

Bogan, Ersel. Interviewed by Kyle DeCoste. Personal interview. Ersel's residence, April 10, 2016.

Bogan, Ersel. Interviewed by Kyle DeCoste. Personal interview. Kyle's residence, June 25, 2018.

Cannon, John, and Ellis Joseph. Interviewed by Kyle DeCoste. Personal interview. Historic St. James A.M.E. Church, July 12, 2018.

Cotton, Chris. Interviewed by Kyle DeCoste. Personal interview. Rue de la Course, March 22, 2016.

Cotton, Chris. Interviewed by Kyle DeCoste. Personal interview. Café Reconcile, July 25, 2018.

Gordon, Eric. Interviewed by Kyle DeCoste. Personal interview. Rook Café, January 20, 2016.

Gordon, Eric. Interviewed by Kyle DeCoste. Personal interview. Kyle's residence, July 19, 2017.

Growe, Al. Interviewed by Kyle DeCoste. Personal interview. Half Shell Oyster Bar, December 14, 2015.

Growe, Al. Interviewed by Kyle DeCoste. Personal interview. Al's truck, March 3, 2016.

Growe, Al. Interviewed by Kyle DeCoste. Personal interview. Kyle's residence, June 21, 2018.

Growe, Al, Ersel Bogan, and Mike Jones. Interviewed by Kyle DeCoste. Personal interview. Livin Swell Studio, June 13, 2017.

Honore, Chad. Interviewed by Kyle DeCoste. Personal interview. Rook Café, March 22, 2016.

Honore, Chad. Interviewed by Kyle DeCoste. Personal interview. Chad's residence, July 26, 2018.

Jackson, Flash. Interviewed by Kyle DeCoste. Personal interview. Livin Swell Studio, June 14, 2017.

Jackson, Flash. Interviewed by Kyle DeCoste. Personal interview. Livin Swell Studio, July 28, 2018.

Jones, Mike. Interviewed by Kyle DeCoste. Personal interview. Kyle's residence, July 17, 2017.
Jones, Mike, Abdule Muhammad, and Javan Carter. Interviewed by Kyle DeCoste. Personal
     interview. Javan's cousin's residence, May 24, 2016.
Macklin, Arian. Interviewed by Kyle DeCoste. Personal interview. Jackson Square, May 20,
     2016.
Macklin, Arian. Interviewed by Kyle DeCoste. Personal interview. Arian's truck, corner of St.
     Louis and Dauphine , July 13, 2017.
Perkins, John. Interviewed by Kyle DeCoste. Personal interview. Rook Café, March 16, 2016.
Ramsey, Ashton. Interviewed by Kyle DeCoste. Personal interview. Mr. Ashton's residence,
     November 17, 2015.
Ramsey, Walter. Interviewed by Kyle DeCoste. Personal interview. Livin Swell Studio,
     November 4, 2015.
Ramsey, Walter. Interviewed by Kyle DeCoste. Personal interview. Livin Swell Studio, June 3,
     2016.
Ramsey, Walter. Interviewed by Kyle DeCoste. Personal interview. Brooklyn Bowl, New York,
     January 13, 2018.
Ramsey, Walter. Interviewed by Kyle DeCoste. Telephone interview. September 19, 2018.
Ramsey, Walter, Andrew Baham, Virgil Tiller, Al Growe, and Brian Gerdes. Interviewed by
     Kyle DeCoste and Matt Sakakeeny. Personal interview. Livin Swell Studio, October 18,
     2015.
Ramsey, Walter, and Elliot Slater. Interviewed by Kyle DeCoste. Personal interview. Newton
     Park, Johns Creek, Georgia, July 22, 2017.
Smith, Clifton. Interviewed by Kyle DeCoste. Personal interview. Melba's Old School Po-
     Boys, April 2, 2016.
Smith, Clifton. Interviewed by Kyle DeCoste. Personal interview. Chad Honore's residence,
     July 31, 2018.
Tiller, Virgil. Interviewed by Kyle DeCoste. Personal interview. Rook Café, January 14, 2016.
Tiller, Virgil. Interviewed by Kyle DeCoste. Personal interview. Rook Café, June 9, 2017.
Tiller, Virgil. Interviewed by Kyle DeCoste. Personal interview. The Well, 1600 Basin Street,
     July 12, 2018.
Westley, J'mar. Interviewed by Kyle DeCoste. Telephone interview. July 11, 2018.

Discography

Hot 8 Brass Band. 2015. *Vicennial.* Compact disc. Brighton, England: Tru Thoughts.
Lil Rascals Brass Band. 2001. *Buck It Like a Horse.* Compact disc. Metairie, LA: Mardi Gras
     Records.
Partners-N-Crime. 1995. *Pump tha Party (Puttin' in Work).* Compact disc. Kenner, LA: Big
     Boy Records.
Rebirth Brass Band. 2001. *Hot Venom.* Compact disc. Metairie, LA: Mardi Gras Records.
Stooges Brass Band. 2003. *It's About Time.* Compact disc. New Orleans: Gruve Music.
Stooges Brass Band. 2013. *Street Music.* 33⅓ rpm. New Orleans: Sinking City Records.
Stooges Brass Band. 2016. *Thursday Night House Party.* Compact disc. New Orleans: Livin
     Swell Music.
T.I. 2003. *Trap Muzik.* Compact disc. New York: Grand Hustle/Atlantic.

Secondary Sources

Adams, Thomas J., and Steve Striffler. 2014. *Working in the Big Easy: The History and Politics of Labor in New Orleans*. Lafayette, LA: University of Louisiana at Lafayette Press.

Adams, Thomas Jessen, and Matt Sakakeeny, eds. 2019. *Remaking New Orleans: Beyond Exceptionalism and Authenticity*. Durham, NC: Duke University Press.

Alexander, Michelle. 2012. *The New Jim Crow: Mass Incarceration in the Age of Colorblindness*. New York: The New Press.

Anslinger, Harry. 1964. *The Protectors: The Heroic Story of the Narcotics Agents, Citizens and Officials in Their Unending, Unsung Battles Against Organized Crime in America and Abroad*. New York: Farrar, Straus and Company.

Barnes, Bruce "Sunpie," and Rachel Breunlin. 2014. *Talk That Music Talk: Passing on Brass Band Music in New Orleans the Traditional Way*. New Orleans: University of New Orleans Center for the Book.

Bejarano, Carolina Alonso, Lucia López Juárez, Mirian A. Mijangos García, and Daniel M. Goldstein. 2019. *Decolonizing Ethnography: Undocumented Immigrants and New Directions in Social Science*. Durham, NC: Duke University Press.

Benjamin, Walter. 1988. "Theses on the Philosophy of History." In *Illuminations: Essays and Reflections*, edited by Hannah Arendt, translated by Harry Zohn, 253–64. New York: Schocken Books.

Berry, Jason, Jonathan Foose, and Tad Jones. 2009. *Up from the Cradle of Jazz: New Orleans Music Since World War II*. Lafayette: University of Louisiana at Lafayette Press.

Bird, Sharon R. 1996. "Welcome to the Men's Club: Homosociality and the Maintenance of Hegemonic Masculinity." *Gender and Society* 10 (2): 120–32.

Breunlin, Rachel, and Helen A. Regis. 2009. "Can There Be a Critical Collaborative Ethnography? Creativity and Activism in the Seventh Ward, New Orleans." *Collaborative Anthropologies* 2: 115–46.

Brothers, Thomas David. 2006. *Louis Armstrong's New Orleans*. New York: W. W. Norton.

Bruno, R. Stephanie. 2017. "2 New Orleans Public Schools Are Demolished in Post-Katrina Rebuilding Campaign." *NOLA.com*. May 29, 2017. http://www.nola.com/education/index.ssf/2011/09/2_new_orleans_public_schools_a.html/.

Burns, Mick. 2006. *Keeping the Beat on the Street: The New Orleans Brass Band Renaissance*. Baton Rouge: Louisiana State University Press.

Buttle, Francis A. 1998. "Word of Mouth: Understanding and Managing Referral Marketing." *Journal of Strategic Marketing* 6: 341–254.

Cape, Roy, and Jocelyne Guilbault. 2014. *Roy Cape: A Life on the Calypso and Soca Bandstand*. Durham, NC: Duke University Press.

Chenier, Kenny A. 2000. *Bended Knees: The Story of the Marching 100*. Cierra Films. https://www.youtube.com/watch?v=mrb2vBCNW78/.

Cherrie, Lolita Villavasso. 2014. "The Right to Read . . . The Dryades Street Library (1915–1965)." *CreoleGen* (blog). March 22, 2014. http://www.creolegen.org/2014/03/22/the-right-to-read-the-dryades-street-library-1915-1965/.

Cotton, Deborah "Big Red." 2009. "Big Nine and the Battle of the Bands—Old vs New Guard." *Gambit* (blog). December 30, 2009. https://www.theadvocate.com/gambit/new_orleans/news/the_latest/article_ffib8ca7-02cf-5896-9cfb-4fd6e7968fec.html/.

Davis, Angela Y. 2012. *The Meaning of Freedom*. San Francisco, CA: City Lights Books.

DeCoste, Kyle. 2015. "Street Queens: The Original Pinettes and Black Feminism in New Orleans Brass Bands." MA thesis, Tulane University, 2015.

DeCoste, Kyle. 2016. "Decolonizing the Discipline through Archival Repatriation: A Conversation with Aaron Fox." *SEM Student News* 12 (2): 38–40.

DeCoste, Kyle. 2017a. "The 'Pre-Postmodern' Ethnomusicology of Zora Neale Hurston." *SEM Student News* 13 (1): 31–33.

DeCoste, Kyle. 2017b. "Street Queens: New Orleans Brass Bands and the Problem of Intersectionality." *Ethnomusicology* 61 (2): 181–206.

Dowd, Nancy E. 2000. *Redefining Fatherhood.* New York: New York University Press.

Edwards, Ezekiel, Will Bunting, and Lynda Garcia. 2013. "The War on Marijuana in Black and White." American Civil Liberties Union. https://www.aclu.org/sites/default/files/field_document/1114413-mj-report-rfs-re11.pdf/.

Foucault, Michel. 1991. *The Foucault Effect: Studies in Governmentality.* Edited by Graham Burchell, Colin Gordon, and Peter Miller. Chicago: University of Chicago Press.

Germano, William. 2016. *Getting It Published: A Guide for Scholars and Anyone Else Serious About Serious Books.* 3rd ed. Chicago: University of Chicago Press.

Greene, Robert. 1998. *48 Laws of Power.* New York: Penguin.

Hari, Johann. 2015. *Chasing the Scream: The Opposite of Addiction Is Connection.* London: Bloomsbury.

Harris-DeBerry, Kelly A., Denese Shervington, and Rashida Govan. 2014. *Crooked Room: Stories from New Orleans.* New Orleans: Institute for Women and Ethnic Studies. http://iwesnola.org/assets/downloads/2015/04/crooked- room3_final_web1.pdf/.

Harris-Perry, Melissa. 2011. *Sister Citizen: Shame, Stereotypes, and Black Women in America.* New Haven, CT: Yale University Press.

Hasselle, Della. 2015. "Kennedy High School Alumni Call for Its Rebuilding." *The Advocate.* March 31, 2015. https://www.theadvocate.com/new_orleans/news/education/article_69331a97-7c44-5a0d-bea2-b997d6e8ff61.html/.

Heerden, Ivor van. 2007. "The Failure of the New Orleans Levee System Following Hurricane Katrina and the Pathway Forward." *Public Administration Review* 67 (1): 24–35.

Heller, Nathan. 2017. "Is the Gig Economy Working?" *The New Yorker.* May 15, 2017. https://www.newyorker.com/magazine/2017/05/15/is-the-gig-economy-working/.

Hobbs, Holly. 2015. "'Shake Fo Ya Hood': Rap Performance, Disaster and Recovery in New Orleans." PhD diss., Tulane University.

jackbrass. 2005. "New Orleans Musicians—Head Count." Forum Post. *Rebirth Brass Band Forum: Fan Forum.* https://web.archive.org/web/20051218034800/http://www.rebirthbrassband.com:80/messaging/cutecast.pl?forum=1&thread=432.

Johnson, Cedric, ed. 2011. *The Neoliberal Deluge: Hurricane Katrina, Late Capitalism, and the Remaking of New Orleans.* Minneapolis: University of Minnesota Press.

Jordan-Zachary, Julia S. 2009. *Black Women, Cultural Images and Social Policy.* New York: Routledge.

Kelley, Robin D. G. 1997. *Yo' Mama's Disfunktional!: Fighting the Culture Wars in Urban America.* Boston: Beacon Press.

Kennedy, Al. 2002. *Chord Changes on the Chalkboard: How Public School Teachers Shaped Jazz and the Music of New Orleans.* Lanham, MD: The Scarecrow Press.

Klein, Naomi. 2008. *The Shock Doctrine: The Rise of Disaster Capitalism.* New York: Picador.

Knowles, Richard H. 1996. *Fallen Heroes: A History of New Orleans Brass Bands.* New Orleans: Jazzology Press.

Lassiter, Luke Eric. 2008. "Moving Past Public Anthropology and Doing Collaborative Research." *National Association for the Practice of Anthropology Bulletin* 29: 70–86.

Lewis, Ronald W., Rachel Breunlin, and Helen Regis. 2009. *The House of Dance and Feathers: A Museum*. New Orleans: University of New Orlean Press.

Linden, Amy. 2007. "Put It Down: New Orleans Brass Band Marches On." *XXL*, July 2007.

Lorde, Audre. 1984. *Sister Outsider: Essays and Speeches*. Trumansburg, NY: Crossing Press.

Meintjes, Louise. 2003. *Sound of Africa!: Making Music Zulu in a South African Studio*. Durham, NC: Duke University Press.

Merriam, Alan P. 1977. "Definitions of 'Comparative Musicology' and 'Ethnomusicology': An Historical-Theoretical Perspective." *Ethnomusicology* 21 (2): 189–204.

Muller, Carol Ann, and Sathima Bea Benjamin. 2011. *Musical Echoes: South African Women Thinking in Jazz*. Durham, NC: Duke University Press.

Mutua, Athena D. 2006. "Theorizing Progressive Black Masculinities." In *Progressive Black Masculinities*, edited by Athena D. Mutua, 3–42. New York: Routledge.

Neal, Mark Anthony. 2003. *Songs in the Key of Black Life*. New York: Routledge.

Nice, Brice. 2013. "Street Music Is the Second Full-Length Album and First Vinyl Release for New Orleans Legendary STOOGES BRASS BAND." Sinking City Records. July 19, 2013. http://sinkingcityrecords.com/journal/detail/4/Street-Music-by-the-Stooges-Brass -Band/.

Nine Times Social Aid and Pleasure Club. 2009. *Coming Out the Door for the Ninth Ward*. New Orleans: University of New Orleans Press.

O'Rourke, Matthew J. 2003. *Between Law and Hope: St. Augustine High School New Orleans, Louisiana*. New Orleans: The Josephite Fathers.

Oyola, Osvaldo. 2013. "Calling Out To (Anti)Liveness: Recording and the Question of Presence." *Sounding Out!* (blog). September 9, 2013. https://soundstudiesblog.com/2013/09/ 09/liveness-and-recorded-music/.

Pembleton, Matthew R. 2015. "The Voice of the Bureau: How Frederic Sondern and the Bureau of Narcotics Crafted a Drug War and Shaped Popular Understanding of Drugs, Addiction, and Organized Crime in the 1950s." *The Journal of American Culture; Malden* 38 (2): 113–29.

Perry, Marc D. 2015. "Who Dat?: Race and Its Conspicuous Consumption in Post-Katrina New Orleans." *City & Society* 27 (1): 92–114.

Raeburn, Bruce Boyd. 2009. *New Orleans Style and the Writing of American Jazz History*. Ann Arbor: University of Michigan Press.

Raeburn, Bruce Boyd. 2013. "Jamming with Disaster: New Orleans Jazz in the Aftermath of Hurricane Katrina." In *Forces of Nature and Cultural Responses*, 169–84. Springer, Dordrecht. https://doi.org/10.1007/978-94-007-5000-5_9.

Red Bull. 2010. "Red Bull Street Kings: Four Bands March In . . . One Band Marches On— Glen David Andrews to Host New Orleans Brass Band Blowout Under the Claiborne Bridge." PRWeb. September 10, 2010. https://www.neworleansonline.com/pr/releases/ releases/Red%20Bull%20Street%20Kings%20Present%20Brass%20Band%20Competi tion.pdf/.

Regis, Helen A. 2001. "Blackness and the Politics of Memory in the New Orleans Second Line." *American Ethnologist* 28 (4): 752–77.

Regis, Helen, Rachel Breunlin, and Ronald Lewis. 2011. "Building Collaborative Partnerships through a Lower Ninth Ward Museum." *Practicing Anthropology* 33 (2): 4–10. https://doi .org/10.17730/praa.33.2.mu53h77518u285pt/.

Bibliography

Sakakeeny, Matt. 2010. "'Under the Bridge': An Orientation to Soundscapes in New Orleans." *Ethnomusicology* 54 (1): 1–27.

Sakakeeny, Matt. 2012. "Why Dey Had to Kill Him." *Oxford American* 79: 142–48.

Sakakeeny, Matt. 2013a. *Roll with It: Brass Bands in the Streets of New Orleans.* Durham, NC: Duke University Press.

Sakakeeny, Matt. 2013b. "Running with the Second Line: How New Orleans Brass Band Went Hip Hop." *Red Bull Music Academy Daily* (blog). October 15, 2013. http://daily.redbullmusicacademy.com/2013/10/running-with-the-second-line-how-brass-band-went-hip-hop/.

Sakakeeny, Matt. 2013c. "Street Queens Bury Competition in Brass Band Blowout." *NPR.org* (blog). October 28, 2013. https://www.npr.org/sections/therecord/2013/10/28/241401570/all-female-brass-band-buries-the-competition/.

Sakakeeny, Matt. 2015a. "Playing for Work: Music as a Form of Labor in New Orleans." *Oxford Handbooks Online.* http://www.oxfordhandbooks.com/view/10.1093/oxfordhb/9780199935321.001.0001/oxfordhb-9780199935321-e-23/.

Sakakeeny, Matt. 2015b. "Music Lessons as Life Lessons in New Orleans Marching Bands." *Souls* 17 (3–4): 279–302.

Schneider, Saundra K. 2005. "Administrative Breakdowns in the Governmental Response to Hurricane Katrina." *Public Administration Review* 65 (5): 515–16.

Sharkey, Patrick. 2007. "Survival and Death in New Orleans: An Empirical Look at the Human Impact of Katrina." *Journal of Black Studies* 37 (4): 482–501.

Shiels, Justin. 2013. "A Report on the New Orleans Center for Creative Arts." Paper 156. Arts Administration Master's Report. New Orleans: University of New Orleans. https://scholarworks.uno.edu/cgi/viewcontent.cgi?article=1156&context=aa_rpts/.

Sublette, Ned. 2009. *The Year Before the Flood: A Story of New Orleans.* Chicago: Lawrence Hill Books.

Szwed, John, and Sally Banes. 2005. "From 'Messin' Around' to 'Funk Western Civilization': The Rise and Fall of Dance Instruction Songs." In *Crossovers: Essays on Race, Music, and American Culture*, 131–52. Philadelphia: University of Pennsylvania Press.

Tucker, Sherrie. 2001. *Swing Shift: "All-Girl" Bands of the 1940s.* Durham, NC: Duke University Press.

Van Syckle, Katie. 2012. "Stooges Brass Band to Manage Hi-Ho Lounge." *NOLA.com.* March 26, 2012. http://www.nola.com/music/index.ssf/2012/03/stooges_brass_band_to_manage_h.html/.

Walter, Evan, Laura Sibert, and Jessica Rocco. 2012. "Young Men Olympians." *MediaNOLA.* October 29, 2012. http://medianola.org/discover/place/842/Young-Men-Olympians/.

Woodward, Alex. 2013. "Hi-Ho Lounge Gets Facelift, New Ownership." *Gambit Weekly.* February 8, 2013. https://www.theadvocate.com/gambit/new_orleans/news/the_latest/article_3d30948d-4784-53d4-a437-9a6a5240b554.html/.

Wyckoff, Geraldine. 2004. "The Stooges: Sweet on the Street." *OffBeat Magazine.* February 1, 2004. http://www.offbeat.com/articles/the-stooges-sweet-on-the-street/.

Young, Tara. 2004. "Suspected Truck Thief Shot and Killed by N.O. Officers." *Times-Picayune.* August 4, 2004.

INDEX

Jackson, Michael, 224
Jackson, Mississippi, 166
Jackson, Royce "Flash," 124, *157*, 169–70, *171*,
  175, 230; biography of, 226–28; flying
  on tour, 176; police interactions while
  touring, 172
Jackson Square, 50, 197, 200–201, 238n4
  (chap. 12)
Jadakiss, 66, 234n10
James, Kerwin, 13, 205
Juárez, Lucia López, 231n5
Jay-Z, 121, 234n1
Jazz and Heritage Foundation, 199–200
"Jazz Fest Johnny." *See* Driver, John "Jazz
  Fest Johnny"
Jazzland Theme Park, 213
Jeanerette, Louisiana, 101
Jena Street, 159
John F. Kennedy Senior High School, 27,
  206, 211; after Hurricane Katrina, 233n5
  (chap. 1); location of, 14; practices
  at, 198; reunion of class of 1978, 106;
  rivalries with, 21; Stooges membership
  from, 14, 19; talent shows at, 16, 17;
  training at, 15
Johns Creek, Georgia, 170
Johnson, Adam, xiv
Johnson, Cedric, 89
Johnson, Fred, 138, 148
Johnson, Pableaux, photos by, xiii, 5, 96, 97,
  118, 131, 134, 140, 155, 163, 189
Jones, Benny, Sr., 138, 148–49
Jones, Dorian "Tank," 13, 184, 229
Jones, Herman, 214
Jones, Mike "Dizzle," *xiii, 167*, 169, 170, *175*,
  188, 190, 230; biography of, 224–25;
  connection to Flash Jackson, 227–28;
  hazards of touring, 174–76
Jones, Tyesha, 140–42
Jordan, Kidd, 15
Jordan-Zachary, Julia S., 234n3
Joseph, Ellis "Ejo," *14*, 15–16, 20, *25*, 33, 181,
  229; beefs with other bands, 36–37;
  biography of, 208–9; connection to
  J'mar Westley, 210; connection to John
  Cannon, 213; connection to Virgil
  Tiller, 218; founding of Free Agents

Brass Band, 91–98; next generation
  of musicians, 199–200; rap career of,
  66–67; recording albums, 63–65; in Red
  Bull Street Kings competition, 138–40,
  144
Joseph, Patrick, 208
JumpShive, 91, 93, 95–96, 98, 100, 217, 227;
  origin of term "shive," 236n9
Junior Buckjumpers Brass Band, 19
"Just a Closer Walk with Thee" (traditional
  song), 183, 184, 238n1 (chap. 12)

Kabuki. *See* Shezbie, Derek
Katrina. *See* Hurricane Katrina
K-Ci and JoJo, 28
Kelley, Robin D. G., 234n8, 237n5 (chap. 10)
Kennedy, Al, 234n12
Kennedy High School. *See* John F. Kennedy
  Senior High School
Kenner, Louisiana, 71
Kerr, Clyde, Jr., 15, 42, 208, 233n7, 234n12
Kin Folks Brass Band, 127, 158
Kinko's, 108
Klein, Naomi, 184–85, 238n2 (chap. 12)
"Knock with Me—Rock with Me" (Lil
  Rascals Brass Band song), 62
Knowles, Richard H., 232n6, 232n7 (intro.)
Krewe du Vieux, 33

labor, 215, 226; academic, xi, xii, xiv, 88,
  153; in capitalism, 46, 89, 194, 234n8;
  in collaborative book writing, xiii;
  in families, 161–62; in gig economy,
  107, 209; leisure and, 237n5 (chap. 10);
  masculinity and, 45; music as, 22, 44–45,
  83, 153–56, 160, 188, 210, 237n3 (chap. 10),
  237n5 (chap. 10); music production as,
  69–71; support for, 212; touring as, 222
Lady Buckjumpers. *See* Original N.O. Lady
  and Men Buckjumpers
Lady Jetsetters, 161
Lady Rulers Social Aid and Pleasure Club,
  22
Lake Pontchartrain. *See* Pontchartrain,
  Lake
Lasalle Street, 236n3 (chap. 7)
Lassiter, Luke Eric, 231n6

ABOUT THE AUTHORS

Credit: Pableaux Johnson

The Stooges Brass Band is a New Orleans, Louisiana, brass band. The group was formed in 1996 after bandleader Walter Ramsey saw a performance by the Rebirth Brass Band. The Stooges Brass Band is known for incorporating elements of hip-hop, funk, and R&B into a more traditional brass band framework. In April 2011, they won the Best Contemporary Brass Band award from the Big Easy Music Awards. Kyle DeCoste is a PhD student in ethnomusicology at Columbia University, where his research interests include African American music, intersectionality, queer theory, collaborative ethnography, and popular culture, among others. His dissertation explores the cultural politics of childhood in Black popular music in the United States.

Printed in the United States
By Bookmasters